CERTAIN, LIVELY EPISODES

CERTAIN, LIVELY EPISODES

The Articulation

of Passion in

Eighteenth-Century

Prose

ALAN T. MCKENZIE

The University of Georgia Press

Athens and London

© 1990 by the University of Georgia Press
Athens, Georgia 30602

Designed by Mary Mendell
Set in Garamond No. 3

The paper in this book meets the guidelines for
permanence and durability of the Committee on
Production Guidelines for Book Longevity of the
Council on Library Resources.

Printed in the United States of America
94 93 92 91 90   5 4 3 2 1

Library of Congress Cataloging in Publication
Data

McKenzie, Alan T.
Certain, lively episodes : the articulation of
passion in eighteenth-century prose / Alan T.
McKenzie.
p. cm.   Bibliography: p.   Includes index.
ISBN 0-8203-1167-7 (alk. paper)
1. English prose literature—18th century—
History and criticism.   2. Emotions—History—
18th century. 3. Emotions in literature.   I. Title.
PR858.E46M35   1990   CIP
828'.50809'353—dc19   89-4826

British Library Cataloging in Publication Data
available

FOR ANN,
WHO HELPED

CONTENTS

ACKNOWLEDGMENTS

BEGAN THIS PROJECT DURING A SABBATICAL
year at Oxford, where I studied the abstractions in
eighteenth-century prose. A Mellon Fellowship to
the William Andrews Clark Library enabled me to
recognize the role of Le Brun and to sharpen my eye
for physical manifestations of the passions, even in *The Rambler*. The
chapter on Fielding was finished, and that on Hume begun, during
my tenure as a Leverhulme Fellow at the University of Dundee. A
National Endowment for the Humanities Summer Seminar at the
British Art Center at Yale University provided an opportunity to
study Benjamin West and Hogarth. A semester as a fellow in the
Humanities Institute at Purdue University supplied the incentive
and the occasion to put the work into final shape.

Many colleagues and students at Purdue have offered help and
encouragement, none more so than Hugo Reichard. Extramurally, I
must single out Paula Backscheider, William Epstein, David
Fleeman, Gwin Kolb, and Howard Weinbrot.

Some of the material in chapter 1 appeared in the *Georgia Review*,
32 (Winter 1978). An earlier version of chapter 6 appeared in the
Dalhousie Review, 62 (1982), and of chapter 7 in *Eighteenth-Century
Studies*, 20 (1986–87).

CERTAIN, LIVELY EPISODES

1

READING THE PASSIONS ON PAGE,

STAGE, AND CANVAS

ARLY ONE MORNING IN 1771 DAVID GARRICK went to see Benjamin West's recent sensation, *The Death of General Wolfe,* on exhibit at the Royal Academy. When a young woman in the crowd that had already gathered objected to the languid expression on Wolfe's face, Garrick lay down in front of the painting and assumed Wolfe's pose and expression. Then, in one of the "turns" for which he was famous, he altered his features, perhaps the most plastic and articulate features ever to grace the English stage, into "that transient rapture which history records the dying hero felt."[1] Convinced and impressed, the crowd burst into applause.

Many elements of the system of the passions figure in this incident: the elaborate vocabulary of the passions underlying the distinction between languor and rapture; the conventions of manifestation that allowed West and Garrick to represent both passions; the informed and sympathetic participation of the viewers in the recognition and discrimination of those passions; and the assumption on everyone's part that there is an essential connection between the expression on the face and the mind within. (All parties were, I assume, much more interested in the state of Wolfe's mind than in the aesthetics of the disposition of his features.) A nearly contemporary description of this painting, so fulsome that West's own hand has been suspected in it, read Wolfe's face as expressing a "serenity . . . somewhat infringed by that sense of pain, and that only, which must be inseparable from the human frame sinking into immediate dissolution."[2]

This is not the place to review Wolfe's military career and subsequent apotheosis, the various sources, allusions and personages in West's painting, or the controversy with Reynolds over the use of modern costume.[3] I do, however, suggest that West's then controversial depiction of a contemporary scene in contemporary uniforms makes his reliance on the traditional depiction of the passions all the more striking. The first viewers of this painting expected anguish to look exactly the way West depicted it here, but they expected the body undergoing that anguish to be clad in a toga. If, to us, the red coats seem both familiar and expected, the expressions on the various faces are too often barely noticed and only vaguely recognized. The Garrick incident ought to instruct us to take the passions in this painting, and in this age, more seriously.

While Garrick imitated and altered passions in successive episodes, West, working in a spatial rather than a temporal medium, surrounded a central passion with others that—for those who can read them—set off and clarify the focal passion:

> The various expressions on the faces of Wolfe's attendants gave depth and variety to the emotional effect of a hero's death in his moment of victory, and served to draw the spectator by sympathy into the company. Each character makes his own contribution: the impersonal grief of the grenadier standing on the right with folded hands; the anxious solicitude of the surgeon wiping Wolfe's brow; the mixed emotions of Sir William Howe stretching out his hand to welcome the victory and regretting that Wolfe will not live to enjoy it; the unwitting eagerness of the soldier running up with the news; and the aloof calm of the Cherokee Indian, indifferent to victory and lost in contemplation of mortality. [Mitchell, 30]

As this reading by an attentive and well-informed art historian indicates, the central episode exfoliates into subsidiary, corresponding passions, which in turn clarify and intensify the focal passion. The articulation of passions throughout this painting suggests a system of signification, clarity, and response; Garrick's performance confirms and extends the suggestion.

The contemplative, dispassionate expression on the face of the Indian emphasizes the passions on the faces of those around him in ways that must have baffled Garrick and his audience. While there had been, in fact, no Indians in Wolfe's party, West had seen a good many of them in western Pennsylvania, where he grew up, and had made the depiction of Indians an intriguing and lucrative hallmark. Something of West's own Quaker background underlies that calm contemplation of death and indifference to a victory in which the Indian cannot share—the Bromley reading quoted above treats him like one of the natives from Montaigne's "Of Cannibals." But if this Indian had not been schooled in the passions, West had been; he had studied passionate incidents from Plutarch and other traditional sources—sources he had already put to use in *Agrippina Landing at Brundisium with the Ashes of Germanicus* and *Pyrrhus When a Child Brought to Glaucias, King of Illyria, for Protection.*[4] Everyone else in the painting, and in that exhibition room in Pall Mall where West hung his work and Garrick staged his performance, had clearly had something of the same education.

Garrick himself had conducted much of the schooling of his con- temporaries: "Garrick will put his head between two folding-doors, and in the course of five or six seconds his expression will change successively from wild delight to temperate pleasure, from this to tranquillity, from tranquillity to surprise, from surprise to blank astonishment, from that to sorrow, from sorrow to the air of one overwhelmed, from that to fright, from fright to horror, from hor- ror to despair, and thence he will go up again to the point from which he started."[5] This display adds to a vocabulary both large and minutely discriminated a syntax unavailable to painting. Garrick begins with an intense response to a great good, moves to a milder one, and then shifts to tranquillity. Next he advances from surprise to more intense astonishment. Finally, and all in the course of a few seconds, he displays five responses to evil, responses that increase in intensity from sorrow to despair and succeed each other in time as the evil approaches and then passes (fright-horror-despair). Those who sat through the performance in a Parisian drawing room must have been every bit as fluent in the language of the passions as those who admired the performance in front of West's painting. I propose to show how they acquired such fluency, what it enabled them to understand, and how much their having done so allowed those who wrote for them to convey.

I want to call attention to this prevalent and significant element in eighteenth-century prose and, in the process, to restore some of the force and clarity which once accompanied every appearance of a passion. In doing so I shall treat each incident of passion as an episode with a brief but cogent, complex, and almost narrative existence of its own, differing from every other passion but comparable in numerous components and considerations to every other episode of the same passion. Thus the rapture that Garrick supplied for Wolfe is strictly comparable to episodes of rapture in Raphael, Shakespeare, Le Brun, and Racine and sufficiently well constituted to withstand the playfulness of Fielding and the scepticism of Gibbon. As we examine the components and sequences from which each such episode is constituted, we will discover that episodes of passion are commensurate as well as intricate and that it is useful and informative now and again to pause to take their measure, as Garrick was encouraging, and enabling, the first viewers of West's painting to do.

Passions, like other episodes, are preceded by events that help determine their nature. In addition, passions have consequences. Wolfe's anguish, for example, is an incident in his life, in the French and Indian War, and in the Battle of Quebec as well as being an episode of anguish. It was followed by his death, his emergence as a national hero, and historic, political, and aesthetic consequences, all of which it helped, in some sense, to precipitate. Yet as both West's painting and Garrick's performance suggest, it was momentarily possible to isolate that anguish from such considerations. It was capable of being manifested, recognized, understood, and analyzed as a separate episode.

Each such episode had, implicitly or explicitly, one or more causes, an object that precipitated it, sensations of pleasure or pain and estimations of good or evil somewhere inside the body of the person who felt it, and manifestations outside that body. The circumstances within which it occurred included calculation of past, present, and future as well as duration and, for some passions (though not, perhaps, the ones Wolfe is here experiencing), comparisons of the rank and power of the person feeling the passion with other persons he considers involved. Finally, each episode had a name that helped link it to other episodes like it, by distinguishing it from comparable episodes with different components. While not every account of every such episode elaborates all of these components, most such accounts, especially those that are written rather

than staged or painted, do elaborate, or at least take into consideration, several of them.

In the pages that follow I will show that such episodes were
rendered and understood fully in the paintings and plays of the
period. Garrick's audience and West's viewers knew exactly how
anguish and rapture looked because they had seen so many clear
episodes of them—on walls and stages, as well as on the faces of
those with whom they lived and dealt. The rest of chapter 1 reviews
some other accounts of the passions in recent scholarship, criticism,
philosophy, and sociology. In chapter 2 I study the process whereby
the various components entered into traditional analyses of the soul
and the various emphases and elaborations they received. Chapter 3
deals with the modifications of that tradition in the hands of theorists and physiologists in the seventeenth and early eighteenth centuries. The remaining chapters inspect the treatment given by five
different writers to the possibilities inherent in every episode of
passion. In these chapters I quote some long but highly significant
passages in which the passions figure. In these passages, I trust, the
reader will notice and appreciate the force and intricacy of the episodes. I quote them in support of the thesis that in the eighteenth
century the passions were conceived and regarded as having meanings clearer, more elaborate, and more systematic than any they now
retain. It is not, I think, a matter of recovering what our ancestors
have wisely discarded to reconstruct the lines along which these
episodes were drawn and developed.

II

While the nature of the passions had long fascinated philosophers,
the clarity of the passions was imparted largely by paintings (and
treatises on painting). The stage developed and elaborated them,
and then writers of prose learned how to explore their intricacy.
With the treatises of Leonardo, Lomazzo, and della Porta and the
paintings of Raphael, Dürer, Caravaggio, Titian, Poussin, and others, depictions of the human countenance became truly expressive.
As Leonardo put it, paintings which did not show forth the passions
vividly were "twice dead."[6] The expression of passion was an essential tenet of humanism, in both the Renaissance and the eighteenth

century. As such it found its source in the classics, its inspiration in human experience, and its confirmation in the emotions stirred in the audience. The codification of this expressiveness in the hands of the French Academy put the passions at the disposal of a public so wide that their signifyings could be taken for granted by painters, actors, and writers alike.

Charles Le Brun (1619–1690), the founder and eventually the director of the Académie Royale de Peinture et de Sculpture, presided over this codification and much else, dispensing the patronage and proclaiming the rules that made the art of his time so thoroughly academic.[7] As director of the Gobelins factory, he designed most of the furnishings for Versailles, creating not only the splendor of the court of the Sun King but also the background against which the passions he schematized were most often displayed. His positions of authority and his own grand canvases, frequently engraved and reprinted, established him as the most powerful and influential artist of his day: "'L'art, c'est moi,' eût pu dire Lebrun," observed a contemporary, more in envy than in admiration.[8] His own paintings received and repaid study along the lines he dictated, and his canvases depict all the right passions in all the likely places: veneration, sadness, and dejection in the numerous martyrdoms, ascensions, and depositions, and hatred, fear, and anguish in the battle scenes. A passage from Félibien's elaborate reading ("ekphrasis") of *The Tent of Darius* manifests the care and accuracy with which the passions were once painted and read:

> But 'tis in the Wife of Darius that Grief is most Wonderfully Express'd; We may see in her Eyes and thro' her whole Countenance, the Manifest Dissatisfaction she Receives from the Condition she is Reduced to. However as She is Young and Beautiful, she Preserves in the midst of so much Grief & Dissatisfaction, a Decency & Majesty becoming a Great Queen. And we may also Discover in her Eyes and all the Features of her Face, the Hopes she has in the Clemency of so Generous a Conqueror. We see likewise very well, that in Beholding ALEXANDER, She Endeavours even with her Looks which are the Interpreters of her Grief, to Affect the very Soul of that Prince of Compassion.[9]

Both depiction and reading employ elements important in West's painting—the overall clarity and complexity of the episode, the modification of one passion by others surrounding it, the contribution of previous circumstances ("she Preserves in the midst of so much Grief & Dissatisfaction"), and the projecting of this episode into the future ("the Hopes she has"; "She Endeavours . . . to Affect the very Soul"). The canvas is resonant, and articulate, with passions and fraught with temporal ramifications that extend both back over the centuries and forward into the moments immediately succeeding the action depicted. And all of this complexity, as Félibien's reading makes clear, was available to the original audience.

The codification for such depictions and interpretations is to be found in the *Conférence de M. Le Brun sur l'expression générale et particulière*—a lecture delivered before the Académie Royale in 1668 and published in 1698, and frequently thereafter.[10] Based on Descartes's *Les passions de l'âme,* which I will consider in chapter 3, the *Conférence* illustrates with passionate expressions from his own canvases Le Brun's theory that the eyebrow is the key to the passions. For *La frayeur,* for example, he took a figure, turban, plume, and all, from his own *La bataille d'Arbelles.*[11] The text reads, in part:

> FRIGHT, when excessive, raises the Eye-brows exceedingly in the middle; the muscles, that conduce to the motion of those parts, are very visible and swelled, pressing against each other, and lowering towards the Nose, which, as well as the Nostrils, ought to appear drawing upwards; the Eyes must look wide open, the Upper-Eye-lid be hid under the Brow, the White of the Eye surrounded with red, the Pupil appear wild, and situate more to the bottom of the Eye than upwards, the lower Eye-lid swelled and livid, the Muscles of the Nose and Nostrils also swelled. . . . [*A Method to Learn to Design the Passions,* 31]

Le Brun analyzed the expression of twenty-four passions along these same lines, borrowing from Descartes and considering a great many paintings. Le Brun's coopting of Cartesian philosophy in his art involves two ironies, first, that Descartes's dualism prompted a detailed and vivid *embodiment* of the passions, and second, that one of the essential tenets of eighteenth-century humanism depended upon so highly academic a schematization for its promulgation. We will return to both of these considerations in chapter 3.

The influence of Le Brun swept over the continent and crossed the

Channel in many forms. In addition to several French and Dutch editions, there were English translations in 1701 (dedicated to Kneller) and 1734 (quoted above) and an Italian one in 1751. The work continued to appear in various guises and languages well into the nineteenth century. Le Brun's battle paintings are commended by Archer in *The Beaux Stratagem* (1707; IV.1); his students had a hand in the furnishing of Blenheim (!); Fielding cites one of his Alexandrian tableaux in *Tom Jones* (V.xii); and Dodsley included illustrations from the *Conférence* in the chapter on drawing in his *Preceptor* (1748), a work in which Samuel Johnson took an active part. William Wordsworth was thrilled by the expression of Le Brun's Magdalene in the Louvre (*The Prelude*, IX, 76–80). Indeed, Le Brun's hand is to be seen in West's painting, where the head of the grenadier is said to be taken from Le Brun's "Compassion" and Wolfe's expression from "Acute Pain."[12]

Generally, the English treated Le Brun's work as they treat any French theories that they elect not to greet with contempt—flexibly, humanely, and with reservations. Many of them found the Raphael "Cartoons" of the Acts of the Apostles every bit as expressive as, and notably less rigid than, the work of the French academicians. *The School of Raphael; or, The Student's Guide to Expression in Historical Painting . . . with . . . The PASSIONS, as characterised by RAPHAEL in the Cartoons, Described and explained by BENJAMIN RALPH*, for example, asserts that "a Person who has only studied Le Brun, will be at a loss when he views some of the Characters in the Cartoons to know what Passions are expressed in them, and yet the Ideas will be found to be in the highest degree, exalted, just, and significant."[13] Ralph's reading of *Elymas the Sorcerer, Struck with Blindness* indicates that, while Raphael's graphic vocabulary was larger than Le Brun's, both men were certainly painting in the same language: "Though Terror and Astonishment are strongly expressed in this Picture, yet it appears of a different Kind, and produces a different Effect from that in the *Cartoon* of the Death of *Ananias*. The Punishment of *Elymas* was to him dreadful and grievous, and to the Beholders terrifying and wonderful; but is apparently considered by them not otherwise than as it relates to this Instance of the divine Judgment inflicted on him. The Death of *Ananias* inspired Horror also, not without a Mixture of Pity for the Sufferer" (19). The index to the plates lists more than fifty passions or combinations of passions that Raphael managed to depict and Ralph to discern.

William Hogarth's contemporaries frequently praised and appreciated his subtle and skillful depiction of the passions. The epitaph that Samuel Johnson proposed for him praised his "curious eyes / That saw the manners in the face," and Horace Walpole, who had strong personal reasons not to like Hogarth, collected him avidly, comparing his work to the comedies of Molière, in part because it was "animated by proper and just expressions of the passions."[14] Walpole quotes Gilpin's praise, words which remind us that the passions must be understood as well as embodied, before they can be appreciated: "Of his Expression, in which the force of his genius lay, we cannot speak in terms too high. In every mode of it he was truly excellent. The passions he thoroughly understood, and all the effects they produce in every part of the human frame" (152).

While his contemporaries acknowledged his genius in depicting the passions, Hogarth himself seems to have regarded the received system as too schematic, arbitrary, and dehumanizing, impaired by the visual and aesthetic prepossessions he regarded as beams in the eyes of his contemporaries—in a word, academic.[15] The strong narrative component in his work depends on actions as well as expressions—no artist with the subtle tales to tell and the complex images Hogarth had in mind could have done otherwise. His practice of taking his subjects and their expressions from life or the stage rather than from the canvases or treatises of the masters rendered his delineations of the passions more supple, more problematic, and more human than those sought by the "connoisseurs" whom he detested. The following passage on the face depends on the fascination with variety and the insistence on empirical scrutiny evident throughout the *Analysis*. Notice that, even though the turns of expression are "numberless," the mind can always follow them. Hogarth called for a larger vocabulary, but he depended on the same syntax:

The face indeed will bear a constant view, yet always entertain and keep our curiosity awake, without the assistance either of a mask, or veil; because vast variety of changing circumstances keeps the eye and the mind in constant play, in following the numberless turns of expression it is capable of. How soon does a face that wants expression, grow insipid, tho' it be ever so pretty?—The rest of the body, not having these advantages in common with the face, would soon satiate the eye, were it to be as constantly exposed. . . . [53]

While his graphic vocabulary was certainly larger and more supple than Le Brun's (and coarser than Raphael's), Hogarth himself recommended Le Brun as useful in learning to distinguish the passions (138) and incorporated several of his expressions in his own works. Critics have detected Le Brun's horror in Rakewell's grimaces, his sadness in the face of the bride and love in that of Counsellor Silvertongue (*Marriage-à-la-Mode*), and his fright (and tent) in *Mr. Garrick in the Character of Richard III.*[16]

Sir Joshua Reynolds's elevation of character and dignity over passion offers something of another counterexample to the schematics of Le Brun. Nevertheless, Reynolds paid his compliments to the passions throughout the *Discourses,* especially the Fifth, where he objects to mingling them in the same expression. Reynolds annotated his copies of *The Tent of Darius Explained* and Du Fresnoy's *Art of Painting,* but his grandest acknowledgment is on canvas, whence Le Brun's "Compassion" and "Fright" peer out over the shoulders of *Mrs. Siddons as the Tragic Muse.*[17]

III

With Mrs. Siddons we return to the stage, where we will again encounter: Le Brun, numerous treatises and handbooks setting forth schemes of the passions, much contemporary evidence that these schemes were well employed and widely recognized, an abundance of recent scholarship to this effect, and, of course, David Garrick.[18] Le Brun's frontispieces for editions of the plays of Corneille (1647) and Racine (1697), for example, display the prominent emotions that fill the plays and, one supposes, characterize contemporary performances of them.[19]

Aaron Hill's *An Essay on the Art of Acting; in which, the Dramatic Passions are Properly Defined and Described,* to single out one treatise, discusses the ten dramatic passions enumerated in its poetic (or at least, rhymed) foreword:

> Ten strong-mark'd passions, signs external bear,
> And stamp assum'd distinctions on the play'r;
> *Joy, Grief, Fear, Anger, Pity, Scorn,* and *Hate,*
> *Wonder, Shame, Jealousy,* and *Love's* soft weight.
> These, when he paints, did he but first conceive,
> Each, on his fancy, would its image leave;
> Thence, ductile fibres catch th'expressive spring,
> And the eyes dart it, and the accents ring.[20]

Hill has combined the control of the medieval faculty of "fancy" over the passions with recent physiology ("ductile fibres") and phraseology ("catch th' expressive spring") and emphasized the actor's opportunity to go beyond facial expression and flashing eyes to the effects of passion on the voice.

In keeping with the findings of contemporary physiology, and in order to enlarge each episode of passion, Hill instructs the actor or actress to begin each episode by conceiving a "strong idea" of every passion. Only then can the passion be conveyed to the muscles of the face and body, and thence into the gestures and voice, and finally, though Hill does not bother to mention it, to the audience, which will have been schooled in the same conventions. He accompanies each set of instructions with passionate passages, as both illustrations and exercises. Here is his analysis of pity, appended to a speech of Belmour's from *Fatal Extravagance:*

> If an actor should endeavour to touch the expressiveness of the passion conceived in this speech, without having previously adapted his look to the sensation peculiar to pity, he would never (though his voice were the finest and most musical in nature), be able to succeed in his purpose: for, his tone would be sometimes too earnest, and sharp, and sometimes too languid, and melancholy.—But let him, first, strain his muscles into the tension, above required for expression of *joy,* and if, then, he adds the look that is proper to *grief,* the result of this mixed co-operation of contraries (of a visage peculiar to sorrow, with a spring on the muscles adapted to joy) will immediately produce the gesture, the voice, and the feeling expression of *pity.* [27–28]

Any number of other contemporary accounts prove that eighteenth-century actors followed these elaborate procedures for episode after episode and that many, perhaps most, members of their audience followed them when they did so. Several passages from *The Spectator* that I will consider in chapter 4 and the account of Partridge's reactions to *Hamlet,* to be discussed in chapter 6, are in themselves ample proof. I mention in addition two careful and contemporary inspections of Garrick's stage performances. Samuel Foote studied, not always without envy, the expressions of passions of most of his rivals, and even when he did not agree with the passions they were manifesting, he knew exactly which ones were being displayed. Here he is on Garrick's version of Lear's recovery: "The Passions of Joy, Tenderness, Grief, and Shame are blended together in so masterly a Manner, that the Imitation would do Honour to the Pencil of a *Rubens,* or an *Angelo.*"[21]

Georg Christoph Lichtenberg, an academic (Göttingen), a physicist, and an exact scrutinizer of passions on the stage, proved that the language of the passions was spoken, and understood, across the Continent as well as across the footlights—an innovation, incidentally, recently brought back from the Continent by Garrick so that audiences could follow his successive expressions. Lichtenberg's account of Garrick's Hamlet shows Garrick converting several episodes into tableaux, holding the expression as if in a painting, and then "turning" to the next one. To heighten the effect of his Hamlet, Garrick had a wig wired to raise his hair as he faced the ghost— an effect lost on neither Lichtenberg nor Partridge.[22] These vivid articulations of passion were recorded, again and again, in paint and in prose.

That Garrick himself knew very well what he was doing is evident in his own treatise, *An Essay on Acting.* Here is his analysis of how Abel Drugger should react to the broken urinal, an episode that exploits the dramatic presence of an "object" in the technical sense we will soon come to appreciate:

When *Abel Drugger* has broke the *Urinal,* he is *mentally absorb'd* with the different Ideas of the *invaluable* Price of the *Urinal,* and the Punishment that may be inflicted in Consequence of a Curiosity, no way appertaining or belonging to the Business he came about. Now, if this as it certainly *is,* [is] the Situation of his Mind, How are the different Members of the Body to be agitated? Why Thus,—His *Eyes* must be revers'd from the Object he is most intimidated with, and by dropping his *Lip* at the some [*sic*] Time *to* the Object, it throws a trembling *Languor* upon every *Muscle,* and by declining the right Part of the Head *towards* the *Urinal,* it casts the most *comic Terror* and *Shame* over all the *upper* Part of the Body.[23]

Famous as he was for his *body* language, Garrick's prose is equal to the analysis of this episode; he had been, after all, a student, though an irreverent one, of Samuel Johnson. Actors did not, of course, want to communicate all of the deliberateness prescribed in these treatises, nor did they have to take into account many components of the passions other than their manifestations. They themselves paid some attention to physiology, but there was neither reason nor means for conveying such concern to their audiences. The writer of prose, and the reader, had more components, more complexities, and more possibilities to contend with.

Paintings of the passions, then, whether by Raphael, Le Brun, or West, freeze the passions and capture only a part of each episode. Painters clarify the passions by schematizing them and surrounding them with attendant passions and, sometimes, the objects that have stimulated them. Paintings of actors exhibiting the passions, a genre in which the age seems to have specialized, sometimes manage to suggest the narrative elaboration of these episodes that the stage conveyed so effectively. Actors specialized in "turns" from one passion to another, emphasizing the sequence and complexity of each separate episode, and then allowing the consequences to emerge first among others on the stage and then among the audience, as Garrick's performance in front of West's painting attests. But only the sentence (especially the periodic sentence) could designate, depict, and analyze all of the components of these complex episodes. Moreover, the episodes of passions articulated in prose remain before us, where they can repeat themselves whenever an informed reader studies them with an attentive eye.

The passions seem to me far less satisfactorily deployed in eighteenth-century poetry, where they are often displayed rather than explored. They were, of course, exhibited repeatedly and variously in the poetry of the period, from the declamations of Dryden through the distillations of Thomson to the broodings of Young and the villagers of Crabbe. Poetic episodes, however, were often merely exhibitions. Some employed a fixed emphasis, as in the pulsations of Eloisa and the "ruling passion" of her poet and the heroic posturings of Pope's *Iliad.*[24] Elsewhere the passions acquire picturesque attitudes and attributes, as in Collins, where they drift through poems in procession rather than sequence, deprived of their objects, impelled only by occasion, and animated only by a Capital Letter ("Come, Capitalization, heavenly pow'r").[25] As sensibility came to dominate theory and practice, poets invoked the passions increasingly and sought to provoke them by resorting to marvelous objects found only within the mind itself:

> The appetite for ideal representation haunted the imaginings of mid-century critics, who desired poetry not merely to awaken the passions but to apprehend them visually, as if through the magic lantern of poetry the entire interior landscape of the mind would be illuminated and the panoply of unsubstantial qualities comprising our humanity be made known. To put the matter in this way was to recognize that the wondrous subject was man himself, not God or gods, not antiquated fictions, but embodiments of powers hidden within man, his essential reality. [Jackson, 35]

Too often merely addressed or depicted in poetry, in prose the passions were articulated, their external circumstances evoked, and their traditional components enumerated or considered. In order to demonstrate and study this articulation in sufficient detail, I have concentrated on six writers whose works display some of the intricacies achieved by the passions. I acknowledge that the passions are to be found in many other writers who doubtless ought to be inspected. I am sorry not to have found room for Mandeville, Swift, Burke, Kames, and Eliza Haywood (*Life's Progress through the Passions; or, The Adventures of Natura* [London: T. Gardner, 1748]). In Haywood's *Life's Progress,* the hero proceeds didactically through the entire catalogue of traditional passions, encountering them in chronological order according to the age at which they beset the individual. Thus book 3, chapter 2: "Shews at what age men are most liable to the passion of grief: the impatience of human nature under affliction, and the necessity there is of exerting reason, to restrain the excesses it would otherwise occasion."[26] I probably ought to have considered Shaftesbury, Richardson, Adam Smith, and some of the Scottish Common Sense philosophers.[27] Others have done so or perhaps will do so.

No single explanation will account for the prevalence, clarity, and force of the passions in the prose of the eighteenth century, but the presence of the same features in its paintings and plays surely accounts for much. Recent philosophers, sociologists, and literary critics have dealt, directly or indirectly, with the passions in ways that suggest other explanations for them or other considerations to be kept in mind in examining their undeniable force in the passages that we will encounter.

IV

Modern philosophers, especially those concerned with perception, epistemology, logic, and morality, continue the discussion of the passions which began, as we shall see in the next chapter, before Plato. The problems of motives and will, of mind and body, and of perception and evaluation have been neither solved nor abandoned. In the course of refuting previous systems and pointing out the errors and inadequacies of one another's schemes and accounts, several philosophers have insisted on useful distinctions between such entities as motives and intentions, on the one hand, and inclinations, agitations, propensities, moods, feelings, and occurrences, on the other. Others have offered such insights as that "causes are assigned to particular emotions, and objects to unspecified emotions" because "emotions are specified by their objects" and made such pertinent pronouncements as: "Only beings who are capable of manifesting a particular emotion are capable of experiencing it." Others have sought to introduce or elaborate the concept of intentionality, while a recent tendency to unite philosophy and biology has made a most intriguing contribution to the continuing discussion.[28] At the end of this chapter I turn to several works which, in combining philosophy with literature and intellectual history, offer several promising explanations and illuminations.

The practice of extracting philosophical implications from grammatical constructions and intuitions suggests that the discussion continues in seminar and Senior Common rooms:

> To feel anger may be to feel angry, but to feel a lump is not to feel lumpish;
>
> When a man is described as being both very avaricious and rather fond of gardening . . . ;
>
> If S is angry about the fact that p, then S's believing that p is sufficient for S to be angry, given some existing conditions that are not themselves sufficient for S to be angry.[29]

These investigations are usually based on general, ordinary locutions that anyone might say rather than on the exacting texts with which I have chosen to deal. They are not episodes but illustrations.

Gilbert Ryle's influential *The Concept of Mind* posits and condemns the ascribing of passions to the "Ghost in the Machine," an error it blames on Descartes and dismisses as a myth and a category mistake (83–115). For Ryle, episodes of passion (and volition) do not give us access to the "workings" of the mind or soul; they *constitute* those workings and are not, therefore, separable occurrences: "To put it quite dogmatically, the vain man never feels vain. . . . there is no special thrill or pang which we call a 'feeling of vanity.' Indeed, if there were such a recognisable specific feeling, and the vain man was constantly experiencing it, he would be the first instead of the last person to recognise how vain he was" (87; see also 58, 83). But this Ghost never haunted the writers dealt with in chapters 4–8. They repeatedly made their own and others' passions both "direct intimations of consciousness" and "objects of introspection" (115). Moreover, we seek access not to the workings of their minds but to the meanings of their prose, in which the passions form separable, observable, and impressive occurrences.

The passions have caught the attention of those social scientists who have turned their eyes to the past, many of whom connect them in one way or another with capitalism. Thus Hirschman has suggested that the idea of "countervailing" passions began in the seventeenth century with Bacon, continued in Spinoza, culminated in Helvetius and Montesquieu, and then devolved with Adam Smith into the doctrine of "interest."[30] This is an idea useful to those who then constructed, and to those who now study, political and economic systems rather than specific humanist texts; it is a notion perhaps more evident in French texts than English. Avarice has *always* been the least interesting of the passions to moralists, and none of these tracts does anything to make it more so. Hume withdrew an early, empty essay on it, and Gibbon's dismissal is both curt and representative: "If avarice were not the blindest of the human passions, the motives of Rufinus might excite our curiosity."[31]

Other social scientists have dealt suggestively with changes in the conventions of passion produced by the unsettling growth of the city and the resulting increase in encounters between strangers:

> By contrast, under a system of expression as the presentation of emotion, the man in public has an identity as an actor . . . , and this identity involves him and others in a social bond. Expression as a presentation of emotion is the actor's job. . . . When a culture shifts from believing in presentation of emotion to representation of it, so that individual experiences reported accurately come to seem expressive, then the public man loses a function, and so an identity. As he loses a meaningful identity, expression itself becomes less and less social.[32]

Such speculations require a different sense of "identity" and "role" than the one I think prevailed in the eighteenth century. They would, in any case, take us too far from the texts into which I propose to enter more closely. Such instability as was beginning to enter into "identity" constituted as yet only a concern, not a crisis. It did not extend to the passions, which, given their nature and their tradition, added constancy and clarity to that concern.[33]

Some of the social disruption of the period may, in fact, have consolidated the tradition of the passions, a tradition most available to those whose wealth and power was beginning to be called into question:

> But in performing such functions their visibility was formidable, just as their formidable mansions imposed their presence, apart from, but guarding over, the village or town. Their appearances have much of the studied self-consciousness of public theatre. The sword was discarded, except for ceremonial purposes; but the elaboration of wig and powder, ornamented clothing and canes, and even the rehearsed patrician gestures and the hauteur of bearing and expression, all were designed to exhibit authority to the plebs and to exact from them deference.[34]

The passions had always been most effectively articulated by and for a narrow band of the social structure. Now they had become even more important to those who belonged to that band and to those who, for whatever reason, "rehearsed" in prose the patrician gestures and expressions of that group.

The discussion of the passions has been continued along different lines by psychobiologists, whose alembics have dissolved the animal spirits into hormones and "hippocampal afterdischarges" and turned episodes of passion into sequences from which all the humanism has been siphoned off:

> A crude but not impossible instance might be, say, depression over the collapse of one's career: this might be identified as the sequence beginning with the belief that one's career has indeed collapsed, the quite strong preference that it hadn't, a consequent depletion of norepinephrine, the effects of that depletion upon the nervous system, consequent further changes in cognition . . . , followed by still further depletions of norepinephrine, and further effects of this still greater depletion, various portions of this sequence being accompanied, perhaps, by that unmistakable qualitative feel. Some emotions, of course, might consist of shorter, simpler sequences.[35]

Such investigations have yet to find an Addison to usher them into polite company. These and similar recent investigations, however intriguing in themselves, do not in any case seem applicable to the texts under investigation here.

At a rather different level of analysis, also with its own methods and vocabulary, the passions have succumbed to the speculations and experiments of sociologists: "When an elicitor is automatically appraised, the affect program is set off, and organized complex emotional responses begin, interference is still possible. The emotional responses may be interrupted, diminished, amplified, or masked with the appearance of another emotion."[36] Robert Solomon has discriminated thirty-four separate passions in the "emotional register" and has reached a conclusion that would surprise, and perhaps dismay, an eighteenth-century humanist, namely that the function of the emotions is the "maximization of self-esteem."[37] Attempts to quantify the passions had to await the present century and the confidence in numbers evident in such works as Lennart Levi, M.D.,

Emotions: Their Parameters and Measurement (New York: Raven Press, 1975), and Paul Ekman, ed., *Darwin and Facial Expression: A Century of Research in Review* (New York: Academic Press, 1973) and *Emotion in the Human Face,* 2d ed. (Cambridge: Cambridge University Press, 1982). Much of this research seems to follow from the James-Lange theory, that the emotions are only the perception of bodily processes.[38]

V

While I shall be content to have proven that the passions were more frequently, consistently, effectively, and intricately articulated in eighteenth-century prose than has previously been realized, I suspect that the reasons will be found in the humanistic conjunction of literature and philosophy rather than in the realm of the social sciences. For the writers of the eighteenth century, the passions constituted an inherent and essential component of human nature, one that had always been there. They produced instability, both psychological and social, but their definitions, components, and complications were preternaturally stable, offering invaluable possibilities of combination and development, possibilities both syntactic and moral. It was, I suggest, the universality and long tradition of the passions, together with their stable nature and unstabilizing effects, that led the writers of the eighteenth century to turn to them so often and so well.

Douglas Lane Patey's discussion of the passions as "probable signs" in logic and testimony is most helpful, especially the logical connection of "semiology" with medicine. When the passions become "diagnostic" signs, their links with the body on the one hand and with rhetorical strategies on the other will make them forceful as well as prevalent. Patey, however, goes beyond these "local matters of language and spectacle to larger concerns of character and action, where despite their more complex applications, the same procedures of relating effect to cause, of mediating body and spirit, obtain" (Patey, 98; 35–74). I think any movement away from these self-contained episodes to larger issues of unity and structure ought to be made, if at all, with great caution and due attention to the full force inherent in each episode. Only then should one move to larger, more remote concerns.

As the most dynamic, as well as consistent, feature of the Aristotelian and Scholastic philosophy of substances and essences, their dynamism carried the passions over into the new philosophy of rationalism and empiricism: "Their problem as writers, then, is to balance a profoundly individualistic epistemology with a cultural and literary habit of mind that suspects individuality and self-definition and insists upon the presence of an audience for meaningful discourse."[39] The passions offered writers an invaluable element in this discourse, a set of terms consistent, traditional, exchangeable, and individually verifiable. They could, because of their uniformity, do a lot more to circumvent "wayward individuality" than the tropes that John Richetti goes on to discuss and that eighteenth-century writers regarded somewhat circumspectly.

In this context, two works, Martha Nussbaum's *The Fragility of Goodness: Luck and Ethics in Greek Tragedy and Philosophy* and Alasdair MacIntyre's *After Virtue: A Study in Moral Theory* are extraordinarily useful and suggestive. Both combine the disciplined inquiry of philosophy with informed historical speculation and the inspection of texts. Their analyses of the Greek and Roman periods suggest to me that, by the eighteenth century, the passions had just enough abstraction, vividness, and complexity to retain their traditional semantic force. That force would be especially valuable in an age that sensed that most of its moral and other evaluative expressions were losing theirs.[40] The fragile "goodness" that Nussbaum delineated in Greek philosophy and tragedy and the evanescent "virtue" whose disappearance MacIntyre chronicled and lamented were entities at which the writers of the eighteenth century looked longingly. But they, too, knew that these abstractions were volatile, increasingly fragmentary, and perhaps even outmoded. If they were to be rescued and carried through the eighteenth century with moral and stylistic vigor, it might have to be by seizing upon their most potent component, the passions.

Thus the connections of the passions with the body attracted the physiologists, their connections with good and evil invigorated the moralists, their role in perception absorbed the empiricists, and their operations in the minds, breasts, or wherever of every civilized person (namely the reader) enabled, indeed obliged, writers to exploit them. The evaluative language of eighteenth-century culture became more incoherent, in the sense in which MacIntyre shows the same thing happening in Sophocles' Athens (131–36), but the language and the understanding of the passions retained the coherence and cogency acquired through many centuries of invocation and investigation.

These considerations may account for the noticeable unwillingness of eighteenth-century writers to use the passions as a means of prediction. These writers repeatedly invoke the passions to account for present or past actions but never suggest that, uniform and constant though they are, the passions can predict how a given person will act in any given set of circumstances. The closest anyone comes to predicting is the "suppositions" of Hume, and even these are made much more for the sake of argument than to predict actual behavior. The writers I have studied are all, it must be acknowledged, fairly conservative (even Hume in this respect). Whether this conservatism obliged them to retain and develop the received tradition of the passions or, equally possible, their conviction that, given the certain and well-understood existence of the passions as an essential component of human nature, conservatism was called for I cannot say.

In any case, the moral component of the passions resident in their origins as responses to good or evil made them especially attractive to the prose writers of the eighteenth century:

> For the history of the word "moral" cannot be told adequately apart from an account of the attempts to provide a rational justification for morality in that historical period—from say 1630 to 1850—when it acquired a sense at once general and specific. In that period "morality" became the name for that particular sphere in which rules of conduct which are neither theological nor legal nor aesthetic are allowed a cultural space of their own. It is only in the later seventeenth century and the eighteenth century, when this distinguishing of the moral from the theological, the legal and the aesthetic has become a received doctrine that the project of an independent rational justification of morality becomes not merely the concern of individual thinkers, but central to Northern European culture. [MacIntyre, 39]

The passions would have a considerable role to play in this justification. The component of good and evil made them detachable from specific, outmoding systems of philosophy and theology but still potent in energizing and validating nascent or partial systems. Furthermore, the passions allowed considerations of good and evil to be carried into society, where they were, or so these writers thought, much needed.

Once there the passions demonstrated their traditional strengths and inherent power. The still strong but shaking sense of social structure responded to and participated in every episode of passion. Just as "any adequate account of the virtues in heroic society would be impossible which divorced them from their context in its social structure" (MacIntyre, 123), so the passions, at a less abstract and much more visible level, are always measuring and asserting the relative power of self and others, as, for example, in reverence, friendship, and pity (responses to a superior, an equal, and an inferior, respectively). These and most of the other passions drew on and spoke to the enormous concern with social structure evident throughout eighteenth-century society and the essays and novels written for it, but they did so from within the nature and the language of the humans who constituted that society.

While other evaluative expressions lost their coherence and their force (whether through the decay of the institutions which authorized them, the attacks of the philosophers, the emphases of empiricism, the growth of a market economy, or some other force, we do not know), the passions retained their clarity, validity, and potency. Empiricism, for instance, will *always* be incompatible with teleology, but the passions were admirably constituted to function forcibly in both systems—not only to function but also to allow good writers to move convincingly from traditional teleological systems to empirical and social ones. Thus the "object" that had always been a component of each episode of passion became, with the new epistemology of empiricism, a place where passions and ideas converged. As such, the object became not just unavoidable but central to every episode, psychologically, morally, aesthetically, and syntactically.

Here I should perhaps insert a disclaimer, or an apology, for attempting to deal, throughout this book, with the passions as they affect *human* nature without attending to implications (or programs) of gender. Attention should sometime be paid to such issues as the Greek expectation that women should control their passions (the virtue of Sophrosyne), carried over into *The Spectator,* and to Hume's hope that women would help men to refine theirs.[41] I have elected, instead, to concentrate on the passions that men and women share and provoke as human beings while acknowledging that the analyses and exploitations I have studied were all conducted by spokesmen. All modern readers may regret that women were supposed to feel (and control) only those passions that belonged to a repertoire designated by a long and undeniably patriarchal tradition. It cannot have been easy or natural to live out one's life as the sane woman in the drawing room.

For these reasons, and doubtless for others as well, then, the passions exerted considerable force throughout the eighteenth century. They were clearly manifested in the paintings of the period, were convincingly performed in its plays, were frequently invoked in its poetry, and were intricately articulated in its prose, where, I assert, they will bear watching. If, as MacIntyre argues and Nussbaum demonstrates, the epic is the ideal narrative form for the ideals and characters of the heroic age, while tragedy (Sophoclean tragedy) works brilliantly for the more troubled selves and less coherent virtues of a classical age, the essay, the novel, and the historical narrative, it would seem to follow, become the essential forms for an age in which the social structures have also been called into question. These forms will also be the ones to exploit all of the possibilities of the passions, and on them I have chosen to concentrate.

2

CLASSICAL ANALYSES OF THE PASSIONS

T HE PASSIONS THAT FIGURE SO PROMINENTLY IN the prose of the eighteenth century had been refined by several thousand years of analysis and illustration at the hands of philosophers, theologians, and artists. The length, clarity, consistency, intricacy, and coherence that they drew from this tradition imparted force to every episode of the passions. I propose to review the tradition here, mentioning the major figures and issues in it and drawing attention to those features that survived in the works of the humanists of the seventeenth and eighteenth centuries. Of necessity, I have dealt with the tradition both selectively and derivatively, combining translations of primary materials with a judicious dependence on intellectual histories and surveys and individual commentaries.[1] While the discussion of the passions was continuous, various, and widespread, I have concentrated on Plato, Aristotle, the Stoics, Aquinas, and Descartes, slighting (indeed sometimes ignoring) important thinkers, schools, and eras and all of the early writers and artists who conveyed the tradition to a wider audience.[2]

I do not maintain that the writers of the eighteenth century turned directly to Zeno or Aquinas whenever they had occasion to write about envy or esteem, but I do think that it is evident, in passage after passage, that they had absorbed the tradition and expected their readers to have done likewise. Thus I offer a straightforward survey of the development of that tradition and of the components of the passions that remained constant in it. As we shall see, several concerns recur throughout the centuries, while most of the features that appeared early in the tradition survived through to the end. The connections between soul and body, for example, exercised every commentator from Plato to Hume, and the process of estimating the good and evil in every external stimulus was examined, or taken for granted, in every discussion of passion for several thousand years. Whether because of the quality of the insights of the early philosophers or the continuity of human nature, the classical passions operated in both the souls and the prose of the Enlightenment, and questions that vexed the early theorists continued to occupy the novelists and essayists of a later age.

HIPPOCRATES

It is convenient to attribute numerous treatises consolidating the theory of humours to the pragmatic physician Hippocrates.[3] The Hippocratic soul was very much responsive to its immediate environment, especially the weather, and to the regimen and diet of the body it inhabited. Hippocrates' emphasis on the body's effects on the soul and his attention to symptoms everywhere in the body informed all but the most cosmic of subsequent speculations. In addition, good health and temperament were matters of proportion among the four humours (Blood, Black Bile, Yellow Bile, and Phlegm). An excess in one of these raised or lowered the temperature of the brain and induced passion. Once Galen had established the connections between humours and temperaments, the four humours persisted into the Renaissance. Then they yielded slowly to the more intricate possibilities of the passions.

For Hippocrates, the brain was the primary organ, subject to physical changes that took place in the heart which produced differing quantities of air and blood in the veins and arteries. While Hippocrates had no concept whatsoever of nerves, he did think that the texture of the structures through which the changes in heat and moisture that produced passion were communicated partially determined both health and temperament. Thus excessive bile "flushes" the face and heats the brain, producing fear, while excessive phlegm cools the brain, producing anxiety and grief. Few other early analyses of the passions were equally systematic, but the rigid symp-

tomatic basis of the system rendered it less accurate and less exploitable than subsequent ones. A passage from Hippocrates' account of
leprosy reflects his symptomatic emphasis while proving that the
passions had been vividly articulated very early in the tradition:

> Men ought to know that from the brain, and from the brain
> only, arise our pleasures, joys, laughter and jests, as well as our
> sorrows, pains, griefs and tears. Through it, in particular, we
> think, see, hear, and distinguish the ugly from the beautiful,
> the bad from the good, the pleasant from the unpleasant, in
> some cases using custom as a test, in others perceiving them
> from their utility. It is the same thing which makes us mad or
> delirious, inspires us with dread and fear, whether by night or
> by day, brings sleeplessness, inopportune mistakes, aimless
> anxieties, absent-mindedness, and acts that are contrary to
> habit.[4]

Already the passions have divided themselves into responses to good
and evil, a division that invites both enumeration and antithesis
(pleasures/sorrows, joys/pains, laughter/grief, jests/tears). There is
evidence of an aesthetic component ("the ugly from the beautiful")
and the considerations of custom and utility that Hume, among
others, will develop so provocatively. Most important, however, is
the firm rooting of the mind in the body, evident in the correlation
of sleeplessness, mistakes, anxieties, and acts.

Hippocrates' emphasis on bodily symptoms was transmitted by
numerous subsequent commentators, most notably for our purposes
by Thomas Sydenham, "the English Hippocrates," of whom Samuel
Johnson wrote: "He could not but know that he rather restored than
invented most of his principles, and therefore could not but acknowledge the value of those writers whose doctrines he adopted
and enforced."[5]

After Hippocrates the Greeks treated the passions as they treated
every other subject of investigation, speculatively and argumen-
tatively. They were interested more in cosmic connections than in
introspection and more in political implications than in social consequences. Empedocles seems to have first enumerated the four elements and considered the physics of sensation, Democritus gave us
atoms and motion, and Pythagoras contributed mathematical forms

and a transmigrant soul. These thinkers seldom thought specifically about the passions, and when they did so, their speculations were absorbed and reshaped by Plato or Aristotle. Plato, for example, took much of his doctrine of pleasure and pain, a doctrine heavy with unexamined material causes, from Heraclitus, Empedocles, Democritus, and the cynics.[6]

PLATO

Plato's discussions of the passions, always metaphysical and distrustful, are early, influential, various, and contradictory. Wherever they appear, the passions interfere with the efforts of the soul to apprehend ideal forms. "Desire is a condition of the [Platonic] soul, and all desire is ultimately of one kind, the creature's recognition of incompleteness. Desire may be either physical or psychic in respect of its origin; but its satisfaction requires an idea of the object, and must therefore depend on the mind. The will . . . depends upon the mind's grasp of an end" (Brett, 92). Thus the passions figure in Plato's repeated efforts to relate pleasure to the good, but his compelling idealism, metaphysics, and ethics, and the weight of his name, made his contributions to psychology more influential than the profundity, consistency, or even plausibility of his analyses warranted. He was most fortunate, at least as far as the passions were concerned, in the quality of his interpreters, translators, and commentators, many of whom imparted new energy and clarity, along with considerable changes of direction and emphasis, to his theories. The place of the passions in the Platonic system was neither lofty nor significant; they were motes in the eye of the soul, to be looked through rather than at in its cosmic search for a transcendental and ideal beauty.

The soul in the *Phaedo* manifests a cognitive faculty with which it reaches for the truth, which it can do only when undisturbed by bodily sensations. As elsewhere in Plato, the disruptions of the soul extend well beyond the self and into the state: "Besides, the body fills us with loves and desires and fears and all sorts of fancies and a great deal of nonsense, with the result that we literally never get an opportunity to think at all about anything. Wars and revolutions and battles are due simply and solely to the body and its desires. All wars are undertaken for the acquisition of wealth, and the reason why we have to acquire wealth is the body, because we are slaves in its service."[7]

The sensations which disrupt the perceptions of the soul and the politics of the state are to be purged rather than controlled by discriminating management: "The true moral ideal, whether self-control or integrity or courage, is really a kind of purgation from all these emotions, and wisdom itself is a sort of purification" (51–52). Throughout the dialogues the Platonic soul struggles to rid itself of passions, which are always associated with the body and are therefore always distrusted.

In *The Republic,* as Robinson shows (36–39), the soul adds to the cognitive a moral capacity, a concern with good and evil, as a function of its affinity with justice. The other, more lasting and more vexing contribution of *The Republic,* the tripartite soul, seems to have been based, rather unfortunately, on the political model with which Plato works elsewhere in the text. The ratiocinative part of the soul is the one "whereby it reckons and reasons the rational" and the appetitive "that with which it loves, hungers, thirsts and feels the flutter and titillation of other desires." The "spirited" part, the one that most concerns us, mediates between the rational and the appetitive parts, imparting calculation and inhibition to the desires and disturbing the reason: "so also in the soul does there exist a third kind, this principle of high spirit, which is the helper of reason by nature unless it is corrupted by evil nurture" (*Republic* I.iv, 435–41; pp. 676–83).

The rest of *The Republic* treats these "high spirits" in conjunction with the virtues. They can, for example, impart greed to the guardians, while the "bravery" that is inculcated in the guardians must be very finely tuned to render them "gentle to their friends and harsh to their enemies" (II.375; p. 622). The passions disturb the state throughout the work: appetite and ambition break out in timocracy, envy leads to extravagance in oligarchy, and democracy is characterized by the indiscriminate indulgence of pleasure by great numbers of people (book 8). The extension of passions from soul to state provides richer narrative possibilities and subtler social insights than one usually finds in Plato, where there are more potent, metaphysical forces operating within and upon the human soul. The true philosopher is the man who has learned to cope with these desires of the soul: "So, when a man's desires have been taught to flow in the channel of learning and all that sort of thing, they will be concerned, I presume, with the pleasures of the soul in itself, and will be indifferent to those of which the body is the instrument, if the man is a true and not a sham philosopher" (VI.485; p. 722).

One other contribution of *The Republic* to the tradition that concerns us is the designation of wisdom, bravery, sobriety, and justice as the four principal virtues (IV.427–34). The connections between the passions and these virtues are murky and inconsistent—here and hereafter. The virtues were more independent, rational, and ideal than the passions. They stand above them, as the humours lay below them, morally, physiologically, and in the possibilities they offer the writer. Plato's virtues are predominantly civic and give rise to something very like "civic Platonism," to be controlled more by institutions and ideals than by analysis. For Plato, wisdom must outwit the passions without thinking too much about them.

The *Timaeus* (the text by which Plato was best known throughout the Middle Ages) offers a cosmic challenge of harmony and rationality to man—a challenge he can appreciate only if he overcomes the distortion of his passions, here partly sorted into pairs of opposites. Failure of the soul to achieve mastery over the passions will lead to reincarnation as a woman; continued failure will lead to successive subhuman reincarnations.[8] The *Timaeus* sets forth such physiology of the passions as Plato provides, without in the least diminishing the distrust:

> around this they proceeded to fashion a mortal body, and made it to be the vehicle of the soul, and constructed within the body a soul of another nature which was mortal, subject to terrible and irresistible affections—first of all, pleasure, the greatest incitement to evil; then, pain, which deters from good; also rashness and fear, two foolish counselors, anger hard to be appeased, and hope easily led astray—these they mingled with irrational sense and with all-daring love according to necessary laws, and so framed man. [69; p. 1193]

Here again the passions are consigned to a lesser, mortal soul, made hard to manage, indeed "irresistible," and listed without principles of classification or organization. Their dangerous power is amply acknowledged and their connections with pleasure/pain and good/ evil established, if not investigated.

Whereas the immortal soul is located in the head, because it is spherical, this "soul of another nature" occupies the breast. The passions gain access to the immortal soul by means of some fanciful biological geography involving the thorax and the neck, an isthmus supposed to make it easier to restrain them when they refuse to take orders from the "citadel" (70; p. 1193). They are caused and communicated by contractions and dilations in the veins of particles of various textures and sizes, which move through the veins in response to perceptions by the several senses (65–66; pp. 1189–90). In another passage, too long to quote, Plato dabbles Hippocratically with the chemistry and the physics of bile, whereby bitter, powerful liquids twist their way through the body in response to the heat generated in the heart by passion or the coolness of it effected by the agency of the lungs.[9]

While this early treatment of the physiology of the passions may be somewhat fanciful, it has been only marginally improved upon by subsequent accounts. We will return to the physiology of the passions as the occasion arises, but we will never find a satisfactory account of exactly what or how, or for that matter where, one "feels" when one is angry.

The struggles of the soul with the potency of desire find their most memorable expression in the *Phaedrus,* with its allegory of the charioteer and two horses, one white and obedient, the other "crooked of frame, . . . hot-blooded, . . . deaf, and hard to control with whip and goad" (253; pp. 499–500). The workings of the Platonic soul in the presence of beauty and the throes of desire are exquisite: "Next, with the passing of the shudder, a strange sweating and fever seizes him. For by reason of the stream of beauty entering in through his eyes there comes a warmth, whereby his soul's plumage is fostered, and with that warmth the roots of the wings are melted" (251; p. 497). Some of this excess returned to the tradition with the Neoplatonism of Ficino, which was especially influential in France (Levi, 42–51).

Other dialogues—the *Philebus,* for example—discuss the passions with varying degrees of thoroughness and consistency. All of the discussions subordinate them to other elements in the Platonic system. The subordination and the distrust combine to make the

Platonic discussion of the passion a peculiarly enervated one. The justice toward which the soul in *The Republic* works by education, institution, and eugenics is too abstract and too social to require investigation of the individual passions, while the good toward which the ideal soul reacts in the other Platonic dialogues is so cosmic that it must be apprehended by revelation rather than analysis, and only a few souls are equal to that task. Plato conferred poetry, potency, and distrust on the passions, but he left definition, analysis, and systematic classification to more pedestrian investigators.

ARISTOTLE

When Aristotle brought his background in biology and his practice in logic to bear on the Platonic passions, he stripped away their metaphysical clouds. In investigating the implications of the passions for psychology, ethics, rhetoric, politics, and logic, he subjected them to such repeated and extensive analysis and description that, by the time he had finished with them, they had begun to acquire solid definitions and to develop subtle distinctions and systematic relationships. They had become the tools and the topics of reasoned argument, and rigorous classification and systematic analysis became both possible and necessary.

Aristotle treated the passions with less distrust than Plato, he distinguished them more carefully from bodily sensations and drives, and he refined their connections with pleasure.[10] His passions are always seeking, with urgency and calculation, some "good"—ideally justice or friendship but often superiority or mere pleasure. His most important contributions to the tradition were the strengthening of the cognitive component in every passion and the refinement of the analysis of causes—the causes of passions and the passions as causes. He established a clear connection between emotional response and intelligent behavior on the one hand and emotional response and reasoned persuasion on the other. Two contributions, lasting but less valuable, were the doctrine of a "mean" between deficiency and excess in every passion and the refinement of the three-part model of the human soul.

I will concentrate on his causal and cognitive contributions and the doctrine of the mean, lingering over the analysis of passion in the *Nicomachean Ethics* and the *Rhetorica* and turning to the *De anima* only to sketch in the source of the medieval picture of the soul. Four long quotations will indicate something of the intricacy and the strength of Aristotle's analyses of this topic, analyses which others would follow for two thousand years. I have omitted most of those distinctions and examples that would concern none but an Aristotelian (for example, the reasons for grouping together the incontinent and the self-indulgent; *Nicomachean Ethics* 1148a).

For Aristotle the passions have causes and themselves become causes; he analyzed both processes. In the *Topics*, for example, he deals with the causes of anger, an analysis he extends and refines in the *Rhetorica*. Then, in the *Organon*, he puts anger vigorously and logically to work as the efficient cause and the middle term in a syllogism that unfolds the consequences of the Athenian attack on Sardis: "Let *A* be war, *B* unprovoked raiding, *C* the Athenians. Then *B*, unprovoked raiding, is true of *C*, the Athenians, and *A* is true of *B*, since men make war on the unjust aggressor. So *A*, having war waged upon them, is true of *B*, the initial aggressors, and *B* is true of *C*, the Athenians, who were the aggressors. Hence here too the cause—in this case the efficient cause—is the middle term."[11] The Platonic passions could not have survived such syllogistic rigors, much less participated as energetically in the workings of the instrument as "Anger" surely does here. A glance at the treatment of anger in book 4 of *The Republic* will prove this point.

A passion as clearly defined and as well understood as anger is here can contribute forcibly to the analysis of other passions. As Fortenbaugh says (15), "the efficient cause became a powerful tool for distinguishing the logical boundaries between related emotions." Indeed, the psychological and semantic possibilities inherent in the making (and constant remaking) of such distinctions enabled the passions to outlast the various psychological and moral systems in which they figured. Having survived the metaphysics of Plato and the logic of Aristotle, they were sturdy enough to come through the rigors and fancies to which the Stoics, the Schoolmen, and the French rationalists subjected them.

Aristotle's philosophy, and perhaps his temperament, led him to emphasize the "practical" emotions, those that produced direct action. This accounts, for example, for his continued interest in anger, which seeks revenge immediately. Shame, on the other hand, is impractical, as it cannot lead to action, though it may indirectly and eventually do some good as a check on unworthy desires. Similarly, indignation, as Aristotle analyses it, does not lead to moral choice or action, and pity is also in this sense impractical and not especially virtuous or interesting (Fortenbaugh, 79–83). These last three passions—shame, indignation, and pity—will assume greater power in the writers of the eighteenth century. Doubtless passions like anger were more frequent and forcible in the public debates, academic, legal, and political, which concerned Aristotle and Cicero, while shame and indignation recommended themselves to the social and moral occasions of the writers of the eighteenth century, and pity became Christianized rather than aestheticized.

Three assumptions underlie the discussion of the passions in the *Ethica Nicomachea,* one of the most influential of all texts in the tradition that concerns us: first, "that all knowledge and every pursuit aims at some good"; second, that the contemplation and pursuit of good is an "activity of the soul in accordance with virtue" which provides the man who is truly good and wise with all the pleasure he needs; and third, that the way to control passion is to aim at the "mean."[12] Implicit in all of these, and equally evident in the following central statement, is the assumption that the passions are temporary and transient states (that is, episodes) and that they are responsive to praise and blame—attributes that account for much of their appeal for moralists of every age:

Next we must consider what virtue is. Since things that are found in the soul are of three kinds—passions, faculties, states of character, virtue must be one of these. By passions I mean appetite, anger, fear, confidence, envy, joy, friendly feeling, hatred, longing, emulation, pity, and in general the feelings that are accompanied by pleasure or pain; by faculties the things in virtue of which we are said to be capable of feeling these, e.g. of becoming angry or being pained or feeling pity; by states of character the things in virtue of which we stand well or badly with reference to the passions, e.g. with reference to anger we stand badly if we feel it violently or too weakly, and well if we feel it moderately; and similarly with reference to the other passions. [1105b]

One might wish for a more comprehensive and better organized list of the passions, one in which the principles of inclusion and classification are both evident and instructive. As it stands, this one must be regarded as indicative rather than exhaustive or analytical. The offhand definition ("in general the feelings that are accompanied by pleasure or pain") treats pleasure and pain as the essential attributes and suggests that the passions were already so well established as to be recognized without analysis or elaboration. Everyone knew what they were, but no one knew quite what to make of them.

Such analysis as does appear in the *Nicomachean Ethics* takes the form of an attempt to indicate where the mean lies in each passion: "For instance, both fear and confidence and appetite and anger and pity and in general pleasure and pain may be felt both too much and too little, and in both cases not well; but to feel them at the right times, with reference to the right objects, towards the right people, and with the right motive, and in the right way, is what is both intermediate and best, and this is characteristic of virtue" (1106b). In this passage, the passions have taken on components they will retain for centuries: the moral element evident in the repeated "right," the essential stimulus of an "object," and the participation of others ("towards the right people"). But it soon became clear that it is simply not possible to establish, lexicographically, psychologically, or morally, a "mean" for every passion. The passions do not submit to arrangement in sets of three. [13]

Later in the *Ethics* Aristotle was obliged, perhaps by personal experience, to distinguish the hot tempered, who neither restrain nor retain their anger, from the sulky, who repress it. This analysis offers some of the physiology, psychology, and insight that one expects from Aristotle. In addition, the intricate considerations of duration and the comparisons of self and others that will figure so strongly later in the tradition are implicit here: "*Sulky* people are hard to appease, and retain their anger long; for they repress their passion. But it ceases when they retaliate; for revenge relieves them of their anger, producing in them pleasure instead of pain. If this does not happen they retain their burden; for owing to its not being obvious no one even [ever?] reasons with them, and to digest one's anger in oneself takes time" (1126a; notice that the pursuit of the mean is abandoned in the course of this analysis).

At the very end of the *Nicomachaean Ethics* (1179b), Aristotle mentions the capacity of the passions to interfere with argument—for him a major inconvenience. In the *Rhetorica,* the passions are treated in detail as one of three ways of persuasion, a moving alternative to logical and ethical means: "There are, then, these three means of effecting persuasion. The man who is to be in command of them must, it is clear, be able (1) to reason logically, (2) to understand human character and goodness in their various forms, and (3) to understand the emotions—that is, to name them and describe them, to know their causes and the way in which they are excited."[14]

While naming may be the simplest part of knowing, it is the one on which all the others depend, and in the *Rhetorica* the definitions and analyses (both strong and thorough) take precedence over any schematic list. The causes of the passions are good or bad qualities, usually in the actions of others, and the ways in which they are excited almost always depend primarily on the relative rank between those others and the self in which the passion is "stimulated."

The rhetorical occasion may account for the passions with which Aristotle chooses to deal as well as the emphasis on converting one passion into another—the conversions are all suggested for the sake of argument rather than as therapy or theory:

> The Emotions are all those feelings that so change men as to affect their judgements, and that are also attended by pain or pleasure. Such are anger, pity, fear and the like, with their opposites. We must arrange what we have to say about each of them under three heads. Take, for instance, the emotion of anger: here we must discover (1) what the state of mind of angry people is, (2) who the people are with whom they usually get angry, and (3) on what grounds they get angry with them. It is not enough to know one or even two of these points; unless we know all three, we shall be unable to arouse anger in any one. The same is true of the other emotions. [1378a]

Aristotle subjects seven pairs of passions to this three-part analysis: Anger and Calm, Friendship and Enmity, Fear and Confidence, Shame and Shamelessness, Kindness and Unkindness, Pity and Indignation, and Envy and Emulation. He shows no concern whatever with establishing a "mean" here—an indifference which considerably strengthens his analysis. The oppositions between the pairs are steady, almost automatic, so that he treats only one passion in each pair, dismissing the other somewhat perfunctorily ("So much for Shame; to understand Shamelessness, we need only consider the converse cases, and plainly we shall have all we need," 1385a).

The definitions of the various passions, thoroughly Aristotelian in their reliance on genus and differentia, contain strong hints of the elements to be developed in the ensuing analyses. Thus "anger may be defined as an impulse, accompanied by pain, to a conspicuous revenge for a conspicuous slight directed without justification towards what concerns oneself or towards what concerns one's friends" (1378a). This definition includes the essential element of pain, the incidental conspicuousness of both slight and revenge, and the element of interest: the slight must have been directed at one's self or one's friends; Aristotle does not permit the possibility of disinterested anger. The lines along which the analysis must be conducted are, in the best Aristotelian tradition, laid out in the definition with which one begins. The discussion of anger proceeds to the complex and intriguing component of comparative status, where each class represents a different relative stratification: "Further, [we are angry] with those who slight us before five classes of people: namely, (1) our rivals, (2) those whom we admire, (3) those whom we wish to admire us, (4) those for whom we feel reverence, (5) those who feel reverence for us" (1379b; see also the treatment of shame at 1384a).

The discrimination of differences between similar passions, one of the most fruitful and impressive features of the tradition, is at work in several of Aristotle's examples. Thus, in contrast to anger, hatred does not require a personal offense, may be directed against classes rather than individuals, cannot be cured by time, and is not accompanied by pain. And subtlest of all, "The one aims at giving pain to its object, the other at doing him harm; the angry man wants his victims to feel; the hater does not mind whether they feel or not" (1382a).

Distinctions such as this one between anger and hatred, complex, intricate, and full of both possibilities and truth, kept the tradition of the passions alive for centuries. Aquinas got into some absorbing tangles in trying to align this distinction with his assignment of hatred to the concupiscent and anger to the irascible passions. It contributed to his assumption that the cognitive soul apprehended universals, and the sensitive one particulars (*Summa theologiae,* Ia.2ae.29.6).

Book 2 of the *Rhetorica* concludes with a brief discussion of the passions to which several types of character are susceptible (1389a–90b): the youthful are quick tempered, hopeful, and angry, regulated more by moral feeling than by reason, and quick to pity others, while the elderly are cynical, small minded, selfish, cowardly, feeble, shameless, and querulous. When he reaches "Men in their Prime," Aristotle reverts to the idea of the "mean": "To put it generally, all the valuable qualities that youth and age divide between them are united in the prime of life, while all their excesses or defects are replaced by moderation and fitness" (1390b).

Those well versed in the Aristotelian system might be able to account for his comparative indifference to one component of the passions that later grew into considerable significance—the temporal one. He does mention such incidental temporal considerations as that "time puts an end to anger" (1380b) and that *recent* riches produce indignation (1387a). He dismisses the Platonic concern with motion because duration has nothing to do with pleasure, but he is not nearly as attentive as later theoreticians to the temporal component of each passion. On the other hand, his physics and cosmology obliged him to give considerable importance to motion, and his doctrine of the "unmoved mover" later became fused with theology rather than psychology. [15]

These and other rhetorical concerns with the passions were taken up by Cicero (*De inventione,* I.xxv, lv, II.lii–lvi; *De oratore,* II.xliv–xlv, III.lii, lix); the *Rhetorica ad Herennium* (book 3); Quintilian (*Institutes,* VI.ii, XI.iii); and Longinus (*On the Sublime*) and others. [16] I defer my remarks on the role of rhetoricians in the study of the passions until the next chapter.

Just as the *Rhetorica* kept the passions active for those who became its disciples, the *Poetics* so aestheticized the passions of pity and fear that they continued to fascinate dramatists and aesthetic theoreticians for centuries, though they became less complex and less interesting to moralists. The idea of catharsis has been plausibly connected with the "concocting out" of spirits in Hippocrates; others have discussed the ceremonial nature of the purification—an element that removes it from the tradition of the passions (Gardiner, 51–52; Ross, 282).

The *De anima* is the text by which Aristotle's three-part model of the human soul was conveyed to the Middle Ages. The links between passion and body are strong here—they are treated as movements of the heart (403a, 408b, 432b)—and the connections between movement and the soul are advanced with more clarity than elsewhere. The definition of passions as "enmattered formulable essences" (403a) might well stand as an emblem for the whole theory and manner of the *De anima*. Throughout the tract Aristotle distinguishes carefully between soul and mind, treating the mind as both indestructible and independent of the passions, whose peculiar property it is to make it possible for the soul to be moved by sensible things (406b, 414b). The three souls, nutritive-generative, sensitive, and rational, on which later ages so elaborated, are introduced (415b–32b). The passions inhabit the second of these and supply the soul with the possibility of movement and desires for objects that appear, and appeal, to it. They operate out of the heart. We will return to these three functions of the soul when we come to consider the elaborations they underwent in the hands of the Arabian doctors and the Scholiasts.[17]

THE STOICS

The original Stoics, Zeno, Cleanthes, Chrysippus, and Diogenes, left only fragments of their philosophy; the materials are not much better for later, divergent figures such as Paenates and Posidonius.[18] The Stoics were thus more fortunate than their philosophy would have allowed them to hope in both their opponents (Plutarch, Sextus Empiricus, and Galen) and their adherents (Seneca, Cicero, and Marcus Aurelius). The sad lucidity of the Stoic soul has always been known through the compilations and incidental quotations of writers such as these rather than from original theoretical tracts. Their doctrine was so striking and so coherent that there has been general agreement as to the Stoic treatment of the passions: they were to be extirpated as irrational perturbations of the soul.

This being the case, I offer a summary of essential tenets, omitting extensive quotations and passing over the central Stoic doctrines on Virtue and Nature to come at once to their essential and difficult, indeed infuriating, distinction of things into "morally good" and "morally indifferent" (Sandbach, 28–31). The large class of objects, actions, and events to which they steadily refused to allow the validity of passionate responses included poverty, illness, and the death of loved ones. This refusal stimulated the passions and the pens of numerous subsequent commentators. The Stoics analyzed the passions repeatedly, the better to eradicate them, and these analyses were of service even to those who were scandalized by the tenet of indifference.

The Stoics seem to have been the first philosophers to have concentrated on understanding the process of self-awareness and the recognition and analysis of the relationship between the self and others (Sandbach, 35; Rist 43–44). Inasmuch as they wanted only to eradicate the passions, the isolation of the component of self from the component of others within each passion (envy, for example) was of little moment to the Stoics, but those who later contended with the same passions would find this an essential distinction.

For the Stoics, as for other Greek philosophers, the passions were an incitement to action in response to the "presentation" of an object to the mind by one of the senses. The mind was, technically, at liberty to assent or not to such objects, but too often it assented unreasonably, unnaturally—in short, passionately. The Stoics divided these "unnatural" responses into four categories: fear; desire (strong desire—perhaps better translated as "lust"); mental pain; and mental pleasure. All of these classes represent, I repeat, excessive responses to morally indifferent objects, so that "desire" is felt for a supposed good that is actually morally indifferent (for example, wealth). The Stoics were especially good at distinguishing various species of desire to be extirpated, producing numerous elaborate lists of the passions. Andronicus of Rhodes, we are told, enumerated "twenty-seven kinds of appetite, thirteen of fear, five of joy, and twenty-five of sadness or grief." Cicero reproduced some of these subdivisions, evidently from Chrysippus, in book 4 of the *Tusculan Disputations;* such enumerations earned the Stoics their lasting reputation for pedantry.[19] Several Stoics wrote whole tracts on specific passions. Seneca, Plutarch, and Cicero, for example, all wrote, in general agreement and at considerable length, on anger. These tracts solidified later notions of these passions and hardened the attitudes of many toward the school that issued them.

The first pair of the four basic Stoic passions (fear/desire) is for imminent, rather than present, good and evil (*supposed* good and evil, they would insist), while the second pair (mental pain/mental pleasure) has to do with present instances. Though slight, this is the first systematic incorporation of a temporal component—another one, as we shall see, that was subject to much development. Mental pain, to indicate the contents of but one of the categories, included such passions as envy, jealousy, grief, and pity—each of which was separately analyzed but was similarly regarded. The presence of pity in this category raised many eyebrows over the centuries: "If sorrow or resentment are not to be felt at one's own sufferings, why should they be felt for those of another?" (Sandbach, 61–62). The person pitied has simply mistaken the moral significance of some object and must not be allowed to disturb someone else's judgment. The Stoics were careful, as subsequent commentators have not always been, to distinguish mental pleasures which they distrusted as passions from sensual physical pleasures, to which they were, theoretically, equally indifferent. (Archedemus compared sensual physical pleasures to the hairs in the armpit!).

To the four classes of passions to be extirpated, the Stoics added three good emotions: wish, a well-reasoned opposite to desire; avoidance, a well-reasoned opposite to fear; and joy, a well-reasoned enjoyment of true pleasure. There is no well-reasoned substitute for the fourth class, mental pain. Seeing no rational cause for distress, the Stoics did not need to posit a rational alternative to it. The humanists of the eighteenth century, as we shall see, diverted themselves with this tenet repeatedly.

Sometimes the episodic passions grew into, or grew out of, more permanent mental states, for example, anger and irascibility or greed and avarice, where the first of each pair is a passion, an irrational response to a single "presentation," and the second a proclivity or propensity of the mind or character and of much longer duration. The Stoics were not the last to try to distinguish fleeting passions from more permanent mental states, episodes from temperaments.

The Stoics agreed that the passions corrupted both perception and judgment, sometimes by distorting the estimate of an object's good or evil (for the Stoics such estimates were all but certain to be mistaken) and sometimes by disturbing the rational, natural response to that presentation. Their main contribution to the tradition with which we are concerned, in addition to provoking extensive clarification and rethinking by a long line of opponents, was to separate distorted perceptions of an object's nature from the estimate of good and evil inherent in that object.

From the time of Zeno, the Stoics had made perception a central issue in the quest for truth. The doctrine of "cataleptic phantasm" held that the mind was able to grasp external objects immediately and in their true nature, without any subjective modifications or limitations. The "New Academy" to which Cicero subscribed insisted that there were subjective limitations to perception but accepted "probable" calculations in the place of perceptive and moral certainty—anticipating, but never reaching, the extreme views on this subject put forth by Hume. Cicero held not that man was incapable of true perceptions but that he had no means by which to distinguish the true from the distorted.[20] These reservations about perception contributed considerably to the analysis of passions by requiring that stimulus be separated from response.

If passions depended on responses subject to the distortions of sensation as well as on judgments of the good or evil inherent in the objects that stimulated them, they could be analyzed, even by those who lacked sufficient "wisdom" to extirpate them. Thus the Stoics treated the passions, theoretically and rhetorically, as diseases of the soul and saw themselves as doctors, first analyzing and then curing these diseases. They replaced the Aristotelian mean with "apatheia"—the state of being without excessive responses to mistakenly supposed good or evil. Virtue for them was an absolute, indeed the only good, so they spurned the notion of a "mean" between excessive and inadequate response.[21] Assenting mildly and correctly to whatever his senses presented to him, the passionless sage of the Stoics would hold a stylus languidly, if at all. The eighteenth century wanted, and got, more passionate sages.

The Stoics differed among themselves on such matters as the existence of the soul after it was separated from the body and whether the passions contaminated the judgment by supervention, succession, replacement, or opposition. These differences were so dispassionately put forward that they strengthened the system rather than destroying it. Subsequent commentators were not inclined to probe the cracks in the Stoic monolith. When it came to physiology, the

Stoics depended on an unexamined and largely undeveloped spatial, nearly muscular, model of a soul governed by "pneuma," whereby the psyche swelled at the presentation of supposed good and shrank in the face of supposed evil. Some Stoics expanded the role of pneuma to constitute the entire soul and, indeed, regarded it as the soul of the universe, too.[22]

Having no social program of their own (Chrysippus said that bad politics would displease the gods and good politics the citizens), but counting a fair number of leaders among their students and adherents, the Stoic philosophers remained both influential and attractive for centuries. If they did not manage to eradicate the passions, or even to make them manageable, they at least succeeded in showing most of the elements of analysis that were essential for discussing them. The attention to perception and the adjusting of estimates of good and evil became more important than the division of passions into four basic classes or the innumerable subdivisions of those classes. These dispassionate analyses stimulated and disciplined more passionate and more sympathetic, that is, more human, responses.

CICERO

The most effective transmitter of the terms and theories we have considered was undoubtedly the digressive, eclectic, and declamatory Cicero, who admired and translated the *Timaeus,* subscribed generally to the teaching of the "New Academy," and maintained a blind Stoic as a resident member of his household.[23] Determined to discuss both (and often more) sides of every question (*Tusculan Disputations* II.3.9), Cicero incorporated these arguments and numerous others into the diffuse work he wrote to console himself for a turn in public events and a check to his own career. He attempted to find, with Antiochus, an intermediate philosophical position between the peripatetic mean and Stoic eradication of passion. In the process he set forth an assortment of arguments against fear of death, pain, and all sorts of "distress" (*aegritudo*), attaching innumerable examples of his own to an astonishing number of arguments drawn from others.

In bringing together and forward the views of others on the passions, Cicero clarified and extended some of the definitions of individual passions and supplied many examples of their working. And in his struggles to reconcile the separate systems with which he was familiar, he proved that "reason does grapple with the emotions and is concerned with things" (Hunt, 193). The passions had to be kept in mind by anyone who looked to Cicero for an account of classical ethics, philosophy, or psychology. Here is his version of the four Stoic passions, as an indication of his effectiveness as a transmitter:

> For as all disturbance is a movement of the soul either destitute of reason, or contemptuous of reason, or disobedient to reason, and as such a movement is provoked in two ways, either by an idea of good or idea of evil, we have four disturbances equally divided. For there are two proceeding from an idea of good, one of which is exuberant pleasure, that is to say, joy excited beyond measure by the idea of some great present good; the second is the intemperate longing for a supposed great good, and this longing is disobedient to reason, and may be rightly termed desire or lust. Therefore these two classes, exuberant pleasure and lust springing from the idea of good, disturb the soul just as the two remaining, fear and distress, cause disturbances by the idea of evil. For fear is the idea of a serious threatening evil and distress is the idea of a serious present evil.[24]

Cicero omits little and is correct about what he includes. Notice the orthodox Stoic clash between reason and passion, the assumption of good or evil, the estimation of the nearness of that good and evil, and, especially, the emphasis throughout on "disturbances" (*perturbationes*).

Not evident in this passage but enormously influential was Cicero's concern with, and illumination of, the social function of the passions and various devices for their social control. The *De officiis* assumes that the passions will respond to social control: "Somehow man's interests as a social creature were supposed to absorb his self-seeking impulses" (Hunt, 168). The same text introduces the notion of private property but without considering its connections with the passions (Hunt, 166–68; Sandbach, 123–25). The civic humanists of the Renaissance would see to those connections.

It would be difficult to decide which of the writers dealt with in chapters 4–8 was the most Ciceronian. *The Spectator* dropped his name repeatedly, Fielding turned to him for consolation, Hume took his catalogue of virtues from the *De officiis,* and Gibbon began his mastery of Roman literature with Cicero. Even Johnson admired his oratory and considered his ethics. Cicero's consolidation of the tradition of the passions was the most influential of all.

GALEN

The Hippocratic, Platonic, Aristotelian, and Stoic theories of the passions converge in the work of the irascible and encyclopaedic Galen, whose father had taken pains to educate him in each of these traditions.[25] He consolidated these, forcefully and logically, with his experience as surgeon to the gladiators at Pergamon and physician to the courts of Marcus Aurelius and Commodus. His work with the wounds of gladiators enabled him to modify the physiology of Aristotle, while his presence at court must have sharpened his eye for various manifestations of passion and workings of temperament. His own analytical powers were evidently considerable, and his physiological speculations determined the way the passions would be envisioned well into the Renaissance.

Galen filled each part of Aristotle's tripartite soul with its own decoction of the Stoic *pneuma.* The liver distills a vapor from the blood that governs nutrition, growth, and reproduction. The heart mixes this with air to produce "vital spirit," which courses through the veins to regulate vital functions. The brain further refines the vital spirit into "animal spirit," subtle enough to move through the arteries and to govern thought. For Galen the brain takes over some of the physiological powers that Aristotle had located in the heart, using the highly refined animal spirits as the source of three separate powers, or faculties: *phantasia, cogitatio,* and *memoria,* each of which occupies its own ventricle in the brain.[26]

Galen and his followers accommodated, without notable difficulty, *two* separate physiological systems, one based in the heart, with its blood vessels connected to all the extremities, and the other in the brain, which reached into the body by way of the spinal cord. The "pneuma" of Erisistratus and the Stoics passed between the two systems, relying on the increasing refinement, or "decoction," of spirit described above. This exchange of spirit, the crucial communication between body and soul, took place in the *rete mirabile,* a "marvelous network" of arteries at the base of the brain in oxen which Galen carried over, by analogy (and by mistake), into humans. Vesalius abolished this organ, reluctantly, in 1543, and transferred its function to the choroid plexus in the front ventricles. Until the discovery of electricity and the development of biochemistry made other theories of transferral possible, philosophers, doctors, and writers all used vital and animal spirits to ferry the passions back and forth between the body and the soul. While they were not always careful to associate "vital" spirits with the "sensitive" soul and "animal" spirits with the "rational" one, spirits continued to carry passions long after their places of derivation had been abandoned or relocated.

The spirits moved through the veins, which were assumed to be hollow tubes. While Galen could distinguish veins from arteries (Alexandrian anatomists had differentiated them and had located the ventricles of the brain by about 300 B.C.), he arbitrarily called "all blood vessels going from the liver, veins, and all those from the left ventricle of the heart, arteries" (Harvey, 10; Watson, 76) and "could not differentiate nerves from tendons" (Sarton, 47). This primitive, even confused, model worked for centuries, adapting itself, as we shall see in the next chapter, to various shifts in doctrine and developments in physiology. While the resumption of dissection by Vesalius and Paracelsus brought the findings of Galen under attack, his consolidation survived for several more centuries. There is, for example, much Galen in the physiology of Descartes (Riese, 125–27). Consider, in this context, the definition of "nervous" in Johnson's *Dictionary:* "Well-strung; strong; vigorous," and the supporting quotation from Pope's Homer, "What *nervous* arms he boasts, how firm his tread."[27]

Galen's "On the Passions of the Soul" was not as available or as influential as the scattered observations I have just summarized from elsewhere in his numerous works. Concentrating on anger, especially as manifested in the striking of slaves (an example dear to many classical philosophers) and greed, it suggests that one needs the help of someone else to see and name his own passions and recommends the "conscious verbalization" of what that observer sees (Riese, 112). He showed some awareness of the distinction of passions into "concupiscent" and "irascible" that we will take up shortly. Elsewhere this "eclectic dogmatist" demonstrated a predilection for the *Timaeus* and a willingness to draw upon the Peripatetics for theories of sensation and the "mean" (Sarton, 38, 71). His greatest contribution to the tradition, however—more influential even than his physiology—was his connection of the four temperaments to the Hippocratic humours, so that the sanguine were hot and moist, like the air; the choleric hot and dry, like fire; the phlegmatic cold and moist, like water; and the melancholic cold and dry, like earth (Baker, 278).

Others soon appropriated for the construction and analysis of character what for Galen had been primarily a matter of pathology. His strong theistic tone and his skill in demonstration combined with the plausibility and ingenuity of his works to impart lasting influence, practical as well as theoretical, to the system he compiled. After they had passed through the skilled hands of several Arab physicians, his works reached the Renaissance in Greek in the Aldine edition (Venice, 1525) and in six Latin translations (1517–1524) by Linacre.

AUGUSTINE

The works of Galen treated too much of the body and too little of the soul to recommend themselves to the theologians of the early Christian church. The saintly and scholastic writers did, however, deal with the passions. They kept the tradition alive and made three important contributions to it—two divisions and a connection: the division of the mind into separate "faculties," the division of passions into "concupiscent" and "irascible," and the connection of the passions to sin—a connection evident in the naming of the seven deadly ones. While the doctrines of the incorporation of Christ and an afterlife, as well as the moral offices soon assumed by the church, obliged them to consider the connections between body and soul repeatedly, they did so without theoretical rigor, empirical investigation, or noticeable success. Their contributions to the tradition were spiritual and rhetorical, rather than physiological and were not, ultimately, either very helpful or very influential.

The doctrines of sin and redemption and the peculiar division of soul and body that follows on such eschatological concerns govern the works of Paul and St. Augustine.[28] This is not the place to deal with the genius of Christianity for touching upon and speaking to the deepest human fears and hopes or its potent elevation of the passion of love. While the passions had little to contribute to the *theology* of salvation, early Christians (and later ones, too) specialized in a few simple passions:

> The early Christians . . . had a clear mandate from their master to carry the glad and simple tidings to the whole world. Until they succumbed to the exigencies of theology, dogma, and ecclesiastical administration they brought a new ethics and a new hope to the ancient world: God is love. The soul is holy, able to know God, and therefore of ultimate significance. Love, as it is interpreted in the fourth Gospel, is the primary fact of the universe which clarifies the relation between God and man. As God loves us, so must we love Him and each other. [Baker, 132]

But specialization is one thing and thoughtful analysis another. It is not to the early Christians that we must look for careful analyses of individual passions. The institutionalized ethics of the later church were interminably, rather than eternally, concerned with sins and penances and are even less resonant and less edifying (Baker, 178–79).

Augustine's analysis of the passions is of a different order altogether, informed throughout by his faith in introspection and revelation. He treats them as part of the incorporeal soul created (like everything else) by God. He posited a soul that acts upon the body by means of diverting the "animal spirits" to the three ventricles in the brain—one each for sense, motion, and memory. His extensive analysis of each of these functions of the soul makes him "implicitly the founder of faculty psychology"—a term which I pause to define as the ascription of the various operations of the soul or mind (memory, will, reason, and imagination) to separate powers, or "faculties," usually occupying separate organs, or at least locations, in the body. The passions do not figure extensively in the midst of his eternal concerns, though Augustine felt them acutely and transcribed their effects vividly. The self, whose consciousness he was among the first to establish, was meant to overcome them quickly, before they could contaminate the will and the love of God with which he identified that will. The human mind, as Augustine saw it, had more eternal entities to contemplate than the passions, and the human will had to submit to the Divine will without regard to experience or passion.[29]

The City of God, relying on Cicero, asserts that the Platonists, the Peripatetics, and the Stoics held essentially the same views of the passions (9.4), an opinion repeated, less testily, by Aquinas (*Summa theologiae,* Ia.2ae.24,3). Quibbles over the meanings of words annoyed Augustine, who does not doubt that the religious mind will become angry, sad, fearful, or piteous—his own had certainly done so. He insists that these and the other passions can be put "into keeping of the mind, to be so regulated and restrained as to be converted into servants of righteousness."[30] More willing to introspect than to attribute, Augustine acquits God of all passion, suggesting, rather scholastically, that the anger attributed to him in the Old Testament "is used to indicate the consequences of his vengeance and not any violent emotion on his part" (9.5; p. 121).

ARABIAN TRANSMITTERS

In turning briefly to Haly Abbas and Avicenna, I pass over such intriguing figures as Nemesius, Bishop of Emesa, sometimes credited with first dividing the passions into concupiscent and irascible; John Gerson, perhaps the first to fuse their cognitive and conative components; and Peter of Spain, "the psychological Pope" (John XXI), who published a history of psychology and conducted, or at least called for, psychological experiments.[31] Most of the discussion of the passions in this era was perfectly Scholastic, devoted to the making of distinctions and the multiplying of terms. Some of both survived for centuries after the makers and the multipliers had been discredited.

The Arabs, on the other hand, were primarily physicians who concentrated on the structure of the human body. They returned to the West a physiology of the passions more elaborate, and a little more accurate, than the one they had taken over from Galen. Haly Abbas set forth the essential process of the decoction of animal spirits from vital spirits in more detail than he had received it, but he retained the *rete mirabile,* which continued to mislead anatomists for centuries.

The vital spirit, made by the heart out of the coarser, "natural" spirit produced by the liver, carries the passions with it as it courses out into the body or back into the heart in response to external stimuli. Though produced by the vital spirit, the passions are, every philosopher insists, both capable of disturbing the more refined animal spirits which operate in the brain and subject to them. Haly

Abbas recommended treating one passion by stimulating its opposite, thus taking advantage of the direct connections between body and mind.[32] I must also mention, if only because its name is so resonant to readers of heroic couplets, the "chiasma." According to the astronomer and optician Alhazen, this is the place in the brain where the spirits concerned in vision cross and thus the place where comparison and judgment take place (Brett, 253).

Avicenna, whose *De anima* was translated into Latin in the twelfth century and was published in Venice in 1508, was more philosophical than Haly Abbas and more Aristotelian. He tried to restore primacy to the brain, and he extended the analysis of a *dispositio* to one passion or another, developing an especially elaborate correlation between the consistency of the blood and the susceptibility to anger, sorrow, and hatred and the workings of the imagination. Without going further into the intriguing details of this system, we should notice the essential contribution of the Arabic medico-philosophers in reestablishing the connections between body and mind and the effects of those connections on the workings of the passions. Avicenna also complicated the analysis of the sensitive soul, the home of the passions, and provided the first complete treatment of its inner senses. The *vis aestimativa,* the one that will most concern us, concerned him least, because it had no chamber, or ventricle, of its own. It became, nevertheless, essential to later theorists as the means whereby the soul attained an intellectual grasp of the objects presented to it. Finally, Avicenna encouraged the division of the passions into concupiscent and irascible. His analysis was taken over in its entirety by Thomas Aquinas, the last and the strongest exponent of the medieval tradition of the passions.

AQUINAS

For Augustine's introspection into his own passions, Aquinas substituted the works of Aristotle, recently recovered by way of the Arabs. He had direct access to the *De anima*—not perhaps, the most fortunate of texts—through the Latin translation of his friend William of Moerbeke.[33] Though both an academic and a clergyman, Aquinas was so dispassionate as to have been angry only twice in his life. Having few passions of his own to analyze, he worked as the diligent synthesizer of the systems of others. He struggled to reconcile faith and reason and to fuse the soul with the body, on which he made it depend for the sensory experience through which it could achieve blessedness: "In sensation, the organs belong to the body and the power to the soul; the whole process introduces the external world in all its detail to the incorporeal intellect, which deals in abstractions."[34]

Aquinas located the passions in the middle, sensitive, soul together with the organs of sensation and divided them according to Avicenna's elaboration of Aristotle: "One sees then that there are three pairs of emotions belonging to the affective orexis [D'Arcy's translation of *concupiscibilis*]: love and hatred; desire and aversion; pleasure and sadness. There are also three in the spirited orexis [*irascibilis*]: hope and despair; fear and courage; and anger, which has no contrary. The emotions therefore comprise eleven distinct species, six in the affective orexis and five in the spirited."[35] Table 1 represents this system schematically. The concupiscible passions are stimulated by objects that offer simple pleasure or pain; the irascible ones occur "when the soul finds that the acquisition of some good or the avoidance of some evil is possible only with difficulty, or even by fighting; it is beyond our ready power and control" and thus "arduous of attainment or avoidance" (23.1–2).

The absence of a contrary passion for anger, which this schematic diagram makes obvious, offers a reasonable example of what the Scholastic mind could do with such a scheme: the evil that stimulates anger is already at hand, so one cannot convert it into an arduous good. One must either capitulate, converting it into the concupiscible sadness, or attack it. There is no hope of converting it into a pleasurable good, and thus it has no contrary (23.3).

The most thorough and intricate system of differentiation and

Table 1. The Passions as Categorized by Aquinas

Concupiscible		Irascible	
Good	Evil	Good	Evil
Love	Hate	Hope	Despair
Desire	Aversion	Courage	Fear
Pleasure	Sadness	—	Anger

arrangement we have yet encountered, this one incorporates an estimation of good and evil, an assessment of difficulty, and, somewhat less explicitly, a temporal component, especially in the case of concupiscibles ("not yet possessed," "not yet befallen," "already," "no longer," "already in process," "is"). The analysis of irascible passions was especially complex: "Now an arduous good has a twofold aspect: *qua* good it attracts us, and arouses the emotion of hope; *qua* arduous it repels us, and arouses the emotion of despair" (23.2). I supply but one example of the numerous elaborate analyses the system gave rise to:

> If, however, we compare the spirited emotions with those affective emotions which involve movement, the latter clearly take precedence, for the former add something to them; just as the object of the spirited orexis adds to that of the affective the note of arduousness or difficulty. Hope adds to desire a certain drive, a buoyancy of spirit about winning the arduous good. Fear adds to aversion or disgust a sense of defeatism because the threatened evil will be hard to avoid.[36]

This distinction between concupiscent and irascible was too much even for some of the Schoolmen; Duns Scotus especially objected to it. And while it was of little interest to the moral essayists of the eighteenth century, it did serve to sharpen the definitions and to sustain many of the components of the tradition that served them so well.[37] Two other elements of Aquinas's system, the estimative and the conative, will be more important for our analysis.

The motion that constitutes so subtle a component of the irascible passions is carried over from Aristotle, where it was central to his teleological metaphysic. For Aquinas, whose metaphysic was one of existence rather than motion, the passions stimulated this motion physically rather than metaphysically. They provided "modifications" of both soul and body, and in doing so, they confirmed the existence, indicated the nature, and proved the power of that soul. And for Aquinas, one must add, they confirmed the wisdom of the Creator.[38]

The *vis aestimativa,* the power by which the soul assesses the property of good and evil in the objects it encounters, also taken over from Aristotle, and again by way of Avicenna, is the only power to which Aquinas assigns an organ. Through it the passions participate with both the reason and the will. They do so in this way: To the *vis aestimativa*, which responds to particular objects in the sensitive soul, human beings add a *vis cogitativa*, which reasons about universals in the rational soul. In this way the sensitive soul can move the will, but the will is free to embrace or reject the objects presented to it (*Summa theologiae* Ia.2ae.77,1–8). Thus the *Summa* becomes the ultimate source of the potent fusion of the cognitive and conative components of the passions, the capacity of the soul to estimate good and evil and to move toward one and away from the other.[39]

If the soul is dependent on sensation for all the information by which it works its way toward universals then those with more refined means of sensation will have more refined souls (Copleston, 156–57). For Aquinas, it is *good* for the soul to be united with the body, and the passions that emerge from and confirm that union are part of God's plan for mankind. The refinement of sensation, and thus of the passions, is part of the control of the passions by reason and an essential element of moral goodness (24.3). The implications for those more interested in social structure than in salvation were not lost on the essayists of the eighteenth century, especially those who combined refined sensation with the power of estimation in a potent concept they called "taste."

The *Summa* proceeds to a lengthy, Scholastic (the terms overlap) analysis of each of the eleven passions, setting forth such "points of inquiry" as which takes precedence and which are finite and infinite, as well as numerous and subtle contrasts in their objects, all with proofs and examples drawn from Aristotle, Augustine, and Scripture and with a strong emphasis on the innate and intense love of the good. These analyses entwine the passions in considerations of "material" and "pre-accidens" causes and in the connections between the intellect and the will. Aquinas, as I have mentioned, tried to align the notion of hatred as a concupiscent passion and anger as an irascible passion with his ingenious and necessary assumption that the cognitive soul apprehends universals and the sensitive one particulars (*Summa theologiae*, Ia.2ae.29,6).

Aquinas is most often associated with the elaboration and establishment of the division of passions into concupiscent and irascible and the analysis of love and will.[40] But as we proceed we will want to keep in mind his lively assessment of good and evil, his complex

Benjamin West, *The Death of General Wolfe*. Engraving by William
Woollett. Yale Center for British Art, Paul Mellon Collection.

Charles Le Brun, *The Tent of Darius: The Queens of Persia at the Feet of
Alexander*. Engraving by Simon Gribelin. Frontispiece to Collonel [*sic*]
Parsons' translation of Félibien's explanatory pamphlet (London, 1703).
By permission of the Houghton Library, Harvard University.

Charles Le Brun, "Fright," *Methode pour apprendre a dessiner les passions* (Amsterdam, 1702). The Elmer Belt Library of Vinciana, Art Library, University of California, Los Angeles.

32

Compation.

Fig. 40.

Charles Le Brun, "Compassion," *Methode pour apprendre a dessiner les passions* (Amsterdam, 1702). The Elmer Belt Library of Vinciana, Art Library, University of California, Los Angeles.

Raphael, *Elymas the Sorcerer Struck with Blindness*. Engraving by Elisha Kirkall. Yale Center for British Art, Paul Mellon Collection.

William Hogarth, *Mr. Garrick in the Character of Richard the III^d*. By permission of the Harvard Theatre Collection.

Sir Joshua Reynolds, *Sarah Siddons as "The Tragic Muse."* Engraving by
H. Dawe. Reproduced by permission of The Huntington Library, San
Marino, California.

Johann Zoffany, *Garrick as Abel Drugger, with Burton and Palmer, in "The Alchemist."* Engraving by J. Dixon. By permission of the Harvard Theatre Collection.

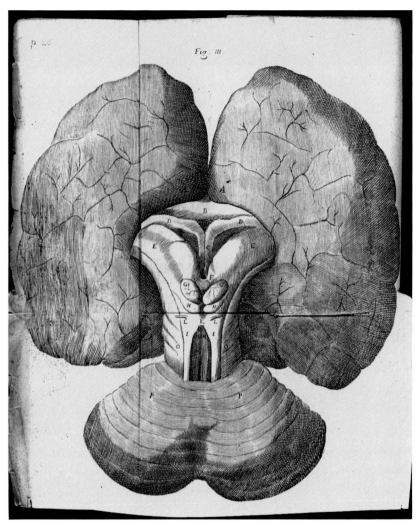

The human brain (drawn by Christopher Wren) from Thomas Willis, *Cerebri Anatome: Cui accessit Nervorum Descriptio et usus* (London, 1664). By permission of the William Andrews Clark Memorial Library.

TAB. IV.

1

James Parsons, "A Countenance of Scorn and Derision," *Human Physiognomy Explain'd: In the Crounian Lectures on Muscular Motion, a Supplement to the Philosophical Transactions of* 1747 (London, 1747).
Reproduced by permission of The Huntington Library, San Marino, California.

estimation of difficulty of attainment, and above all, the fusion of will and desire.

In leaving the Scholiasts, it seems worth suggesting, with Brett (266), that nominalism favors the senses and the feelings, while realism, in distinguishing implicitly between the soul and the body, eliminates them or at least seriously depreciates them. The tension resulting from this rigorous theoretical separation—a tension evident to those who felt passion as well as to those who wrote about it, disturbed the French rationalists and the British empiricists, who found, by observation, that the number of the passions had to be increased, the theory adjusted, and the mechanics refined. At a more practical level, the categories that the ancients had found so convenient and fruitful for interpreting all experience were especially useful in coping with states of mind. The passions came out of their Scholastic pigeonholes fraught with possibilities and potencies, entailed with half a dozen obligatory considerations, and well able to enter into certain well-established combinations. But given the medieval preoccupation with theology, the passions seemed too brief, too physical and social, to acquire great significance. What is an episode in the face of eternity? Even in the Renaissance, they assumed real significance only when they were exaggerated. It would remain for the prosaic and reasonable writers of the eighteenth century to develop all the possibilities that they had been so long in accumulating.

As yet, these possibilities were merely considerations. The symptomatic interrelationship between soul and body described by Hippocrates and the likelihood that any worldly object will disturb the moral and cognitive capacities of the Platonic soul intensified the distrust with which the passions were regarded, but the systematic treatment of Aristotle was, except for its physiology, of lasting value. After him, the passions could be defined, sorted, and applied. They could operate as causes and as constants in logic and motives in rhetoric. They could be, indeed would have to be, systematically distinguished from each other as well as intricately connected with one another and their circumstances. After Aristotle, in short, the passions became both the subject of repeated analysis and the means by which innumerable other analyses—of character, cause, fitness, and so forth—would have to be conducted.

The Stoics shifted the grounds for distrusting the passions and increased the possibilities for self-awareness and the attention to perception and time. Then Cicero consolidated the names and definitions and certified their power to disturb while suggesting that they might be subject to social control. Augustine contributed introspection and the faculties and emphasized the connections between passions and the will. Aquinas's contribution, if "contribution" is the word for it, of the categories concupiscent and irascible confirmed that the passions had acquired considerable complexity, and it opened up new possibilities for their schematic treatment. With him the component of good and evil became central, and the process of estimation crucial, but the mode of analysis became hopelessly and scholastically complex.

The physiology with which the passions entered the Renaissance was speculative (Plato), schematic (the tripartite soul), spirited (Galen, Haly Abbas), and somewhat confused, especially as to where the passions resided and by what means they were conveyed. Some of these considerations the Renaissance would ignore; others it would exaggerate.

3

QUICKENING FORCES: THEORETICAL AND PHYSIOLOGICAL MODIFICATIONS OF THE TRADITIONAL COMPONENTS

S THE DISCUSSION OF THE PASSIONS CONTIN-
ued into the Renaissance, the stubborn connections
between the passions and the will occupied, and de-
feated, the theorists, while those between the mind
and the body diverted the theorists and absorbed
the physiologists, yielding slowly, but never ultimately, to the re-
searches of the latter. The passions continued to be variously enumerated and divided, becoming more courtly on the one hand and
more physical on the other. The first meant that they were now to
be managed socially rather than politically or theologically, and the
second that they became discernible, almost measurable, forces
moving along paths that were increasingly more exactly visualized
and more confidently described. Much ingenuity went into both
elaborations and investigations. By 1700 the passions were better
understood, better regarded, and more effectively articulated than
ever before.

FRENCH THEORETICAL TREATISES

By the time they fell into the hands of the French theorists, the
passions had been described by Vives and Melanchthon, clarified by
Pomponazzi ("the pivot on which the whole system of academic
psychology turned to face in the new direction"),[1] and anatomized
by Vesalius. The theorists worked a priori, from an unlikely but
influential amalgamation of Platonism and Stoicism (effected in part
by Ficino), to which they added many Scholastic components. In

doing so they confronted, without solving, the problem of the ethical implications of the connections between the passions and the will: "It was to be the part played by the will in Scholastic ethics which particularly complicated the restatement of the Stoic theory of the passions in the late sixteenth century."[2] In constructing their theories and confronting such difficulties, these theorists kept the ideas, the vocabulary, and most of the considerations that we have just examined current throughout Europe for two more centuries.

Thus Guillaume du Vair attempted, not very successfully, to combine the four Stoic passions with the Scholastic list and divisions.[3] Nicolas Coeffeteau, on the other hand (*Tableau des Passions*, 1620), gave primacy to the concupiscible passions because their objects were both abstract and difficult of access—two qualities that fit smoothly into the prevalent *éthique de la gloire*. Coeffeteau's definition of passion as "a movement of the sensitive appetite, caused by the apprehension, or by the imagination of good or evil, which is followed by a change in the body, against the laws of nature" carried forward the "sensitive appetite" and its alternative responses to good and evil.[4] As the "against" and the "laws of nature" suggest, the revival of Stoicism induced Coeffeteau to exaggerate the Scholastic separation between the higher and lower parts of the soul and to posit a rational part absolutely independent of passion. He lodges the physical effects of passion ("followed by a change in the body") "unequivocally" in the heart, describes them at length, and divides and enumerates them exactly the way Aquinas did (Levi, 144–47). In the course of this discussion Coeffeteau mentions mercy, indignation, envy, and shame—passions that were not on the Scholastic list. Other French rationalists also found more than eleven passions to take into account. Thus Cureau de la Chambre added such mixtures of the original passions as shame, impudence, indignation, and jealousy (Levi, 251). The framework provided by the Scholastics supported all the passions the Stoics had enumerated while accepting, even inviting, such additions.

J.-F. Senault's equally influential *De l'usage des passions* (originally published in 1641 and frequently reprinted and translated) testifies, in its contents and its dedication to Cardinal Richelieu, to the increased courtliness of the passions. As Norman Bryson has observed, "Preoccupied with signs, the courtier is always deciphering and never experiencing without suspicion the influx of his sensations, since his ability to survive and the degree of his success equally depend on his virtuosity as a manipulator of signs."[5] Le Brun's emphasis on the eyebrow, discussed above in chapter 1, adds a note of punctuation to Bryson's discussion of the "ocularity" of the court (41–43), and Galen, it will be remembered, watched the passions at work at court at the same time that he was looking into the wounds of gladiators. We shall return to the increased courtliness of the passions in connection with the Elizabethans, *The Spectator,* and Gibbon. Associated with this phenomenon, and perhaps the best indication of the coherence and adaptability of the passions in this era, was their perversion into the ethic of *gloire.* Strictly not for export, this singularly French development separated the passions from innate response, external morality, and divine reason, and yoked them to an ethic of intense personal energy and strenuous development, one whose exaggeratedly courtly code included the "glorious crimes" at the heart of the tragedies of Corneille and Racine—works, as we have seen, published with frontispieces and performed with passions, by Le Brun. This ethic of *gloire* combined with renewed emphasis on *amour-estime* to produce, or at least to reflect, what Levi calls the "rationalist dilemma," the enormous theoretical difficulty of accounting for the appetitive function, once it had been separated from the rational function. That separation had been effected to make an uncontaminated reason at least theoretically possible: "The ethic is Cornelian, and concerns a word sacred to Corneille, to France, and to LeBrun: *gloire;* neither merit nor excellence by themselves, but these qualities caught in a double movement of display and recognition."[6]

Those French rationalists who treated the physiology of the passions at all did so either conservatively and indifferently or with a willingness to speculate and oversimplify. Cureau de la Chambre combined his training in medicine with his interest in morals to produce the physical determinism in *Les caractères des passions* (1640–1662), some of which underlies the second part of Le Brun's *Treatise,* on the correspondence between passions and the animals that a character resembles. "Its most important innovation is perhaps the simplification of the traditional teaching on the spirits so that Cureau could more easily explain how violent passion, diverting the spirits from their proper physiological role, could encompass the destruction of bodily heat."[7] He did this by ascribing some of the functions of the more refined "animal" spirits to the "vital" spirits—functions we have seen moved in this and the other direction previously. At the same time that he was making the spirits simple physical entities, other theorists, under the impetus of Neoplatonism, made them either wholly spiritual or wholly material. Though quite willing to simplify or revise the physiological scheme, they were not willing to incorporate the circulation of the blood into it. In the first place, Harvey was an Englishman, and in the second, the heart would then have become an involuntary organ, and the rationalist dilemma would collapse onto the heads of the materialists.[8]

There was, then, in all their physiology, an eagerness for materialism combined with a distaste for experiment and any but the most superficial observation. The great work in anatomy was done in the Italian universities, at Padua by Vesalius, Fallopio, and Fabricius (Harvey's teacher), while the convincing experiments in mechanics and microscopy were conducted in Italy by Malpighi and Borelli and at Oxford by men we shall consider shortly. The French were content to theorize along lines laid out long since but no longer tied to eternity. They were not deflected from them by the knife or the lens, to the evidence of which no one showed more sublime indifference than Descartes.

DESCARTES

His announced intention to write on the passions as though he were "treating of a matter which no one had ever touched on before" notwithstanding, and radical though his system might have been in other respects, even Descartes did not depart dramatically from the tradition we have been investigating.[9] The passions were central to his metaphysical preoccupations and crucial to his rigorous distinction between mind and body, but his theory retained all of the familiar components and solved none of the familiar problems. In fact, his dualism and his rationalism made some of the familiar problems more awkward than ever. The confusion and conservatism of his physiology, drawn almost entirely from Galen, challenged his ingenuity and diminished his influence. (Descartes was no more willing than other French theorists to accept the circulation of the blood, although he did acknowledge Harvey's work.)

Les passions de l'âme (1649), his last publication, was quickly translated into English as *The Passions of the Soule,* and was published by J. Martin and J. Ridley of London in 1650. It was not translated again until 1911. Its influence was enormous, partly because of the controversies aroused by Cartesian philosophy in general and partly because of effective simplifications of Le Brun. In the first part, Descartes makes a fancy, but not very convincing, distinction between the conceptual passions of the soul and the corporeal passions of the body. The soul is independent of the heat and movement of the body and of perceptions relating to objects outside us (Arts. 5, 25). The body communicates its feelings to the soul by means of the animal spirits, which make presentations in the pineal gland (Art. 34). The animal spirits, busier and more insistently material than ever, conduct all the transactions between the body and the brain: "But these very subtle parts of the blood form the animal spirits; and for this end they have no need to experience any other change in the brain, unless it be that they are separated from the other less subtle portions of the blood; for what I here name spirits are nothing but material bodies and their one peculiarity is that they are bodies of extreme minuteness and that they move very quickly like the particles of the flame which issues from a torch" (Art. 10).

This highly imaginative arrangement allowed the passions to be submitted effectively to the will without violating the duality of body and soul. (The submission of passion to will, though not, of course, the insistent duality, very much recalls the theories of Aquinas, whose influence on Descartes is the subject of much discussion; Watson, 137). Articles 45–47, too long to quote here, depict the "strife" between the passion and the will as fierce but ultimately imaginary.

Dismissing the Scholastic division into concupiscent and irascible because it requires the division of the soul into faculties (Art. 68), he identifies six "primitive" passions: "wonder, love, hate, desire, joy and sadness" (Art. 69). The presence of wonder (*l'admiration*) at the head of this list and the absence of an opposite for desire are its distinctive features. The emphasis on wonder, which reflects the Cartesian emphasis on the physical effects of the animal spirits, may be regarded as Descartes's major contribution to the tradition and a sure hallmark of his influence. The analysis of the responses of the body to new objects, and especially the separating of that response from the good or evil in the object, is both thorough and original (Arts. 70–78).

Yet Descartes's not very romantic description of the "primitive" passion of love indicates how firmly his treatment lies within the tradition:

> These observations, and many others which would be too lengthy to transcribe, have caused me to judge that when the understanding represents to itself some object of love, the impression which this reflection makes in the brain leads the animal spirits, by the nerves of the sixth part, towards the muscles which are around the intestines and stomach in the manner requisite to cause the juice of the food, which converts itself into new blood, to pass quickly towards the heart without stopping in the liver; and that being driven thither with more strength than any that is in the other parts of the body, it enters in greater abundance and excites there a stronger heat because it is coarser than that which has already been several times rarefied in passing and repassing through the heart. And this causes the spirits also to be sent to the brain, whose parts are coarser and more agitated than usual. And these spirits, fortifying the impression which the first thought of the agreeable object there makes, oblige the soul to pause over this reflection; and it is in this that the passion of love consists. [Art. 102]

The "observations" mentioned here depend on the materialistic emphasis and gave rise to careful consideration of the external signs of the passions, changes in color, tremors, laughter, tears, and sighs, all closely observed and fancifully explained (Arts. 112–35). In the course of this analysis Descartes mentions, in passing, the possibilities of dissimulation that these manifestations offer (Art. 113), a possibility that was to become one of the most fruitful of all components in the hands of English dramatists and novelists and a major concern of Diderot.

The distinction between these six "interior emotions" and the "particular" passions enumerated below is typically Cartesian and not very influential. Suffice it to say that these six are clearer than passions because less confused by the nerves and the body and depend more than passions on the worthiness of their objects. The rest of the tract enumerates and analyzes the "particular" passions, the ones that we have been considering all along. Having cut them off from the soul and confined them to the body, Descartes emphasizes the objects that stimulate them and the (highly fanciful) physiology that conveys those stimuli through the body. These stimuli are conveyed toward the pineal gland, where they are then presented to that other set of "real" passions. In fact, most of his analysis is given, as I have suggested, to the manifestations of this conveyance on the body itself—evidence of the materiality of the spirits.

The two emphases on external stimuli and mechanistic response throughout the body are far more important for our purposes than either the central dualism or the elaborate enumeration of "particular" passions, which I list here as an indication of the number and range of episodes now at the disposal of informed writers: esteem, disdain, generosity, pride, humility, veneration, hope, fear, jealousy, confidence, despair, irresolution, courage, emulation, cowardice, terror, remorse, scorn, envy, pity, self-satisfaction, repentance, favor, gratitude, indignation, anger, shame, disgust, regret, and gaiety (Arts. 54–67). This list is not exhaustive, Descartes adds; the passions on it are not all independent of one another, and some of them are, in fact, "virtues" or absences of passion—a blurring of distinctions that should be familiar from chapter 2. Nevertheless, the list does indicate what happens to the passions in the hands of a rationalist rather than a Scholiast: they multiply along well-established lines. The enumeration is distinguished by a shrewd analysis of self-esteem (Arts. 151–56) and the psychology of ridicule (178–81) as well as by a somewhat surprising tolerance for envy (182–84).

Here, representative in its subtlety, accuracy, conservatism, and emphasis on wonder, is Descartes's analysis of scorn:

Derision or scorn is a sort of joy mingled with hatred, which proceeds from our perceiving some small evil in a person whom we consider to be deserving of it; we have hatred for this evil, we have joy in seeing it in him who is deserving of it; and when that comes upon us unexpectedly, the surprise of wonder is the cause of our bursting into laughter, in accordance with what has been said above of the nature of laughter. But this evil must be small, for if it is great we cannot believe that he

who has it is deserving of it, unless when we are of a very evil
nature or bear much hatred towards him. [Art. 178]

The traditional elements of good/evil and self/others, the estimation of the amount of evil, and the renewed emphasis on physical
effects and manifestations are what matter in this enormously influential, but as far as the passions are concerned very traditional,
analysis.

The careful observations of Malebranche, who reverted to Augustine in response to the provocations of Descartes, attest to the
stimulation of his theorizing and the resiliency of the doctrine of the
spirits. For Malebranche the vital spirits took over some of the functions of the animal spirits, especially in their susceptibility to habit
and their role in memory. Working with exactly the same components but insisting on the fundamental unity between body and
mind, and between passion and idea, Spinoza constructed his own
elaborate system, one which connected the will very closely to the
appetite and in which the passions occupy a well-lit middle ground.
With Leibniz, Continental psychology, or rather, philosophy, set off
in earnest in the direction indicated by Descartes and confirmed by
Kant, leaving us to turn, at last, to Britain, and the empirical
tradition.[10]

Most of the elements of the passions that the French discussed
figured, less consistently but more vividly, in Elizabethan literature
and the few English theoretical tracts. Such innovations as the English introduced came either in the contents and workings of the
mind—workings which the traditional passions disturbed in the
traditional ways—or in the process of adapting the animal spirits to
the laws of Newtonian mechanics.

THE ELIZABETHANS

The classical, Scholastic, and French treatments concerned themselves more with the systems into which the passions were to fit
than with the human nature from which they emerged. In Elizabethan England, where the passions flourished along with most of
the other components of human nature, they figured frequently and
vigorously, if not always systematically, in poetry, plays, and treatises.[11] The Elizabethans included them eagerly and vividly in their

world picture, where they provided numerous opportunities for correspondences, analogies, and symbols. They came into it directly and in translations of classical and French theorists, and by way of the innumerable classical and contemporary texts, literary, political, and religious.[12]

Lomazzo's influential compendium, to cite but one example, was translated into English by Richard Haydocke as *A Tracte Containing the Artes of Curious Painting*. It devotes book 2 to "THE ACTIONS, GESTURES, SITUATION, DECORUM, MOTION, SPIRIT, AND GRACE OF PICTURES," combining Scholastic divisions and a Platonic fascination with motion and a Renaissance concern with the humours and the cosmos. It offers psychological analyses, instructions for depicting the passions, and incentives to do so (but no illustrations): "Thus whensoever we represent all these passions in a storie, together with their convenient & proper motions, we set forth that great variety, which worketh such delight & pleasure, that it allureth our mindes ynto it, with a sweete kind of compulsion."[13] Here is part of Lomazzo's entry on envy: "Envie (being a most cruell vexation of the minde, for an other mans good) causeth a man to drawe backe all his limmes, plucke in, and as it were shaddowe his eie-liddes, grinde his teeth, wry his mouth, turne himselfe with a passionate kinde of lookes, as if he meant to prie into other mens actions, being ever talking of other men" (27). The passions emerged from the Renaissance with new vividness and energy, completely adapted to the vernacular. They retained all their old analyses and developed some fresh possibilities. Their theological and political implications became somewhat muted, but the opportunities for social speculation, individual psychology, dramatic tension, poetic embellishment, and prosaic brooding were considerable.

The study of human nature had become important to the Renaissance with the help, or insistence, of educational theories, the printing press, and such emergent professions as that of the lawyer and the courtier, both of which revived the classical interest in the manipulation, manifestation, and rhetoric of the passions. Writers like Castiglione, Sir Thomas Elyot, Thomas Wilson, and Sir Philip Sidney sought to enable the courtier to flourish (rather than to save his soul) by instructing him in the management and display of the passions, with precepts and examples from the established tradition. The "ethics of gentility," of which Sir Philip Sidney was the embodiment, combined the corporeal emphasis evident in most Elizabethan treatments of the passions with the increased refinements of the Renaissance court, with incalculable results for psychology, society, and syntax.[14] The passions had become components to be put to work, rather than extirpated, though they retained their capacity to disturb the soul (especially the imagination) and to disrupt society (especially when they gained possession over the mind of a ruler or hero).

It would require another work longer than this one to study and illustrate the treatment of the passions in Elizabethan and Jacobean literature. I will content myself with a few passages from theoretical treatises and a mention of some places where the literature indicates how forceful and vivid they were for the Elizabethans. Consider, as representative in its theory, content, and manner, the following passage from Burton's *Anatomy of Melancholy*. The passage comes from a section (1.2.3) on the passions and their "instrument," the imagination, as one of the most potent causes of melancholy. In the course of this fantasia Burton quotes Plato, several Stoics, Cicero, the Old and New Testaments, Bernardus Penottus (!), Avicenna, Melanchthon, Vives, Bright, Wright, and several dozen others, all of whom he regarded as authorities:

> Thus in brief, to our imagination cometh, by the outward sense or memory, some object to be known (residing in the foremost part of the brain) which he, misconceiving or amplifying, presently communicates to the heart, the seat of all affections. The pure spirits forthwith flock from the brain to the heart by certain secret channels, and signify what good or bad object was presented; which immediately bends itself to prosecute or avoid it, and, withal, draweth with it other humours to help it. So in pleasure, concur great store of purer spirits; in sadness, much melancholy blood; in ire, choler. If the imagination be very apprehensive, intent, and violent, it sends great store of spirits to or from the heart, and makes a deeper impression and greater tumult; as the humours in the body be likewise prepared, and the temperature itself ill or well disposed, the passions are longer and stronger; so that the first step and fountain of all our grievances in this kind is *laesa imaginatio*, which, misinforming the heart, causeth all these

distemperatures, alteration and confusion, of spirits and humours; by means of which, so disturbed, concoction is hin-
dered, and the principal parts are much debilitated; as Dr.
Navarra well declared, being consulted by *Montanus* about a
melancholy Jew.[15]

All the familiar components are here, from the presentation of the
object to the mind in the front ventricle to the flocking to the heart
of pure spirits, with its attendant tumult and distemperature,
though the emphasis on corporeal effects strikes me as especially
Elizabethan. Here, typically, the humours, in which Elizabethan
writers generally showed more interest than in the passions, complicate the passions and lengthen their effects on the body by disturbing the process of "concoction."

As this passage makes clear, the "humours" were coarser, simpler,
and more organic determinants of character than the passions. The
four basic ones, though subject to numerous subdivisions, lacked
the intricate considerations of object, self and others, the calculations of difficulty of access, and the temporal component that made
the passions a more complex psychological and literary phenomenon. The humours could lengthen the disturbance of a passion and
make one more susceptible to some passions than to others, but they
lacked the differentiations and complications that made the passions
so much more fascinating. And they were much quicker than the
animal spirits to succumb to the discovery of the circulation of the
blood.

Burton's energetic eclecticism and his corporeal emphasis govern
the following passage, in which he hurries over ground we have
already traversed. Notice how well informed Burton was about the
details of the tradition we have just reviewed and how forcibly the
temporal component has begun to emerge from the various taxonomies. Burton alone provided a refresher course in the tradition of
the passions, and many of the writers of the eighteenth century
went to school to him:

Perturbations and passions which trouble the phantasy, though
they dwell between the confines of sense and reason, yet they
rather follow sense than reason, because they are drowned in
corporeal organs of sense. They are commonly reduced to two
inclinations, irascible and concupiscible. The Thomists sub-

divide them into eleven, six in the coveting, and five in the invading. Aristotle reduceth all to pleasure and pain, Plato to love and hatred, Vives to good and bad. If good, it is present, and then we absolutely joy and love; or to come, and then we desire and hope for it. If evil, we absolutely hate it; if present, it is sorrow; if to come, fear. These four passions Bernard compares to the wheels of a chariot, by which we are carried in this world. All other passions are subordinate unto these four, or six, as some will: love, joy, desire, hatred, sorrow, fear; the rest, as anger, envy, emulation, pride, jealousy, anxiety, mercy, shame, discontent, despair, ambition, avarice, etc., are reducible unto the first; and if they be immoderate, they consume the spirits, and melancholy is especially caused by them. [258]

Not content to reduce these (or anything else), Burton then annexes innumerable quotations, illustrations, and observations to all of the passions on his list, on his way to a digression on the miseries of scholars, whose love of learning he treats as a concupiscible passion.

Dissatisfied with the way in which they had been handled by Aristotle and the Stoics, Francis Bacon treated the passions with his customary freshness and eclecticism, and the usual English preference for example over theory:

But to speak the real truth, the poets and writers of history are the best doctors of this knowledge, where we may find painted forth with great life and dissected, how affections are kindled and excited, and how pacified and restrained, and how again contained from act and further degree; how they disclose themselves, though repressed and concealed; how they work; how they vary; how they are enwrapped one within another; how they fight and encounter one with another; and many other particularities of this kind; amongst which this last is of special use in moral and civil matters. [16]

Drawing on Vives, Bacon goes on, not very remarkably, to develop the role of custom in the management of the passions; to recommend care and realism in the choosing of their objects; and to conclude that "there seems to be a relation or conformity between the good of the mind and the good of the body" (30). He expands on these connections between mind and body in the *Sylva sylvarum,* accounting for the manifestations of fear, grief, joy, anger, displeasure, shame, pity, wonder, laughing, and lust by the operations of the spirits on the eyes, heart, and extremities: "Tears are caused by a contraction of the spirits of the brain; which contraction by consequence astringeth the moisture of the brain, and thereby sendeth tears into the eyes. And this contraction or compression causeth also wringing of the hands; for wringing is a gesture of expression of moisture" (2:568). The dualism evident here is partly Stoic and partly alchemical—the passions themselves being largely the former, and the spirits ("the agents and workmen that produce all the effects in the body," 10:83), the latter. The humours figure in the emphasis on moisture. [17]

Bacon ruminates on single passions in his *Essays* (Revenge, Envy, Love, Boldness, Suspicion, Ambition, Faction, Vain-glory, and Anger) and mentions them repeatedly elsewhere. I find especially intriguing his treatment of Desire in the Fable of Dionysius (*De sapiente veterum*, xxiv), where the fermentation goes beyond alchemy toward iatrochemistry, while the latency goes beyond the Stoics toward Freud. The distrust and some of the sensations look in the other direction, backward, toward Plato. Desire hides and is nourished in the lower part of the soul, "where it causes such prickings, pains, and depressions in the mind, that its resolutions and actions labour and limp with it. . . . It is notably said too that Bacchus came to life again after death. For the passions seem sometimes to be laid asleep and extinguished; but no trust can be placed in them, no not though they be buried; for give them matter and occasion, they rise up again." Equally prophetically, and more mischievously, Bacon adds, "It is true also that the Muses are seen in the train of Passion, there being scarce any passion which has not some branch of learning to flatter it" (6:742).

Having ventured into the literature of this age, one could turn unendingly to Marlowe, Shakespeare, Jonson, Donne, and a dozen others for any number of exhilarating passages dealing with the passions. I refer the reader to those writers and to such familiar, intricate, and revealing passages as Alma's "parlour" and the Bower of Bliss in book 2 of *The Faerie Queene* (where various powerful passions hold court, and the distinction between concupiscent and irascible is invoked), Hamlet's soliloquy on the player's passions (where their capacity to disturb and reveal is commingled with the equally disturbing and essentially dramatic possibility of feigning them), and book 9 of *Paradise Lost* (where Adam and Eve are beset and Satan betrayed, by passions).[18] Less well known but equally indicative exempla sometimes mentioned include the Senecan heroes of Chapman, Thomas Walkington's *The Optick Glasse of Humors* (1607), and my own favorite, Sir Philip Sidney's "The 7. Wonders of England," which compares the contents and workings of the mind with a provocative series of natural and man-made, but un-Courtly, wonders, from Stonehenge to a lake, a cave, and a wrecked ship. The passions figure, hauntingly but traditionally, in each analogy.[19]

David Bevington concludes his compelling account of "The Language of Gesture and Expression" in Shakespeare as follows:

> Shakespeare's characters do find something invaluably normative in the gestural language of emotion. The wearing of gesture is in the final analysis a function of role; the gesture must be appropriate and typical because the emotion itself is typical. In love, one acts out the experience of lovers everywhere; in grief, one shares communally with others not only the feelings of sorrow but the gestures through which it is expressed and relieved. *To come fully to terms with one's humanity* is neither to deny one's feelings nor to luxuriate in them, but rather *to respond as others have done* to fear, sorrow, or anger, and thus to grow more wholly aware of one's participation in the natural and social order. [98, my emphasis]

The passions, then, had become terms by which one could exhibit and explore humanity—one's own and that depicted in works of art. In the first place, they were constituted of shared, similar, and commensurate responses to kindred circumstances. In the second place, they had been so thoroughly honed by philosophers and moralists and envisioned by artists that they participated in, indeed partially constituted, "the natural and social order." The passions once occupied an essential intersection between public and private, and the prose of the eighteenth century would pass through this intersection repeatedly. Every time it did so, it would offer an episode of hope, anger, or envy, one's own or someone else's, and thus simultaneous participation in that social and natural order as well as one's own humanity. After a few more philosophers and physicians had taken the passions in hand, they would be able to function with sufficient intricacy and clarity to satisfy the most demanding writer and to inform the most inquiring reader.

Earlier ages had inspected and analyzed the private sensations and their implications for the life of the soul. Classical philosophers asked whether these sensations reflected or were conducive to the good life. The Scholiasts wondered about or asserted their implications for an afterlife. Then, even as physiologists began to follow the paths of these sensations, to locate their whereabouts and designate the organs and muscles whereby they did their work, moralists turned to their public manifestations and consequences. The episodes continued to operate in the same manner and under the same names, but now their public components became increasingly significant, in every sense of that word. Wolfe's passionate death, which would once have been of concern only to the philosopher and the orator, and later to the confessor, would now be able to provide rich material for both painter and actor, and also for the essayist, the historian, and their readers. Several philosophers, mechanical, empirical, and natural, had a voice in the final shaping of these materials. We turn now to them.

HOBBES

Thomas Hobbes, the loudest and most independent participant in the English discussion, came to philosophy late, by way of geometry, and by all accounts, out of fear, though he had the courage to think through and promulgate a disturbing doctrine of materialism, motion, and power.[20] Hobbes had felt his own passions, had studied those of Aristotle and Thucydides, and had seen those of his warring contemporaries, and the passions worried him. They were an essential but troublesome component of human nature. Without them the mind would not be put into motion, and thus would not exist, but with them the mind might well move too fast, too far, and in the wrong direction. The psychology which emerged from this peculiar source infuriated those concerned with theology, and continues to fascinate those concerned with the imagination:

> For the thoughts are to the desires, as scouts, and spies, to range abroad, and find the way to the things desired: all steadiness of the mind's motion, and all quickness of the same,

proceeding from thence: for as to have no desire, is to be dead: so to have weak passions, is dullness; and to have passions indifferently for everything, GIDDINESS, and *distraction;* and to have stronger and more vehement passions for anything, than is ordinarily seen in others, is that which men call MADNESS.[21]

Hobbes lists the objects of the passions as power, riches, knowledge, and honor and, typically and revealingly, reduces them all to the first, "For riches, knowledge, and honour, are but several sorts of power" (61). Thus the passions make some form of external arbitrary power necessary. But for Hobbes, and in dramatic contrast to *The Republic,* the passions themselves provide the basis on which this authority is established: "The desires, and other passions of man, are in themselves no sin. No more are the actions, that proceed from those passions, till they know a law that forbids them" (114; 1.13).

The ensuing treatment of the passions reflects the stubborn deductiveness of his method and the essential materialism of his philosophy. The physics of Galileo and the physiology of Harvey revived for Hobbes the Aristotelian emphasis on motion, to which he then attributed sensation, passion, mind, and will. The materialism that so alarmed his contemporaries is evident early in *Leviathan,* when he discusses the reciprocity between the dreaming mind and the sleeping body: "And hence it is that lying cold breedeth dreams of fear, and raiseth the thought and image of some fearful object, the motion from the brain to the inner parts and from the inner parts to the brain being reciprocal" (7–8; 1.2). This evocation fuses motion with materialism into an episode of fear that is vivid, understandable, and evocative. The mind and its sensations were very much alive in the system of Hobbes—so much so that he found the combination alarming; nevertheless, he was about to make them inseparable.

In chapter 6 of *Leviathan,* dealing specifically with the passions, Hobbes treats them as voluntary, or "animal" (as distinguished from "vital") motions, material responses to given objects, divided initially (and pointlessly for our purposes and perhaps for Hobbes's purposes as well) into appetite, aversion, and contempt. In the ensuing analysis he makes good and evil more relative than his predecessors had done—a relativity that requires the arbitrary power of the Commonwealth to settle. The pleasure and pain that underlie this good and evil are again a function of the motion of material spirits: "*conceptions* and *apparitions* are nothing *really*, but *motion* in some internal substance of the *head;* which motion *not stopping* there, but proceeding to the *heart,* of necessity must there either *help* or *hinder* the motion which is called *vital;* when it *helpeth,* it is called *delight, contentment,* or *pleasure,* which is nothing really but motion about the heart."[22]

For Hobbes the passions are essentially competitive; *Human Nature* includes a chart of the passions as a race in which "To endeavour to overtake the next, [is] *emulation;*" "Continually to be outgone, is *misery,*" "And to forsake the course, is to *die*" (4:53). In all of his analyses he attends to the "signs" of the passions, especially the means of manifesting power and submission, but he does not insist, in spite of his materialism, on the certainty of the connections between these signs and the passions within. The passions are not necessarily settled or uniform: "And because the constitution of a man's body is in continual mutation, it is impossible that all the same things should always cause in him the same appetites, and aversions: much less can all men consent, in the desire of almost any one and the same object" (*Leviathan* 1.6; 3:40–41).

The most original (and most resisted) of Hobbes's twists of the traditional components is his absorption of the will into motion as Deliberation—the last appetite:

When in the mind of man, appetites, and aversions, hopes, and fears, concerning one and the same thing, arise alternately; and divers good and evil consequences of the doing, or omitting the thing propounded, come successively into our thoughts; so that sometimes we have an appetite to it; sometimes an aversion from it; sometimes hope to be able to do it; sometimes despair, or fear to attempt it; the whole sum of desires, aversions, hopes and fears continued till the thing be either done, or thought impossible, is that we call DELIBERATION.[23]

The desires and fears of men might be neither uniform nor trustworthy, but their inner motions were powerful and their external consequences were alarming, so Hobbes counted on the Commonwealth to control them. The materialistic motion with which the passions began and the political control to which Hobbes wished to see them submit were his own contributions (though we have seen something of the former in Hippocrates and Aristotle and of the latter in Plato). He adapted other components, especially the comparative element and the connections with the will, to his own ends. The retention and consistency of so many of its elements in so many strikingly different systems attests to the strength and plausibility of the tradition from which these elements were drawn.

Bishop Edward Reynolds's long, thorough, clear, and derivative *A Treatise of the Passions and Faculties of the Soule of Man* (1640) combined examples drawn from Pliny, Plutarch, and Tacitus with Aristotelian theory and Aquinas's division into concupiscent and irascible. Here is part of his discussion of anger:

> The Fundamentall and Essentiall Cause of Anger, is Contempt from others meeting with the love of our selves. Whether it be disestimation and undervaluing of a mans person, or disappointment of his purposes, or slandering his good name, or any other way of casting injury on him, or any of these particulars being impaired (if by such on whom we may hope to receive revenge) doe worke not only Anxiety and Griefe (which is a motion of slight [?]) but hope also and desire to ease it selfe, if not in the recovery of its own losse, yet in the comfort of another mans.[24]

The consideration of self and others has assumed primacy, even over the estimation of good and evil, and the possibilities of complex recombinations have increased; otherwise, the analysis is quite traditional.

Walter Charleton's *Natural History of the Passions* (1674) shows that Descartes quickly found his way into English treatises and that his supposedly revolutionary doctrine blended effortlessly with the findings of Gassendi and Willis and the pneumatics of Galen. Charleton was especially eager to combine the discoveries of the anatomists with his belief in God:

> For, the *Passions* seem to be in the general, only certain Commotions of the Spirits and bloud, begun in the seat of the Imagination, propagated through the Pathetic nerves to the heart, and thence transmitted up again to the brain: and therefore whosoever would duly enquire into their nature, their first sources and resorts, their most remarkable differences, tides,

forces, symptoms, &C. will soon find himself under a necessity to begin at Anatomy, thence to learn the course of the bloud, the structure of the brain, the origin and productions of the nerves, the fabric of the heart with its pulses, and the wayes by which a reciprocal communication or mutual commerce is so swiftly effected, so continually maintain'd betwixt the Animal and Vital machines.[25]

The imagery of commerce has crept into the tradition, attesting to the exactness with which the cargo could be calculated and transported and the certainty with which it could now be delivered. There is perhaps also a renewed sense of the potential value and incentive of the passions.

LOCKE

The passions scarcely figure in John Locke's reasonable, sensible, and faithful investigation of the human mind. Acknowledging their power to prevail, he emphasizes, like a good empiricist, their dependence on objects, and, like a good Christian, their place in the divine scheme: "It has therefore pleased our Wise Creator, to annex to several Objects, and to the *Ideas* which we receive from them, as also to several of our Thoughts, a concomitant pleasure, and that in several Objects, to several degrees, that those Faculties which he had endowed us with, might not remain wholly idle, and unemploy'd by us."[26] Locke's disregard of the passions extends to his treatment of the vital spirits, which he treats tentatively and only in connection with perception and habit.

The passions are "Modes of Pleasure and Pain resulting in our Minds, from various Considerations of Good and Evil" (232–33; II.20). Locke lists ten of them, complex uneasinesses in the mind emanating from simple ideas of pleasure and pain: Love, Hatred, Desire, Joy, Sorrow, Hope, Fear, Despair, Anger, and Envy. He mentions the mixture in the last two of some "Considerations of our selves and others," the ways by which they influence the will, and the fact that there are many more he could discuss (231). But the passions do not detain Locke. His elimination of innate ideas may have opened the way for a "ruling passion," as Kenneth MacLean suggests, but I do not see the connection.[27] I do suggest that the division of matter into primary and secondary qualities made the passions dangerously dependent on the latter, with consequences for the ideas of good and evil that no one but materialists were willing to consider (until David Hume, to whom I devote chapter 5). After Locke, the passions submitted to analysis as if they were complex ideas, with separable components, essential circumstances, and causes and effects both immediate and remote. But they behaved, syntactically and physiologically, as if they were simple ideas. The combination was to prove most fruitful.

The sermonic compilation of Isaac Watts presented the standard blend of Aristotle and Descartes, buttressed by examples from the Bible and somewhat weakened by his own insipid theology. The power of the object to determine passion seems to have increased after the work of the empiricists, as the following two passages indicate: (1) "The *Passions* may be thus described: They are those sensible Commotions of our whole Nature, both Soul and Body, which are occasioned by the Perception of an Object according to some special Properties that belong to it" and (2) "The *Passions* keep all the natural Spirits and the Thoughts of the Mind strongly intent upon those Objects which excite them, and with a sudden call they awaken and excite all the Powers of Nature to act agreeably to them."[28] Watts never doubts that the properties of good and evil reside in the objects themselves or that they were put there by God.

Watts's specialty was passing judgment on each passion: "But there is a wicked Passion called *Envy,* which stands in direct Opposition to *Pity* and *Congratulation. Envy* takes Pleasure in seeing others made unhappy. . . . 'Tis a most hateful Passion or Temper of Mind, for 'tis not only odious to all others, but it wastes the very Life, and destroys the Comfort of him that carries it in his Bosom" (61–62). It was the duty of the Christian to moderate and subdue his passions. The traditional distinctions and connections between the passions and the body on the one hand and the will on the other had been neither wholly severed nor wholly understood even after two more centuries of theory and research:

Since the *Passions* are made up of the Ferments of the Blood, and the Commotions of animal Nature, as well as the Operations of the Mind, they do not lie entirely under the Command of the Will; we cannot stir up and suppress these Ferments of animal Nature by a sovereign Act of Volition when we please. But it may be done by the *Consideration of Truth:* For as the *Passions* are raised by *Perceptions of the Mind,* so we may by degrees raise or suppress the Passions, by applying our minds to the Perception of those Objects, or those Truths, which are suited to these Purposes. [97–98]

Watts has added the process of perception to the power of the object and kept sufficiently current with physiology to incorporate fermentation, but he has not solved the traditional problems that kept the discussion moving. While much of the force of the passions in the eighteenth century can be attributed directly to the authority of these and other works of philosophy, the rhetoricians of the day added some impetus to that force. It is both easy to overestimate and necessary to review that rhetorical impetus. Having done so, we will be in a position to consider the findings of physiology.

THE RHETORICIANS

Ever since Aristotle, rhetoricians had discussed and invoked the passions as one of the best understood, most readily available, and most effective means of persuasion. If they added little more than emphasis to the tradition, they added an enormous amount of that and thus served as both conservators and promulgators.[29] Such works as Thomas Wilson's *The Arte of Rhetorique* (1553) and John Ward's *A System of Oratory* (1759) consolidated the ideas and methods of Aristotle, Cicero, and Quintilian pertaining to the passions and delivered them to their respective centuries. They did so because it had long since been established that the passions figure significantly in nearly every stage of the rhetorical process and every category of rhetorical discourse. Here is a representative passage from John Ward, full of echoes of Aristotle, Cicero, and Quintilian:

But rhetoric not only directs to those arguments, which are proper to convince the mind; but also considers the various passions and interests of mankind, with the bias they receive from temper, education, converse, and other circumstances of life; and teaches how to fetch such reasons from each of these, as are of the greatest force in persuasion. It is plain therefore that rhetoric not only supplies us with more heads of *invention* than logic, but that they very much differ from each other in the use and design of them; the one imploying them only as principles of knowledge, but the other chiefly as motives to action.[30]

That passage considers the passions of the audience and mentions their usefulness in "Discovery" (a.k.a. "Hermeneutics" and "Invention"). Numerous others could be adduced to testify to the main concern of seventeenth-century rhetoricians, "Style," and to that of eighteenth-century locutionists, "Delivery." Longinus, recently reintroduced and enthusiastically received, had championed figurative language as passionately sublime and had succeeded so well that Sprat and the Royal Society opposed all figurative language, while the concerns of the elocutionists with voice and gesture owe a good deal to Le Brun.

The passions had been run through the "Topics" or "Commonplaces" by rhetoricians for so many centuries that they must have followed the routes of their own accord. The components that we have seen them acquiring seem to have been developed for, if not, indeed, derived from, these topics. I cite Ward's essentially Ciceronian list of the "Common Topics" to show how effortlessly the passions could process through the Topics: "Definition, Enumeration, Notation, Genus, Species, Antecedents, Consequents, Adjuncts, Conjugates, Cause, Effect, Contraries, Opposites, Similitude, Dissimilitude, and Comparison."[31] Every "place" on that list lends itself to the development of some component of the passions, and many of those components seem to be responses to one or more of those places. The "Common Topic" of "circumstance," surprisingly missing from Ward's list, yielded up, or enriched, many episodes of passion.[32] Of the "special topics," the worthy and the good, the *quale sit* (motives), and *all* the special topics for epideictic rhetoric called for considerations of the passions. Long after speakers and writers had abandoned the topics as mechanical, exhausted, and discredited, the passions continued to offer possibilities or obligations along lines that led back to one or another of these common places.

In themselves, however, the derivative truths of the rhetoricians could not have kept the passions current in the eighteenth century. The speculations of the empirical philosophers combined with the findings of the physiologists to make these episodes a little more certain and a little more lively. The exaggerated materialism of the metaphysical theories of Descartes and Hobbes preceded the materialistic physiologies that seemed for a time to vindicate them, almost, indeed, to have been called into being by them. Theory and physiology vindicated one another until dramatic discoveries in the latter finally eliminated the faculties and the animal spirits. It being no longer crucial that the passions be found immaterial, they were much more susceptible to the substantial findings of the physiologists, findings which did not make them unsuitable for the speculations of the theorists or the essays of moralists and humanists.[33]

PHYSIOLOGY

Hippocrates had sought to find the place of human physiology in the cosmic order, and Galen had attempted to identify the physiological functions of the various parts of the body. The physiologists of the seventeenth century, in turn, tried to accommodate the traditional doctrine of the passions to the findings of the Paduan anatomists and the circulation of the blood. They had also to consider the mysterious reactions of iatro- [= medicinal] chemistry and the forceful motions of iatro-mechanics. This they did by extending the atomism of Democritus and Epicurus, as revived by Gassendi, imported by Charleton, and supported by Boyle. The last of these predicted, quite rightly, "Those great transactions which make such a noise in the World, and establish Monarchies or ruin Empires, reach not so many Persons with their Influence as do the Theories of Physiology."[34]

It took longer than Boyle had anticipated for these changes to emerge from the laboratory, and when they did so they did not produce quite the results that he had expected or wanted. Nevertheless, the writers of the eighteenth century were able to effect an accommodation with surprisingly little adjustment. The clarity that the passions had acquired in the process of analysis as elements of matter and form equipped them to serve as dynamic particles in an age when only those elements adaptable to Newtonianism could survive. And the components of volition and estimation were so firmly attached to them that they were not detachable by even the most vehement mechanical philosophers. Perhaps also because they came by way of classical literature as well as theoretical treatises, the passions retained their clarity in spite of such disruptions as the disappearance of the chambers where they had been supposed to originate and reside, successive revisions of the passageways through which they were supposed to travel, and dramatic changes in the substances by which they were thought to have been conveyed.

Writers continued to name, analyze, and depict the passions as they had always been named, analyzed, and depicted, without worrying overmuch about the findings and quarrels of physiologists. For example, the ventricles of the brain, central to all medieval doctrines of the passions, underwent drastic changes in this period, but they survived in literature and a few theories long after anatomy had done away with them. The tradition required places for the spirits to reside and operate, and it was rhetorically and morally convenient to divide the soul into faculties, even though Vesalius had discredited the ventricles by finding similar structures in the brains of many animals, most notably the ass. Even Willis, who did most to transfer the functional centers of the brain from its structures to the substances that surrounded them, retained the ventricles as mental drainage pits. At the same time, the ventricles of the heart gained new but complicated importance with the discovery of the circulation of the blood and Malpighi's proof that the left ventricle of the heart was full of blood rather than spirits. In fact, the blood itself took over most of the physiological functions of the spirits, which became little more than refinements of the blood, no longer needing chambers, or faculties, in which to operate.[35]

The same adaptability is evident in Kepler's relocating of the convergence of rays from the crystalline lens to the retina, which merely moved the point at which the sight impinged on the animal spirits (Brett, 339–40). One way or another, the animal spirits were remarkably persistent. As Philopirio, Mandeville's spokesman and a doctor generally unimpressed by either theory or research, observed: "That there are Animal Spirits, has been the Opinion of all ages Ancient and Modern, all Schools of Physicians, all Sects of Philosophers have agreed in this; and whatever they have differ'd from one another, here they have been unanimous."[36] Perhaps the professional *terminus ad quem* for the animal spirits may be set at 1740, when Cheyne, who had earlier employed them, adopted the assumption that vibration was the operant principle, without aether, fluid, or corpuscles. Even then, writers were not quick to give up the animal spirits.

While Galen supplies most of the physiology needed to read the passages in the chapters that follow, writers and artists that had previously drawn on the findings of cosmologists and theologians began now to absorb those of anatomists and physiologists. Only when physiology fell into the hands of chemists, biologists, and physicists and thus became a matter of hormones and synapses did its contributions become too exact and too technical to continue to strengthen the tradition of the passions. With these discoveries, as we have seen, physiology deserted the library and the drawing room for the laboratory and the lecture hall.

William Harvey's discovery of the circulation of the blood represents the culmination of the explanation of organic functions based on anatomical observation. His *Exercitatio Anatomica de Motu Cordis et Sanguinis in Animalibus* (1628) attends with impressive single-mindedness to the structure of the arteries and veins and the organs they connect. It mentions, in passing, the envy of his detractors and the capacity of cold, alarm, and horror to hasten the return of blood to the heart. Ultimately, however, "his demonstration was the death-blow to the doctrine of the 'spirits.' "[37] The circulating blood now was understood to leave the heart by way of the arteries, which had previously been supposed to carry only spirits (though Galen had, as Harvey mentions, found blood in the arteries), to return to it through the veins, and to pass from one ventricle of the heart to the other not directly, through invisible pores in the septum, but indirectly, through the lungs.[38]

Although Harvey had produced the spirits "inseparable" from the blood, there were numerous ingenious attempts to explain some kind of separation, either chemical or mechanical, in order to retain the traditional means of transmitting sensations, responses, and muscular instructions. The chemical derivations depended on fermentation, the mechanical on increasingly minute particles which obeyed Newtonian laws and traveled along passageways that resembled veins and arteries but were much smaller. By one or another of these means, the animal spirits conveyed the traditional passions into the nineteenth century with renewed clarity and vigor.[39]

Harvey's doctrine had to overcome both inertia and anxiety, the first in the form of the enormous and continuous appeal of Galen, of whose writings the Renaissance prepared nearly five hundred editions (Rothschuh, 48). The anxiety came from within the College of Physicians, who had much invested in Galen (Keynes, 381–82), and from those theologians who could see the effects on spirit and soul of the increasing materialism of the age. The animal spirits, which Galen had depended upon to refute the increasing materialism of the Greeks, continued to be useful for many theorists, not all of them churchmen. It must be pointed out that this increasing mechanism was not incompatible with the medieval and animistic conception of a universe and a human nature created and informed by divine goodness: "The microscope revealed a world no less wonderful than that envisioned by the peripatetics and the schoolmen."[40] While the blood lent itself to these materialistic interpretations, Harvey himself remained a vitalist.

Descartes, as we have seen, was a willful and influential (though strictly theoretical) champion of the spirits and found much work for them to do in his system. Needing, for his philosophy as well as his physiology, a source of heat, an isolatable will, and an uncompromising materialism, he turned the heart into a teakettle instead of a pump, one which propelled an aqueous serum through the body by means of a fire that did not burn, resisting, all the while, the essential innovation of circulation.[41] Other investigators treated the blood less speculatively and developed an understanding of the forces and passages by which it *could* transmit sensations, passions, and instructions through the body. Thus Borelli's nervous fluid flowed through tissues described by Malpighi (like Boerhaave a fellow of the Royal Society). In their laboratories the spirits became corporeal, if not mechanical, and better fitted than ever to convey the passions. These and other findings required new explanations of the functions of the heart, muscles, lungs, and liver and new sources and destinations for bodily fluids.[42] But the men and women who awaited these explanations continued to feel envy, anger, and veneration and to write about them as if they still felt them along traditional lines.

The center of this activity in England was unquestionably Oxford, where much of the work of the "new philosophy" was done and discussed. Harvey was warden of Merton and Thomas Willis Sedleian Professor of Natural Philosophy.[43] Thomas Willis's appointment obliged him to lecture twice a week on Aristotle's physics, biology, and psychology, but in fact he promulgated early versions of the theories he later published as *Cerebri anatome* (1664, with illustrations by Christopher Wren). The lectures survive, in one of the wonderful coincidences of intellectual history, in the notes of a diligent, attentive, and methodical student named John Locke.[44] Given to figurative language and compelling, but often misleading, analogies, Willis associated blood with flame and light, which equipped it splendidly to produce animal spirits and to transmit impulses and passions along solid tissues. He exercised considerable ingenuity in finding ways for the vital spirits to interact with the animal ones, availing himself of analogies with ivy, dew, and fermentation, culminating in a "Nervous Juice" full of properties that were as nearly magical as mechanical (Hall, 1:317–18). The vividness of the farmhouse in many of his analogies, the chemical residue of his replacing the four humours with five chemical agents, and a refreshing combination of intelligence, originality, and common sense mark Willis's work, but it is not always possible to distinguish his figures from those generated by Martinus Scriblerus and Swift's more extravagant physiologists.[45] Nevertheless, it was Willis who finally eliminated the *rete mirabile*, scoffed at the notion that the Pineal gland was the seat of the soul, and established the means and significance of cerebral *circulation*. His major contribution clarified the question of the connection between passion and will by connecting the animal spirits and voluntary motion to the cerebrum and involuntary actions like respiration, digestion, and excretion to the cerebellum. He also discovered reflexes and came very near to depicting the animal spirits as hormones. (His suggestion that they did their work by exploding, which seemed so implausible to his contemporaries, no longer seems very farfetched.)[46]

Willis's style and method are distinctive, as these passages prove: "This causes frequent movements of the lungs, which noisily blow out the soot and vapours along with the breath," and "Vinegary spirits are made of salt elevated and united with spirits. They are of two kinds: first the milder, like spirits of distilled vinegar and spirits of the heavier woods such as box and guiacum."[47] Willis devised an elaborate account of the ways in which the animal spirits affected the muscles, an account evident in the next quotation (and perhaps underlying the passage from James Parsons below). It is a translation of Locke's notes, an example of Willis's physiological emphasis, and yet another instance of the updating of a long tradition:

> Thus when the spirits in the cerebrum are excited by some pleasant or disagreeable object into a sensation of pain or pleasure they communicate the impression of this idea and motion upon the spirits in the cerebellum which minister to involuntary motions. Hence in pleasure there is a dilation of the blood and a pleasant expansion of the vital spirits. Thus, when the nerves have been titillated or affected by some pleasant object, the movement continues to the cerebrum, and thence to the cerebellum and moves the spirits residing there. . . . Meanwhile the cerebral spirits affect the origins of the nerves of the face, causing lifting the eyebrows, parting of the lips, thereby shaping the face into a smile. [Dewhurst, 69]

The Stoics, we recall, attributed pleasure and pain to an expansion and contraction of pneuma. The substances have changed, but the figures continue. Notice also that the effects of the spirits on the body that Descartes had theorized Willis has "explained." He repeats this connection in a later lecture: "Through these interconnections the imaginations and the passions, conceived in the cerebrum, may be communicated through the cerebellum to the praecordia, and similarly the passions from the praecordia may reach the imagination and the cerebrum. Hence, love, anger, etc. cause various praecordial motions accompanied by diverse modulations and fluxes of the blood. Thus, too, the motion of the spirits is communicated to the facial muscles which depict or imitate the passions."[48] The same passions produce the traditional expressions, but now they do so by means which have been given a new, more thoroughly physiological explanation.

Willis mentions, in passing, the special susceptibility of women to certain passions as a result of the peculiar delicacy of their physiology, his alternative to the Greek notion of "hysteria." Willis traces this phenomenon to the richness of female blood in "fermentative particles" (Dewhurst, 89). He treats the passions of virgins and widows in some detail, but along lines since discredited. The theory of the passions was more successful, as I have suggested, when it dealt with the passions of all humans than when it tried to account for or legislate those of a single sex, region, or age (Isler, 135–40).

G. S. Rousseau has elevated Willis's work to the status of "paradigm," arguing that by limiting the seat of the soul to the brain he made that organ absolutely dependent on the nerves for all its functions.[49] This dependence in turn made necessary and possible the concentration of physiology on the structure of the nerves and the emphasis of the "age of sensibility" on their condition. For the writers I have chosen, however, Willis's importance lies elsewhere, in the places I have mentioned. As Rousseau says, it "took imaginative writers like Richardson and Sterne a half century to 'catch up,' as it were; and more importantly, it also took most scientific thinkers like Cheyne, Haller, and Whytt almost as long to understand what had transpired in the interim" (142).

We turn now from the flamboyant Willis to the conservative Dutch physician Herman Boerhaave, the most successful and influential consolidator of these and other discoveries and a man whom Samuel Johnson eulogized (in the *Gentleman's Magazine*, 1739) for his genius, sagacity, industry, and piety.[50] Johnson praised Boerhaave for conserving the tradition of Hippocrates and Sydenham, as well as for refuting, by his careful handling of the relationship between soul and body, Epicurus, Hobbes, and Spinoza.[51] Johnson also commended his pious patience in the face of the torments of disease as preferable to the indifference of Stoicism.

Conversant with the theories of Descartes and Gassendi as well as with the discoveries of Harvey and Willis, Boerhaave was learned in theology, medicine, and physics and willing to become so in chemistry and botany. He was a compelling and industrious teacher who promulgated his consolidations through many years of lectures—four or five hours a day, to students from all over Europe, among them Linnaeus, Haller, Van Swieten, La Mettrie, and even, on one occasion, Joseph Spence.[52]

His publications were reedited with commentaries by his students, were frequently translated, and were regularly pirated. A copy of his central work, *Institutiones medicae* (1708) reached his student and friend Cox Macro in England late in 1707 and went through five further editions in his lifetime.[53] Of his eminence and his influence there can be no doubt: "Boerhaave's great contribution was to construct a polished doctrinal edifice, almost monolithic, that captured men's attention, satisfied their curiosity—and restricted their imagination. Here and there some of his assertions were demonstrated to be false, but in general his teachings persisted without much change throughout most of the century, acquiring in academic circles a revered character and an almost dogmatic authority" (King, 63).

Essentially conservative, even Galenic, his work emphasized the mechanics of bodily fluids, imparting hydraulic emphasis to spirits that had previously been more aetherial. Pressure on the blood as it circulated through the veins refined its particles so that they could enter the very fine (hollow) tubes leading to the brain (which, like Malpighi, Boerhaave regarded as a gland). This system, micromechanical, corpuscular, and a refinement of the one the Arabian doctors had bequeathed to Aquinas, entailed no major revision of the workings of the passions. The connections between mind and body were perhaps more emphatically reciprocal than in some more theoretical systems in that the impact of the body on the mind could be accounted for. Then, as now, those connections eluded perfect understanding and defied exact description. The motion that figured so prominently in Aristotle's analysis of the passions was now more mechanically understood; that force which had always been considerable was now, for a few decades, and in the hands of a few writers, considerably increased.

This corpuscular phase of the spirits, reinforced so strongly by Newtonian mechanics, recent physiology, and most psychological theories, imparted so much vigor to the passions that they held sway even as the philosophical, psychological, and physiological systems in which they figured were modified, questioned, or discarded. At the same time that the corpuscular spirits lent themselves vividly to the findings of mechanical philosophy, they invited the attacks of those worried by materialism. These attacks sought to reaffirm the traditional passions and their traditional means of conveyance, so that, between these reaffirmations and the clever innovations of both theorists and experimentalists, the passions continued to thrive. Hope, fear, and envy remained active and effective in the vocabulary and syntax of the eighteenth century because writers and readers were enabled to picture, even to feel, them as forcible entities making their way through the body along well-established paths in response to well-understood stimuli. That this understanding had been accumulating for several millennia was perhaps more important to writers such as Addison and Gibbon (and to their readers) than that it had been lately vindicated by both theorists and experimentalists.

The strong connections between mind and body that accompanied the transformation of spirits into juices is most evident in the extension of Boerhaave's theories by Van Swieten, who held that strong passions long continued could alter the juices that transported them as well as the vessels through which they moved. Another student, Haller, produced the theory of "irritability" that was so important for physiology, for Hartley, and for "sensibility," while Maupertuis endowed his particles with psychic properties. Earlier, Malebranche, who reverted to Augustine and influenced Watts and Hume, had supplied a remarkably vivid but imaginary account of the ways in which the spirits left traces in the mind. Experimental Newtonians such as James Keill, Robert Whytt, and Stephen Hales confirmed the whole doctrine by calculating the momentum with which the nervous fluid was propelled along the nerves; Whytt even distributed the soul through the organs and substances of the brain and the body.[54]

These extensions of physiology remarkably paralleled the extensions of theory, most notoriously that of Descartes, leading in directions that I see no need, given my present purpose, to follow. By the time the iatro-mechanical tenets of dynamic corpuscularity had been absorbed by the writers of this age, its physicians had discarded it for, by one account, a new medical animism or, by another, aetherial materialism.[55] These distinctions are not discernible in the weaker traces of physiology evident in the texts that concern me.

These were the major voices in the continuing discussion. Other, obscurer voices emanated, often in disagreement, from Pembroke College, Oxford (Conyers Purshall), Clare Hall, Cambridge (Robert Greene), and the Colonies (Cadwallader Colden) (Schofield, 115–33). Some of these were more cosmological than physiological in their anti-Newtonianism, and they did little to diminish the force with which the passions were felt. Of the other voices, I mention the early one of John Bulwer (*Pathomyotomia; or, a Dissection of the Significative Muscles of the Affections of the Minde,* 1649) and transcribe the later one of James Parsons: "On the same Side the *Risorius* draws back the Corner of the Mouth; and the Action of the *Aperiens Palpebram* is remitted, whilst that on the other Side is in its action; so that, tho' one Eye is moderately open, and the other almost shut, the *Pupils* are carried obliquely downwards, by the *Abductor* of the one, and the *Adductor* and *Obliquus inferior* of the other, looking downwards and backwards at the Object of Contempt."[56]

In the same way that earlier writers had accommodated the separate systems of blood and brain, eighteenth-century writers continued to call up and explicate the traditional complications while their more scientifically or theoretically minded contemporaries argued over whether the passions made their way about the body by way of animal spirits, aether, or vibrations, and whether through or along tubes, hollow or solid, or cords, elastic or inelastic, and whether all this was done chemically or by fermentation. We will encounter occasional passages alluding, sometimes playfully, to one or another of these underlying physiologies. Always, however, the usual passions will be called by their customary names and accompanied by their traditional components, whether or not any reference is made to their means of conveyance. Cartesian philosophy, Newtonian physics, and Boerhaave's physiological consolidations combined to give the passions cumulative significance and enormous force. Many centuries of philosophy had made them certain, and a few decades of physiology had made them lively; for the next century they enriched and informed the prose of every thoughtful writer.

Then, before the century was over, the episodes dissolved into spasms, the forces dissipated into tremors, the tubes slackened into fibers, and the vocabulary collapsed, all in the name of "sensibility." Sir John Hill, from whom we heard in chapter 1, urged the actor to expose his nerves to the Miltonic sublime until he could "take in sensations which he was before unacquainted with, *and for which there is no name.*"[57] Or as Foucault put it: "What had been perceived as heat, imagined as agitation of spirits, conceived as fibrous tension, would henceforth be recognized in the neutralized transparency of psychological notions: exaggerated vivacity of internal impressions, rapidity in the association of ideas, inattention to the external world."[58] Thereafter the articulate systems and clear taxonomies gave way to organicism, "identity," and the subconscious, while the schematic manifestations of the eyebrow move from the muscles of Parsons to the bones of phrenology or the upper lip and nostrils of Bell and Darwin. George Henry Lewes, for example, applied recent developments in physiology to the stage, insisting on "fluctuating" and "spontaneous" manifestations of "organic" passions slow to subside rather than on the discrete episodes and careful sequences that we are about to follow.[59] David Garrick's performance would have been lost on an audience schooled by Lewes.

Two thousand years of discussion had provided the passions with enough clarity, force, and continuity to keep them current in the face of dramatic changes in cultural milieu, theoretical context, physiological understanding, and theological orientation. This clarity and force, in turn, imparted continuity to every new context in which they occurred, whether theoretical, scientific, or literary. The writers of the eighteenth century were enabled, and obliged, to write effectively about fear and envy in part because Aristotle, Cicero, Aquinas, and Descartes had already done so.

I have chosen to investigate the force of the passions in a few writers in some detail. For those who want to look elsewhere, I suggest Dryden's extensive discussion, echoing Longinus and anticipating Addison, on the raising and staging of passions in drama (Preface to *Troilus and Cressida*); Thomas Parnell's *Essay on the Different Styles of Poetry* (1713); Mandeville's *Fable of the Bees* (1714); and Charlotte Lennox's "On Reading Hutchinson on the Passions." I have already acknowledged that few poets are more passionate, in the enlightened sense of that word, than Pope, and I know that Richardson and Smollett invoke the passions repeatedly.[60] Extensive quotations will demonstrate that the writers I have chosen took special advantage of the tradition we have reviewed. I show in my analyses that an understanding of that tradition will enhance the reading of those passages. The traditional components of the passions, their stimulation by an object, the good or evil in that object and the pleasure or pain in the person perceiving it, the degree of refinement in the sensibility of that perceiver, the temporal conditions of that perception, the comparative status of the empassioned self in relation to others involved in the transaction, the physiology by which the impressions and responses were conveyed—all these components, usually detached from the systems in which they originated, combined to form new properties in the prose of the eighteenth century. Other writers prove the continuance of the tradition; these writers prove, and improve upon, its significance. Each of them absorbed the passions into his own concerns and deployed them with his own genius, transforming, creating, and adapting the same episodes to different temperaments, styles, and purposes. For two chapters now we have watched the passions idling, as Wittgenstein put it, in the hands of philosophers and physiologists.[61] It is time now to watch them at work in a series of writers well able to exploit their many possibilities.

4

INTO COMPANY AND BEYOND:

THE PASSIONS IN *THE SPECTATOR*

 HE SPECTATOR PROPOSED TO RESCUE PHILOSO-
phy from closets, libraries, schools, and colleges—
bookish, masculine, and solitary locations where the
passions had long been studied rather than felt or
displayed. The clubs, assemblies, tea tables, and cof-
feehouses into which it was to be transferred were sociable places
where the sexes could mingle and the passions rise.[1] As we have seen,
the passions with which philosophy and the Renaissance dealt per-
tained to power and frequented the court. Mr. Spectator wanted to
inspect the passions in company by following them out onto the
street and thence into the sophisticated urban interiors where men
and women of lower (but by no means lowly) spheres congregated:
"We are very Curious to observe the Behaviour of Great Men and their
Clients; but the same Passions and Interests move Men in lower
Spheres; and I (that have nothing else to do, but make Observations)
see in every Parish, Street, Lane, and Alley of this Populous City, a
little Potentate that has his Court, and his Flatterers who lay Snares
for his Affection and Favour, by the same Arts that are practised upon
Men in higher Stations" (no. 49, 1:208).

As this passage suggests, the traditional analyses of the courtly
passions admirably served *The Spectator*'s purpose of inculcating classical values and morals for a new, partly financial and mercantile
public.[2] In seeking, as they saw it, to "humanize" this new public,
and in electing to concentrate on voguish follies, its authors com-
mitted themselves to recurrent passions rather than to profound
ones and to those passions that delight or disturb a coterie rather

than to those that exhilarate an era or fester in the depths of a single self, yet this commitment was not the limitation one might expect.

The passions appear throughout the run. In no. 2 the Templar "is studying the Passions themselves, when he should be inquiring into the Debates among Men which arise from them," and in Addison's final contribution, no. 600, he celebrates the "Variety of Passages, [by which] Joy and Gladness may enter into the Thoughts of Man," urging his readers not to "make those Faculties which [God] formed as so many Qualifications for Happiness and Rewards, to be the Instruments of Pain and Punishment."[3] The early example provides evidence of the tendency to bring the passions into company; the later to project them beyond it, into eternity. Both suggest that they continued to disturb the minds and inform the prose of the eighteenth century.

In the intervening papers episodes of passions abound and signify. Traditional components such as the object and temporal and class considerations figure with regularity and intricacy. The established vocabulary is everywhere invoked and exploited. Episodes are sorted into correspondences and sequences as impressive, if not always as vivid, as the ones Garrick performed and Cicero recounted. Two considerations receive special and consistent emphasis in their treatment, one expected, the other somewhat unlooked for. The first is the operation of the passions in company, an obvious but a significant concern, especially in a series of essays intended for the drawing rooms of so carefully stratified and consciously social a period. This concern will find its most intriguing manifestation in three papers in which a small company of city dwellers removed to the country sends those who cannot control their passions back into the closet. Another passage we will consider combines this concern with the second one; in it, the people in which the passions occur are all in their tombs, provoking some somber reflections on eternity. This second concern, that of the connections between the passions and eternity, draws on the traditional affinities between the passions and eschatology and culminates in the account of the execution of Sir Thomas More with which this chapter concludes.

The aesthetic implications are investigated in ways that look backward to Plato and forward to Hume; the Ciceronian and Stoic sources of the tradition are repeatedly invoked; and the obligations of the stage to articulate the passions are asserted. Addison and Steele knew very well how troublesome the passions could be as they found their way into company. They articulate the difficulties in sober essays dealing with tombs and executions, and in more playful ones where the fan becomes a social engine. We will find *The Spectator* a very instructive document in which to watch the passions at work. It acknowledged their established vitality and exploited their acknowledged complexity. It did so repeatedly and eloquently and frequently managed to impart special considerations of its own in the process.

If the passions bring their established definitions and calculated components to nearly every paper, they emerge with their customary clarity, a new familiarity, some quite subtle socialization, a not very subtle feminization, and, occasionally, theological implications renewed by their refinement in the company through which they are made to pass. Later writers would have to restore some of the profundity and complexity the passions had left behind in the closets and colleges, but they would be able to count on a wider, fresher audience and one that understood their social and syntactic possibilities much better because of the frequency, clarity, and intricacy with which *The Spectator* had treated these episodes. All these considerations make *The Spectator* an ideal place to begin our study of the ways in which the writers of the eighteenth century exploited the enormous social and stylistic possibilities of the passions.

The passions in *The Spectator,* as everywhere else, are governed by their objects: "The Man of Pleasure resolves to take his leave at least [last?], and part civilly with his Mistress: But the Ambitious Man is entangled every Moment in a fresh Pursuit, and the Lover sees new Charms in the Object he fancy'd he could abandon" (no. 27, 1:113). They make their customary appearances in the countenance: "The Muscles of a real Face sometimes swell with soft Passion, sudden Surprize, and are flushed with agreeable Confusions, according as the Objects before them, or the Ideas presented to them, affect their Imagination. But the *Picts* [women who paint their faces] behold all things with the same Air, whether they are Joyful or Sad; The same fix'd Insensibility appears on all Occasions."[4] And especially, they exploit the comparative component into which we will look in greater detail in the next chapter. This component "makes Mr.

Puzzle [an immethodical freethinker] the Admiration of all those who have less Sense than himself, and the Contempt of all those who have more" (no. 476, 4:187).

These traditional components provide the occasion for some subtle turns of phrase and witty defeating of expectations. Thus the definitions of admiration and contempt are reasserted in that last example, but for those who know the system well enough to follow out all the implications, it is Mr. Puzzle who is redefined. And as so often in *The Spectator,* the passions take effect in company ("all those who"), with implications beyond it—Mr. Puzzle was, after all, a freethinker. A little more intricately, shallow pedants who cry one another up repeatedly "are obliged indeed to be thus lavish of their Praises, that they may keep one another in Countenance; and it is no wonder if a great deal of Knowledge, which is not capable of making a Man Wise, has a natural Tendency to make him Vain and Arrogant" (no. 105, 1:438). This passage presupposes separate faculties, one intellectual, the other passionate. That knowledge which ought to inhabit and inform the former faculty inflates the latter, rendering the learned man, with all his knowledge, foolish. In this case, knowledge, which is not episodic, is perverted into an attitude toward the self (vanity) and a behavior toward others (arrogance) which are. That mind which ought to have rendered itself impervious to the passions has indulged them. In this case the passions spoil the mind but enrich the prose.

The scrutinizing persona of these essays exhibits few passions of his own. Except for the familiar and perhaps forgivable vanity of an author, a vanity frequently subject to mortification (no. 4, 1:18), he exhibits but one passion, one not found on most classical lists: "An insatiable Thirst after Knowledge carried me into all the Countries of *Europe,* in which there was any thing new or strange to be seen; nay, to such a Degree was my Curiosity raised, that having read the Controversies of some great Men concerning the Antiquities of *Egypt,* I made a Voyage to *Grand Cairo,* on purpose to make the Measure of a Pyramid."[5] Neither subject to passions of his own nor (usually) the object of the passions of others, the Spectator watches for and comments on the passions of the companies he attends with a quiet, subtle expertise: "I see Men flourishing in Courts and languishing in Jayls, without being prejudiced from their Circumstances to their Favour or Disadvantage; but from their inward Manner of bearing their Condition, often pity the Prosperous and admire the Unhappy" (no. 4, 1:20). Notice, again, the alertness to the courtly tradition of the passions and the eye for circumstance, as well as the ability to rework that tradition in subtle ways: pity is not the usual response to prosperity, nor admiration to misery.

Mr. Spectator has preserved himself from passion by interposing a reasonable, sometimes a frigid, indifference between himself and the customary objects of the various passions. When he looks at beauty, for example, he does so "abstracted from the Consideration of its being the Object of Desire," thus, perhaps, entitling him to the pity, or the contempt, of some readers (no. 270, 2:553). He tells us, in no. 355, that he has let Epictetus help him curb his resentment at criticism, but in no. 442 he allows himself to pity would-be contributors to his paper. Not many of the many passions at work in *The Spectator*, then, are those of the Spectator himself, who achieved, or was given, the dispassion traditionally required of those who articulate such episodes. Mr. Spectator becomes the liaison between the closet and the drawing room, embodying in himself, and in this passage, precisely the differences with which the passions were regarded and understood in the eighteenth century: "He who comes into Assemblies only to gratify his Curiosity [that is, Mr. Spectator], and not to make a Figure, enjoys the Pleasures of Retirement in a more exquisite Degree, than he possibly could in his Closet; the Lover, the Ambitious, and the Miser, are follow'd thither [that is, to the closets] by a worse Crowd than any they can withdraw from. To be exempt from the Passions with which others are tormented, is the only pleasing Solitude" (no. 4, 1:19; Steele then quotes Cicero, *De officiis*).

Addison and Steele sometimes attribute unlikely passions to their persona as a device to isolate and ridicule those readers who have missed the point of previous issues. Sir Roger's tenants, baffled by Mr. Spectator's taciturnity, attributed pride, modesty, and melancholy to him (no. 131), while in no. 158 a "Woman's Man," with wonderful unperceptiveness, accuses Mr. Spectator of envy. Those who once belonged to the charmed set within which *The Spectator* circulated must frequently have smiled at those whose remoteness or dullness kept them outside. Those who now attend to the workings of the passions may add admiration to their amusement.

Addison and Steele often placed their mutual understanding of the passions at the disposal of imagined correspondents, the better to share it with real readers. Consider this passage from a jealous wife: "Hitherto I have only told you the general Temper of my Mind, but how shall I give you an Account of the Distraction of it? Could you but conceive how cruel I am one Moment in my Resentment, and, at the ensuing Minute, when I place him in the Condition my Anger would bring him to, how compassionate; It would give you some Notion how miserable I am, and how little I deserve it" (no. 178, 2:202). The established vocabulary enables this correspondent to comprehend and convey her distraction by following it through a sequence of episodes from resentment to anger and thence to compassion and misery. (If those with more recent and more clinical psychologies in mind wish to look more deeply into her fantasies and motives, the clarity and control of the original vocabulary will enable them to do so.)

Occasionally routine appearances of the passions grow so intricate that they govern the development of entire essays. In no. 185 the Spectator, expressing the usual neoclassical distrust of zeal, and sounding a little like Hume in doing so, analyzes that passion into kindred but less attractive ones: "I would have every Zealous Man examine his Heart thoroughly, and, I believe, he will often find that what he calls a Zeal for his Religion is either Pride, Interest, or Ill-nature." The assumption that one of these states of mind underlies every episode of zeal provides the outline for the rest of the essay, which concludes: "Let me therefore advise this Generation of Wranglers, for their own and for the Publick good, to act at least so consistently with themselves, as not to burn with Zeal for Irreligion and with Bigottry for Nonsense" (no. 185, 2:228, 230). The burning is routine, though justified by both physiology and tradition. It works splendidly with the zeal, reinforcing the catachresis that undermines "bigottry," while their objects, "irreligion" and "nonsense," render the zeal and bigotry they have inspired more passionate than intellectual and thus make themselves the objects of contempt.

Seemingly simple elaborations of the traditional components and definitions of the passions regularly supply such intricate syntactic possibilities. All the antitheses in the following passage, for example, depend on contrasting responses, shame and fear, to the same object, poverty. Notice that the responses of shame to the object it sees as an evil are self-regarding, excessive, futile, and abstract, so much so that Laertes disappears in the midst of his equipage, expense, and entertainments. Fear, on the other hand, focuses Irus's mind so intently in himself that that self figures centrally in every manifestation of it. The ostentatious response produces invisibility as well as the shameful condition it seeks to avoid, while the energetic ("irascible") response produces motivation and thus success—of a sort. Laertes vanishes in the midst of much and splendid company, company which, presumably, will ignore or despise Irus as long as he is unattended, laborious, and intent only on himself:

> *Laertes* and *Irus* are Neighbours, whose Way of living are an Abomination to each other. *Irus* is moved by the Fear of Poverty, and *Laertes* by the Shame of it. Though the Motive of Action is of so near Affinity in both, and may be resolved into this, "That to each of them Poverty is the greatest of all Evils, yet are their Manners very widely different." Shame of Poverty makes *Laertes* launch into unnecessary Equipage, vain Expence, and lavish Entertainments; Fear of Poverty makes *Irus* allow himself only plain Necessaries, appear without a Servant, sell his own Corn, attend his Labourers, and be himself a Labourer. Shame of Poverty makes *Laertes* go every Day a Step nearer to it; and Fear of Poverty stirs up *Irus* to make every Day some further Progress from it.[6]

The rest of this essay recommends a kind of Aristotelian mean between these two passions.

The temporal component of every passion, to look at what happens to one last traditional component in *The Spectator,* is frequently muffled by the concern with modishness. When it does show itself it does so briefly, and usually in the Lockean sense of duration. Thus "the Hours of a wise Man are lengthened by his Ideas, as those of a Fool are by his Passions: The Time of the one is long, because he does not know what to do with it; so is that of the other, because he distinguishes every Moment of it with some useful or amusing Thought; or in other Words, because the one is always wishing it away, and the other always enjoying it" (no. 94, 1:401). Occasionally the Lockean element is added to a Platonic soul—one that then acquires theological motions that transcend this temporal component:

> The *Time present* seldom affords sufficient Employment to the Mind of Man. Objects of Pain or Pleasure, Love or Admiration [note that Addison has confined himself to those passions that emerge from present objects], do not lie thick enough together in Life to keep the Soul in constant Action, and supply an immediate Exercise to its Faculties. In order, therefore, to remedy this Defect, that the Mind may not want Business, but always have Materials for thinking, she is endowed with certain Powers, that can recall what is passed, and anticipate what is to come.[7]

This essay moves to the good internal effects of hope and then on to happiness and devotion, passing from a Plutarchan insight into the efficacy of hope to a conclusion from the Psalms. It is difficult to imagine the shape this essay would have taken without the temporal element of the passions to draw upon. This is also the second time, and by no means the last, we must notice a tendency to endow the passions with theological implications that go beyond social circumstances. Episodes of passion in *The Spectator* usually begin in company, but as we shall see, they often pass through that company into or toward eternity.

Elsewhere time imparts a clever twist to individual passions or to the end of an entire essay. Thus an aging roué, "Jack Afterday," writes of the perversion of his passions by time—the force which ought to have corrected them. He urges Mr. Spectator to write an essay on the art of growing old and laments that he has practiced that art so badly that "I hate those I should laugh at, and envy those I contemn" (no. 260, 2:512). *The Spectator*'s settled distrust of hurry is kindred to this neglect of the temporal component: "This loose State of the Soul hurries the Extravagant from one Pursuit to another" (no. 222, 2:364). In no. 101, on censure and fame (the fame, as it happens, of *The Spectator*), we are told that fame cannot be hurried, as it can be properly distributed only by posterity. So subject is it to the passions and prejudices of contemporaries that it must be bestowed eventually rather than sought hurriedly. Like *The Rambler*, *The Spectator* takes the long view when it deals with the fame of writers.

If its commitment to modishness draws it away from the rich possibilities of the temporal component at one end of the time line, a substantial theological proclivity propels it in the direction of eternity at the other. Mr. Spectator pictures the perpetual satisfaction of curiosity and the perfection of rank as features of an afterlife, and we are assured that, in the course of "the perpetual Progress which the Soul makes towards the Perfection of its Nature," the soul will ultimately "extinguish all Envy in inferior Natures, and all Contempt in superior"—a final triumph of theology over social distinction and Christianity over classical psychology.[8] That the passions were not always extinguished in superior natures is evident in no. 391, where a Menippean Jupiter assesses the passions motivating the prayers that ascend to him. After a while, these motives put Jupiter himself into a passion, and he slams the trap door!

The soul wherein the passions resided was not often brought up in company. If we did not have numerous models of it from earlier works, we would be hard put to picture the one that the Spectator and his readers had in mind. Even with these it is not often possible (or necessary) to say which of several models is supposed to be in operation. We might begin to suspect, as a number of passages I have already cited suggest, that the distinction between soul and mind was beginning to blur and that the passions had entered the mind instead of just interfering with it from somewhere nearby. Such glimpses as we do get suggest a traditional, indeed Platonic, entity, governed by pleasure and pain and thus subject to passion, in need of social correction and, ultimately, divine adjustment. The clearest glimpse we are given comes in an allegorical continuation of the *Phaedrus* which depicts Pleasure and Pain as "constant Yoke-fellows" in the human soul, the "yoke" perhaps taken over from the pair of horses discussed above in chapter 2.[9]

The passions that inhabit and disturb that soul transport it from some Platonic realm into the drawing room, where the human condition is elegantly strung within a chain of being: "Our Superiours are guided by Intuition, and our Inferiours by Instinct" (no. 162, 2:136). The complications endemic to that condition are exacerbated by social circumstance: "Man is subject to innumerable Pains and Sorrows by the very Condition of Humanity, and yet, as if Nature had not sown Evils enough in Life, we are continually adding Grief to Grief, and aggravating the common Calamity by our cruel Treatment of one another. Every Man's natural weight of Affliction is still made more heavy by the Envy, Malice, Treachery or Injustice of his Neighbour" (no. 169, 2:164–65). "Neighbours" (that is, "company") excite one another's passions and increase one another's burdens. Notice how weighty and substantial ("adding," "aggravating," "more heavy") the passions have become in that passage. The syntax can clearly bear that weight, but the tea table was, by design, a fragile structure.

The universe inhabited by these minds and souls is one in which secondary qualities have been thoughtfully, indeed divinely, added to the bleaker primary ones as an eternal stimulant of pleasurable passions:

> If Matter had appeared to us endow'd only with those real Qualities which it actually possesses, it would have made but a very joyless and uncomfortable Figure; and why has Providence given it a Power of producing in us such imaginary Qualities as Tastes and Colours, Sounds and Smells, Heat and Cold; but that Man, while he is conversant in the lower Stations of Nature, might have his Mind cheared and delighted with agreeable Sensations? In short, the whole Universe is a kind of Theatre filled with Objects that either raise in us Pleasure, Amusement, or Admiration. [No. 387, 3:453]

Hume, as we shall see, develops this idea of the stimulation of the passions by secondary qualities, without, however, the thoughtful creator who instilled responses to them in the souls of those he hoped to reclaim.

These stimulating secondary qualities figure throughout the papers on "The Pleasures of the Imagination" (nos. 411–21), where God becomes the ultimate object that our souls have been implanted with a relish to contemplate ("Object," I might add, precisely in the sense developed in the previous two chapters):

> The Supreme Author of our Being has so formed the Soul of Man, that nothing but himself can be its last, adequate, and proper Happiness. . . . Our Admiration, which is a very pleasing Motion of the Mind, immediately rises at the Consideration of any Object that takes up a great deal of room in the Fancy, and, by consequence, will improve into the highest

pitch of Astonishment and Devotion when we contemplate his
Nature, that is neither circumscribed by Time nor Place, nor
to be comprehended by the largest Capacity of a Created
Being. [No. 413, 3:545]

Addison has here incorporated the passions into his aesthetics and
his theology, absorbing the insights of Aristotle and Descartes on
Admiration into a soul that retains Platonic resonances and Senecan
overtones. The rest of these papers concern themselves more with
the operation of ideas which enter the mind through the imagination than with the passions of the soul, which play only a small
aesthetic part, as in no. 418, where they increase the effect of description. In a mind that was rapidly becoming "the sum of its
processes and ideas" and "a space to be filled," episodes of passion
could take on, finally, the psychological, aesthetic, and moral potency for which they had been preparing for centuries.[10] Yet thinking "that the aim of poetry is to increase man's physical and moral
knowledge, as Addison did, he was bound to find passions and the
pleasures of the senses the least informative and the most misleading
of human pleasures."[11] Thus he set out to inform and redirect those
passions and pleasures, and he did so by bringing them into company, and by relegating the imagination to an organ of "taste."

Throughout *The Spectator*, objects that stir up passions within the
soul reach it in the customary way. *Spectator* no. 115 provides a
perfect summary of the unworried simplification of the physiological means by which the Lockean mind and the Aristotelian soul
were supposed to communicate their operations to the English
body:

I consider the Body as a System of Tubes and Glands, or to use
a more Rustick Phrase, a Bundle of Pipes and Strainers, fitted
to one another after so wonderful a manner as to make a proper
Engine for the Soul to work with. This Description does not
only comprehend the Bowels, Bones, Tendons, Veins, Nerves
and Arteries, but every Muscle and every Ligature, which is a
Composition of Fibres, that are so many imperceptible Tubes
or Pipes interwoven on all sides with invisible Glands or
Strainers. [1:471; cf. no. 250, where the eye becomes the por-
tal "to let our Affections pass in and out; Love, Anger, Pride,
and Avarice all visibly move in those little Orbs," 2:471]

This passage adds only urbanity to the tradition of Galen and the findings of Boerhaave, though I suspect that Addison is also toying with Willis's penchant for figurative language drawn from his Oxfordshire farmhouse. [12] No. 417, on the other hand, makes the animal spirits responsible for "association," giving "A Cartesian's" version of the "Traces" they make through the brain. Pleasant ideas, by this account, make wider traces than disagreeable ones—an intriguing metaphor whereby episodes of passion take on spatial implications rather than temporal ones.

Sometimes noble blood, in a combination of the intensified concern with social class and the recent absorption of the passions into that blood, responds to ignoble objects, as in the case of the old, meek, wealthy man who wants (for excellent reasons) to cut the "Pin-money" of his wife, making "her noble Blood swell in her Veins" (no. 295, 3:51). The high spirits in her blood interfere with her reason and demeanor and eventually render her unable to argue calmly. The blood and the prose both carry much meaning throughout this essay.

That *The Spectator* was more amused than intrigued by the findings of anatomists is evident in no. 281, on the dissection of a "Coquet's Heart," the nerves of which are connected not to a brain but only to the muscles of the eye! (2:586). In the corresponding dissection of a "Beau's Head" there is no evidence of a soul at all. Had there been one, it would have been confined to one object— itself: "The *Pineal Gland,* which many of our Modern Philosophers suppose to be the Seat of the Soul, smelt very strong of Essence and Orange-Flower Water, and was encompassed with a kind of Horny Substance, cut into a thousand little Faces or Mirrours, which were imperceptible to the naked Eye, insomuch that the Soul, if there had been any here, must have been always taken up in contemplating her own Beauties" (no. 275, 2:571). The Augustans did not encourage their contemporaries to contemplate the beauty of their own souls. And the English did not like the French, their vanities, their philosopher, or his gland.

Perhaps because of this indifference to physiology, *The Spectator* seldom annexes a physical attribute or another abstract noun to one of the passions. Examples like "This single Consideration would be sufficient to extinguish the Bitterness of Hatred, the Thirst of Avarice, and the Cruelty of Ambition" (no. 289, 3:29) are not numerous. The hint of personification that recommended such a structure to Johnson, for example, does not seem to have appealed to Addison and Steele, whose personifications pale when they come into company. (See the allegorical vultures in no. 159 and the moral exempla in no. 164.)

As repeated references to Plato, Aristotle, and Descartes suggest, *The Spectator* often exhibited the studious origins of the passions it articulated, so that the philosophic tradition lent both dignity and clarity to its analyses of social states of mind. The couching of that analysis in terms drawn from the writers and thinkers of the past and the conducting of it along lines that had been laid down and followed for centuries seemed both to reassure and to edify the minds of the company on whose behalf the passions were now being watched.

One striking passage extends another image from Plato into Christian theology: "When therefore the obscene Passions in particular have once taken Root and spread themselves in the Soul, they cleave to her inseparably, and remain in her for ever after the Body is cast off and thrown aside" (no. 90, 1:381). In no. 93 the consolations of friendship are drawn as much from the *Nicomachean Ethics* as from life (here, again, the ultimate reference goes beyond the classical source): "The Man who lives under an habitual Sense of the Divine Presence keeps up a perpetual Cheerfulness of Temper, and enjoys every Moment the Satisfaction of thinking himself in Company with his dearest and best of Friends" (no. 93, 1:396).

Cicero's name is dropped so often that several correspondents complain of it (nos. 154, 158). *De officiis* figures in no. 104, on decency, by Steele, while Budgell draws on the same source for the active principle in the human soul (no. 116), and Addison turns to it for his examples for the love of animals for their offspring (no. 120). *Spectator* no. 408 (one sometimes claimed for Pope) draws on Cicero, among others, for its analysis of the passions, comparing them to winds driving a ship. It also mentions Plato's charioteer and the Aristotelian passions appropriate to youth and age, as well as the great chain of being and a handful of other philosophical commonplaces. As Bond's notes to this paper make clear, these trains of thought had been followed by so many writers that attribution is simply not possible (3:523–26). No. 491 contains a passionate, indeed operatic, anecdote from another frequent source, Bayle. This anecdote concerns the tyrannical and brutal lust of Rhynsault for the beautiful wife of Danvelt.

Seneca and the other Stoics were brought into company to be berated for pedantry and corrected with Christianity.[13] Paper no. 25 concludes with a Stoic source and sentiment: "If we have this Frame of Mind, we shall take the best Means to preserve Life, without being oversollicitous about the Event; and shall arrive at that point of Felicity which *Martial* has mentioned as the Perfection of Happiness, of neither fearing nor wishing for Death" (no. 25, 1:108). This was followed the next day, Good Friday, by a paper thick with tombs, passions, and Christian sentiments, a paper which must be quoted at length and read with special attention to the passions at work within it. The company through which Mr. Spectator passes here inspires a complex and profound sequence of passions within him. It does so because that company is in touch with eternity:

> But for my own Part, though I am always serious, I do not know what it is to be melancholy; and can therefore take a View of Nature in her deep and solemn Scenes, with the same Pleasure as in her most gay and delightful ones. By this Means I can improve my self with those Objects, which others consider with Terror. When I look upon the Tombs of the Great, every Emotion of Envy dies in me; when I read the Epitaphs of the Beautiful, every inordinate Desire goes out; when I meet with the Grief of Parents upon a Tomb-stone, my Heart melts with Compassion; when I see the Tomb of the Parents themselves, I consider the Vanity of grieving for those whom we must quickly follow: When I see Kings lying by those who deposed them, when I consider rival Wits plac'd Side by Side, or the holy Men that divided the World with their Contests and Disputes, I reflect with Sorrow and Astonishment on the little Competitions, Factions, and Debates of Mankind. When I read the several Dates of the Tombs, of some that dy'd Yesterday, and some six hundred Years ago, I consider that great Day when we shall all of us be Contemporaries, and make our Appearance together. [No. 26, 1:111]

This remarkable passage moves toward a theological resolution that transcends Stoicism while proving that Stoic teachings on the passions continued to provoke thoughtful responses. The path through Westminster Abbey is strewn with passions, or rather, with the tombs of those who indulged and inspired them, those who analyzed and mocked them, and those who felt them. Those who felt them did so in groups (competitions, factions, debates), though they now lie in solitary graves, where they are contemplated by the solitary spectator on behalf of a (presumably) sociable reader. These tombs have become objects that enable the Spectator to manage his own passions and remind him and his readers of the ultimate reason for doing so. The human soul the Spectator has in mind is not, as it comes, ready to enter company or eternity. The more refinement it acquires in the former, the better prepared it will eventually be to enter the latter, at which time it will have transcended both its human limitations and its traditional analyses.

Not all of *The Spectator*'s sources were as recondite as these, nor did they all lead in such somber directions. Itself a convenient, maneuverable vehicle for conveying the passions to a wider, but still select audience, it drew regularly upon the stage, an established medium which for centuries had shown its audiences—Greek, Roman, French, and English—what the passions looked like, what actions they produced in those who harbored them, and what their consequences were when once set in motion: "The Motions of the Minds of Lovers are no where so well described, as in the Works of skilful Writers for the Stage."[14] The links between *The Spectator* and the stage are numerous and strong, though perhaps more reciprocal than causal. Recent performances supplied many characters to stimulate and illustrate passages on the passions: Sir Sampson Legend came readily to hand from *Love for Love* to illustrate the deformed passions of "an unnatural Father" (no. 189), while Malvolio walks directly from the stage into an elaborate analysis of the passions in a paper on flattery. He is so full of envy, self-love, and detraction that he "turns pale at the Mirth and good Humour of the Company, if it center not in his Person; he grows jealous and displeased when he ceases to be the only Person admired, and looks upon the Commendations paid to another as a Detraction from his Merit, and an Attempt to lessen the Superiority he affects" (no. 238, 2:426). These actions and reactions are all noticeably dramatic ones, indicating that we are to picture him in performance rather than in print. That he "turns pale at the Mirth and good Humour of the Company" reminds us that the actor playing Malvolio conceived and displayed these episodes in the midst of one company, and before a larger one. Both were exceedingly well skilled in construing the signs of the passions—a skill *The Spectator* evidently expected to find, and was well equipped to develop, in its own audience.

The genius of the playwright, the talent of the actor, and the insights of the critic were not always so successfully conveyed to the audience. The last time Mr. Spectator saw *Macbeth,* he was "wonderfully taken with the Skill of the Poet, in making the Murderer form Fears to himself from the Moderation of the Prince whose Life he was going to take away" (no. 206, 2:308). Unfortunately, that audience got its own passions wrong and laughed at Lady Macbeth's feigned astonishment. Instead of exhibiting "the Indignation which is natural to the Occasion . . . , They were as merry [as] when a Criminal was stabbed" (no. 208, 2:315).

The Spectator regularly deplores the stage's recent pandering to less discriminating members of its audience, insisting that "Corporeal and Intellectual Actors ought to be kept at a still wider Distance than to appear on the same Stage at all," and thus separate "such as could show all the Postures which the Body is capable of, from those who were to represent all the Passions to which the Mind is subject" (no. 141, 2:56; cf. no. 436, on the passions of the spectators at a boxing match). Its early and repeated distrust of opera originates in the same concern—operas exploited passions which they did not enable their audience to understand: "what may properly express a Passion in one Language, will not do it in another"—because the cadences in Italian are quite different from those in English, their notes of admiration very much resembling English tones of anger.[15] The episodes of passion in opera are bloated rather than articulated. The audience can follow these passions, but it is the business of the stage (and even more so of the essay) to see that they lead somewhere. In the playhouse they should lead, as the passage on the laughter at *Macbeth* suggests, to pity and fear. Thus the objection to the facile use of thunder to induce terror and the handkerchief to call forth pity: "Our Minds should be open'd to great Conceptions and inflamed with glorious Sentiments by what the Actor speaks, more than by what he appears."[16]

The conventions of double plots, poetic justice, and tragicomedy all interfere with the depiction of passions on the stage (no. 40), but the greatest disservice the stage performs is the "clap trap":

> The Poets that were acquainted with this Secret, have given frequent Occasion for such Emotions in the Actor, by adding Vehemence to Words where there was no Passion, or inflaming a real Passion into Fustian. This hath filled the Mouths of our Heroes with Bombast; and given them such Sentiments, as proceed rather from a Swelling than a Greatness of Mind. Unnatural Exclamations, Curses, Vows, Blasphemies, a Defiance of Mankind, and an Outraging of the Gods, frequently pass upon the Audience for tow'ring Thoughts, and have accordingly met with infinite Applause. [No. 40, 1:171; cf. no. 546]

In these episodes, as in those in opera, the passions cease to be controlled, and the company is encouraged to applaud rather than to discriminate. It was not merely to trap cheap clapping that Addison and Steele brought the passions into public view.

They sensed the connection between staging the passions and feigning them, but they did not worry about it, as, for example, Fielding and Diderot did: "Consider all the different Pursuits and Employments of Men, and you will find half their Actions tend to nothing else but Disguise and Imposture; and all that is done which proceeds not from a Man's very self is the Action of a Player. For this Reason it is that I make so frequent mention of the Stage: It is, with me, a Matter of the highest Consideration what Parts are well or ill performed, what Passions or Sentiments are indulged or cultivated, and consequently what Manners and Customs are transfused from the Stage to the World, which reciprocally imitate each other" (no. 370, 3:393). The stage is so necessary in teaching its audience to recognize and manage its passions, and this transfusion so central to the social and psychological conventions of the age, that the issue of sincerity can, for the moment, be overlooked.

Complaining that the stage has sometimes failed to do its part in articulating all the components of episodes of the passions, *The Spectator* sometimes called for connections among performance, passion, and response that only the periodic sentence could set forth and only the attentive and informed reader could follow: "Our Mirth is the

Laughter of Fools, and our Admiration the Wonder of Idiots; else such improbable, monstrous, and incoherent Dreams could not go off as they do, not only without the utmost Scorn and Contempt, but even with the loudest Applause and Approbation" (no. 22, 1:92). Readers, in other words, should be wiser laughers and more intelligent wonderers, scorning those who give their mirth and admiration to unworthy objects. Extended series like this one, less frequent in the *Spectator* than in the *Rambler,* count on, confirm, and continue the system of passions by their precision and syntactic elaboration.

Having found our way back from the theater to the library, we should note that *The Spectator* and its correspondents shared the touching assumption that the passions could be better dealt with by books. In recommending the turn from journalism to history it notes that in the latter "The Reader's Curiosity is raised and satisfied every Moment, and his Passions disappointed or gratified, without being detained in a State of Uncertainty from Day to Day, or lying at the Mercy of Sea and Wind. In short, the Mind is not here kept in a perpetual Gape after Knowledge, nor punished with that Eternal Thirst, which is the Portion of all our Modern News-mongers and Coffee-house Politicians" (no. 452, 4:91). Women, especially, may be edified by good books: "What Improvements would a Woman have made, who is so Susceptible of Impressions from what she reads, had she been guided to such Books as have a tendency to enlighten the Understanding and rectify the Passions" (no. 37, 1:158; cf. no. 79). But if the right books clarify and rectify the passions, the wrong ones can corrupt them. In no. 156 a pretty, silly woman keeps frivolous company and reads frivolous books, and no. 223 suggests that it is better for mankind that the works of Sappho have been lost—because they are reported to have been so passionate.

In the papers on *Paradise Lost,* the book in which he watches the passions most carefully, Addison admires their complication in Satan and considers the effect of those passions on the reader's imagination: "His Pride, Envy and Revenge, Obstinacy, Despair and Impenitence, are all of them very artfully interwoven. In short, his first Speech is a Complication of all those Passions which discover themselves separately in several other of his Speeches in the Poem" (no. 303, 3:84). Addison's own weaving is careful in its sequence and perceptive in the grouping—the first three succeed one another as separate episodes, leading to the next three, which merge into a single one. These are not passions to which Addison's readers would want to have been party. Addison returns to the analysis of Satan's passions in no. 321. He inspects the passions raised in the mind of the reader with great care in no. 315, reflecting the influence of Descartes, perhaps by way of Le Bossu, in his enthusiasm for Admiration. In no. 345 he turns to a careful appreciation of the propriety, and in no. 357 of the succession, of sentiments in the love of Adam and Eve: "Milton has shewn a wonderful Art in describing that variety of Passions which arise in our first Parents upon the breach of the Commandment that had been given them. We see them gradually passing from the triumph of their Guilt thro' Remorse, Shame, Despair, Contrition, Prayer, and Hope, to a perfect and compleat Repentance" (no. 363, 3:357). This is a sequence that writers had spent centuries preparing. It would be a shame if readers were to stop following it. Among the most influential and, as far as the passions are concerned, traditional, of all the *Spectators,* these alone would have seen to it that the discussion of the passions continued along the well-established lines.[17]

The press could once rely on the occasional assistance of the pulpit, whence the traditional powers of rhetoric reinforced the truths of sacred texts: "My Mind was really affected, and fervent Wishes accompanied my Words. The Confession was read with such a resign'd Humility, the Absolution with such a comfortable Authority, the Thanksgivings with such a Religious Joy, as made me feel those Affections of the Mind in a manner I never did before."[18] Well read, these texts can minister to the minds of sizable congregations, warming them to devotion. The problem with the passions stirred up in church, however, is that the company there, as in the theater, is easily distracted. In no. 503 "Ralph Wonder" objects to a succession of ostentatious episodes of goodness, sweetness, humility, gratitude, joy, loneliness, sorrow, triumph, and ecstasy performed by an elegant young lady. The congregation followed her performance more carefully and perceptively than the sermon.

Only once does *The Spectator* acknowledge that painting might also serve as a vehicle for conveying and clarifying the passions. In doing so it chooses the most striking and effective example then available, an example that subsequent historians of the passions have found equally compelling—the Raphael cartoons discussed in chapter 1. Painting, we are told, ought to be used more often for the improvement of manners: "When we consider that it places the Action of the Person represented in the most agreeable Aspect imaginable, that it does not only express the Passion or Concern as it sits upon him who is drawn, but has under those Features the Height of the Painter's Imagination, What strong Images of Virtue and Humanity might we not expect would be instilled into the Mind from the Labours of the Pencil?" (no. 226, 2:378) This paper then "reads" the passions in several cartoons and concludes by confessing that the Spectator, like many of his contemporaries, entered paintings, if he entered them at all, through the passions depicted in them.[19]

The willingness to handle the passions in and of coteries constitutes one of the most indicative and typical features of *The Spectator*. A pair of pipe-smoking friends induce greater tranquillity in one another than the isolated reading of Seneca could have done (no. 196, 2:268); consolation is likely to be found in the company of other sufferers (no. 163); and soldiers master their fear of death by participating in a crowd (no. 152). "The Sad, the Merry, the Severe, the Melancholy shew a new Chearfulness when [Varilas, a man with the "portable Quality of Good Humour"] comes amongst them" (no. 100, 1:421), and Cicero is quoted to the effect that Catiline "lived with the Sad severely, with the Chearful agreeably, with the Old gravely, with the Young pleasantly . . . , with the Wicked boldly, with the Wanton lasciviously" (no. 386, 3:448). Occasionally groups embody a passionate homogeneity, as when the Everlasting Club looks on all other clubs with an eye of contempt (no. 72).

Michael Ketcham has shown how thoroughly the passions participated in the daily transactions whereby self and society were informed and reconstructed.[20] It seems to me, however, that, because they combine roots in the humanistic tradition and felt effects in the self, the passions transcend the other "gestures" that Ketcham studies. *The Spectator* certainly wanted to move its audience "toward a more complex, more novelistic reading of social performances whereby the meaning of a sign must be read according to its context, and toward a theory of sentiment where the meaning of the sign resides in the observer's responses" (Ketcham, 49–50). But of the "signs" available, only the passions brought with them considerations of both context and response, and only the passions offered the fruitful complexity on which the eighteenth-century essay depended. They were the one part of the social and psychological lexicon which did not need, or receive, "continual assessment." In fact, they served to anchor and to guide the assessment of other moral terms. When these episodes entered a semantic field, they retained their established meanings and imparted their own energies (cf. Ketcham, 132–35, 147).

The most revealing, extended, and ingenious manipulation of this concern with the functioning of the passions in groups is the account, spread over three papers (424, 429, and 440) of a small company of city dwellers lent the use of "an absent Nobleman's Seat" during the season when it was fashionable to leave the city. Unaccustomed as they are to such isolated and concentrated company, they create an "Infirmary" for the temporary banishment of those who indulge their passions. Only by removing themselves from company can they render their passions fit to rejoin it: "Whoever says a peevish thing, or acts any thing which betrays a Sowerness or Indisposition to Company, is immediately to be conveyed to his Chambers in the Infirmary; from whence he is not to be relieved, till by his Manner of Submission, and the Sentiments expressed in his Petition for that Purpose, he appears to the Majority of the Company to be again fit for Society. You are to understand, that all ill natured Words or uneasy Gestures are sufficient Cause for Banishment" (no. 424, 4:591). By the time the visit is nearly over, the Infirmary is full, partly because of an Easterly Wind, and partly because the circumstances provide so much occasion for the display of passions and so little for the company in which they are displayed to avoid, ignore, or refine them. In this instance, the passions have been sent back to the closet for the benefit of the company by which they were provoked!

One effect of this reliance on group response for the management of passion is the emphasis, characteristic of the age, on shame, modesty, and impudence. The first of these figures in numerous, but unremarkable, instances of blushing. The latter two of these most social of the passions appear in company in this passage, where the modesty of the reclusive frequenters of closets and libraries is unable to compete with impudence:

I must confess, when I have seen *Charles Frankair* rise up with a commanding Mein, and Torrent of handsome Words, talk a Mile off the Purpose, and drive down twenty bashful Boobies of ten times his Sense, who at the same Time were envying his Impudence and despising his Understanding, it has been Matter of great Mirth to me; but it soon ended in a secret Lamentation, that the Fountains of every thing Praise-worthy in these Realms, the Universities, should be so muddied with a false Sense of this Virtue, as to produce Men capable of being so abused. I will be bold to say, that it is a ridiculous Education which does not qualify a Man to make his best Appearance before the greatest Man and the finest Woman to whom he can address himself.[21]

For Addison and Steele, as for Johnson (*Rambler* nos. 159, 173, 179, 180), those who desert their studies for the tea table will have to adapt their attitudes and accustom their passions to the expectations and conventions of the company gathered there. As it is, they discredit their learning and themselves by bringing only their bashfulness, envy, and despising with them.

To the undiscerning, the impudence of Charles Frankair lends him an air of courtliness. It reminds us that the court was the coterie in which the passions had most often prevailed and had most often been analyzed and anatomized. This venue imparted several features unwelcome in the genteel places that subscribed or aspired to the transitional values of *The Spectator*. Having, out of "invincible Modesty," quit "a Way of Life in which no Man can rise suitably to his Merit, who is not something of a Courtier as well as a Souldier," Captain Sentry often laments "that in a Profession where Merit is placed in so conspicuous a View, Impudence should get the Better of Modesty" (no. 2, 1:11). The courage that had seemed so essential to earlier cultures became inconvenient for later ones, so courts encouraged other, subtler passions. These passions were to be replaced in turn, *The Spectator* hoped, by more refined (*socially* refined) ones. The French court, as we have seen, codified the passions (along with everything else), enabling them to be recognized, analyzed, and, sometimes, simulated. They thus came to *The Spectator* clarified but also heavily contaminated with courtly display. They could be understood, but they needed to be watched, and watch them was precisely what the Spectator did.

The passions at court focused on the lofty object at its center—a focus good for neither that lofty object nor those in whom it inspired ambition and encouraged impudence. *The Spectator* thus deprecates the vicarious, fashionable, and indulgent grief for departed foreign princes (no. 64). For Addison and Steele, as for most writers, courtiers corrupt whatever they do, wear, or say—because they do, wear, or say it with modishness and insincerity. All of their "professions," especially their passions, are artificial: "A Couple of Courtiers making Professions of Esteem, would make the same Figure after Breach of Promise, as two Knights of the Post convicted of Perjury."[22] The sophistication which all courtiers affect obliges them to treat the Spectator and his moral and social program with contempt. One of them objects to Mr. Spectator's emphasis on virtue and his references to an afterlife, his frequent quotations from Cicero, and his general disapproval of courtiers: "I have a great deal more to say to you, but I shall sum it up all in this one Remark, In short, Sir, you do not write like a Gentleman" (no. 158, 2:119).

One court had kept itself free, or so the writers it is convenient to call "Augustan" sometimes liked to think, from the contamination of courtly passions. Augustus had lived "amongst his Friends as if he had his Fortune to make in his own Court" and "assumed no Figure in it but what he thought was his Due from his private Talents and Qualifications, as they contributed to advance the Pleasures and Sentiments of the Company" (no. 280, 2:592). Even the writers (*mirabile dictu*) of this court were free from envy and detraction (see no. 253, an essay that seems ultimately to have led to envy and a quarrel between Addison and Pope). Freed from the passions themselves, writers such as Horace and Cicero were better able to understand their operation in others and to produce works that enabled others to do so. To the extent that the society *The Spectator* was working to cultivate could emulate the candor, affability, recognition of merit, and uniformity of taste and judgment of the Augustan court, to that extent Captain Sentry would be better off at the tea table than in the officers' mess.

Provided, of course, he took his rank with him. The strong comparative component in every passion had lent itself to the political structure of every court; it worked a little more tentatively within the elaborate but negotiable stratification of status in early eighteenth-century urban society. In a clever paper on the uses of the disturbing new art of calculation (no. 174, 2:186–87), comparisons are conducted both horizontally and vertically on social scales that have been compiled into exactly ranked "lists." Those who occupy adjacent places on these lists are only in this cynical sense "neighbors," all equally given to calculation and thus episodes of ill nature and envy. The ill nature runs up and down one scale, while the envy moves between one scale and the other. The soldier and the courtier exchange passions back and forth and up and down and spoil the company when they do so.

The Spectator never undertook to subvert this stratification, socially or psychologically. Indeed, it drew upon the tensions between the passions and the shifting society within which they had to make their traditional comparisons to produce a quickening of the soul that could then serve moral as well as social purposes and produce theological, even eternal, results. Supposing that the souls of those in the upper ranks had quicker admonitions and finer edges than those in the lower ranks, and therefore more refined passions (no. 6), it counted on that refinement to make numerous improvements in this world. More important, it assumed, with no hint of irony that I can detect, that this stratification would be continued, corrected, in a better world: "The truth of it is, Honours are in this World under no Regulation; true Quality is neglected, Vertue is oppressed, and Vice triumphant. The last Day will rectifie this Disorder, and assign to every one a Station suitable to the Dignity of his Character; Ranks will be then adjusted, and Precedency set right" (no. 219, 2:352). Then it will be easy to know whom to treat with reverence and whom with contempt. And evidently, such comparisons and behavior will still be necessary. Perhaps it will be one of the celestial rewards that they will also be effective.

A passage full of physiology will direct us to another typical but less satisfactory aspect of *The Spectator*'s treatment of the passions, a treatment we might expect from someone so full of tendentious fragilities that he had acquired the character of "the Ladies Philosopher" (no. 380, 3:426): "Women in their Nature are much more gay and joyous than Men; whether it be that their Blood is more refined, their Fibres more delicate, and their animal Spirits more light and volatile; or whether, as some have imagined, there may not be a kind of Sex in the very Soul, I shall not pretend to determine" (no. 128, 2:8). The refinement of blood and the motion of the more delicate "animal Spirits" through hollow fibers to produce passion are, as we have seen, taken over directly, and not even metaphorically, from a long tradition. The attitude toward the special physiology, and thus women's special capacity for passion, is continued from the same tradition.

In deploring "Party Rage" in women and enumerating the conventional spiritual and physical effects of anger, *The Spectator* "proves" that this passion is doubly out of place when women bring it into company: "This is, in its nature, a Male Vice, and made up of many angry and cruel Passions that are altogether repugnant to the Softness, the Modesty, and those other endearing Qualities which are natural to the Fair Sex. Women were formed to temper Mankind, and sooth them into Tenderness and Compassion, not to set an Edge upon their Minds, and blow up in them those Passions which are too apt to rise of their own Accord" (no. 57, 1:242). The repugnant passions entered company in the veins of "Camilla" (whose namesake had been dedicated to Diana) when she encountered a heroine named after a Queen of the Amazons: "The Dear Creature, about a Week ago, encountred the fierce and beautiful *Penthesilea* across a Tea-Table, but in the height of her Anger, as her Hand chanced to shake with the Earnestness of the Dispute, she scalded her Fingers, and spilt a Dish of Tea upon her Petticoat" (no. 57, 1:242). Evidently, if the passions were to be brought into company, they would have to be chosen, controlled, and refined to fit that company. And it would be the company that judged the fit (schooled, of course, by the hand and mind of the Spectator).

A few of his numerous female correspondents are permitted to share the Spectator's informed understanding of the workings of the passions—their own, those of other women, and those of the men who admire them. These women combine this special understanding with their special physiological advantages to refine the passions of the men who keep them company. In this latter capacity (one that they exhibit in Castiglione, Pope, and Hume, among others) they appear most often in *The Spectator*. In no. 362 "Belinda" refines the passions of a censorious scholar, and nos. 433–34 describe the good effects of Amazons on Scythians (and vice versa). In no. 53 an elaborate passage on the reciprocal good effects of esteem on both subject and object suggests that, if women will only bestow their love on better objects, they will provoke more refined passions in return.[23]

The greatest refinement, however, occurs when the passions are filtered through both gender and rank. In those special cases, they will have been brought into company to very good effect: "The entire Conquest of our Passions is so difficult a work, that they who despair of it should think of a less difficult Task, and only attempt to Regulate them. But there is a third thing which may contribute not only to the Ease, but also to the Pleasure of our Life; and that is, refining our Passions to a greater Elegance, than we receive them from Nature" (no. 71, 1:304). The early academies had tried to conquer the passions, and later courts had tried to regulate them. Addison and Steele, however, sought to have them refined in company, "to a greater Elegance." The whole essay deals with love and language at various social levels, assuming that passions grow more refined as they ascend the social scale.

Spectator no. 102 depends for much of its success on an understanding of how the passions work, or rather worked, in women and in company. It presupposes, in addition, the temperament and ability to play with language, convention, and human nature. I quote at length because the passions enabled Addison to write at length. The sustained play here indicates both the strength of the tradition and the cleverness of those who toyed with it:

> There is an infinite Variety of Motions to be made use of in the *Flutter of a Fan:* There is the angry Flutter, the modest Flutter, the timorous Flutter, the confused Flutter, the merry Flutter, and the amorous Flutter. Not to be tedious, there is scarce any Emotion in the mind which does not produce a suitable Agitation in the Fan; insomuch, that if I only see the Fan of a disciplin'd Lady, I know very well whether she laughs, frowns, or blushes. I have seen a Fan so very angry, that it would have been dangerous for the absent Lover who provoked it to have come within the Wind of it; and at other Times so very languishing, that I have been glad for the Lady's Sake the Lover was at a sufficient Distance from it.[24]

The playful metonymy of articulate fluttering exaggerates the conventional—that is, well-understood—language of the passions, the body language as well as the English language. It follows several paragraphs of travesty of the language of a drillmaster. These vocabularies combined to provide both social insights and linguistic possibilities to those who were fluent in either language, but they need the syntax of the periodic sentence to flourish into so many lively episodes. Addison exploits the tradition of associating passion with spirit and breath as well as the physiological heat which the fan purportedly dissipated. This social appliance, a peculiarly female one, clarifies, codifies, and amplifies those passions which women contrive to bring into company. The lady with a fan becomes the rival of Garrick—so much so that we must be meant to wonder whether she has been "disciplin'd" to feel and display her own passions or only those of the company before which she displays them.

The division of passions into generations rather than gender had a longer tradition of deliberate analysis. *Spectator* no. 192 analyzes the esteem that ought to unite father and son, and no. 496 the tensions between them, while no. 153 goes beyond its source in Cicero (itself a compendium) to construct intricate patterns of congruity and reaction among generations:

> A young Man whose Passion and Ambition is to be good and wise, and an old one who has no Inclination to be lewd or debauched, are quite unconcerned in this Speculation; but the Cocking young Fellow who treads upon the Toes of his Elders, and the old Fool who envyes the sawcy Pride he sees him in, are the Objects of our present Contempt and Derision. Contempt and Derision are harsh Words; but in what manner can one give advice to a Youth in the pursuit and Possession of sensual Pleasures, or afford pity to an old Man in the impotence and desire of Enjoying them? [No. 153, 2:100–101]

Two pairs of passions, well established and carefully separated, develop in this passage: the correct passions of young and old, where the young hope to be good and wise and the old have outgrown their youthful lewdness, and the incorrect ones of the overeager and indulgent young and the still lecherous and envious old. The final episode takes place in right-minded readers who, in the company of the Spectator, grow contemptuous of both members of the latter pair.

Several passages combine the two concerns of gender and generation in ways that remind us that the age in question did not look as deeply into some passions as ours does. They knew very well with what episodes of the human spirit their prose could cope and were willing to settle for those. While the natural affection of parents for their dependent children formed part of the "Design of Providence," a special vocabulary was needed to capture the peculiar power and focus of this particular passion. The Spectator adopted the Greek *storgé* ("natural Affection to every thing which relies upon us for its Good and Preservation," no. 181, 2:214; see also the note) for this passion, a passion to which Essays 449 and 466 reverted. In no. 520 a widowed father discusses the effects of his daughter on his grief for his wife. The underlying passions inform both vocabulary and syntax:

> I confess to you I am inconsolable, and my Eyes gush with Grief as if I had seen her but just then expire. In this Condition I am broken in upon by a charming young Woman, my Daughter, who is the Picture of what her Mother was on her Wedding-Day. The good Girl strives to comfort me; but how shall I let you know that all the Comfort she gives me is to make my Tears flow more easily? The Child knows she quickens my Sorrow, and rejoices my Heart at the same Time. Oh, ye Learned, tell me by what Word to speak a Motion of the Soul for which there is no Name.[25]

We now have names for that passion as well as clinical diagnoses, costly analyses, and perhaps even smug understandings of its ambivalent images and troubling responses. I am not at all certain that we are to be envied.

I offer as a passage that might well be regarded as the culmination of the passions in *The Spectator* one that returns them to the court from which they came and the humanists to whom they belonged, that attends to their public display as well as their inner significance, that derives a profound reassurance from the troubling connections among soul, mind, and body, and that contains perhaps the ultimate example of Addison's recurrent connection of passion and afterlife. It describes the death of Sir Thomas More:

> He died upon a point of Religion, and is respected as a Martyr by that side for which he suffered. That innocent Mirth, which

had been so conspicuous in his Life, did not forsake him to the last: He maintain'd the same Chearfulness of Heart upon the Scaffold, which he used to shew at his Table: and upon laying his Head on the Block, gave instances of that good Humour with which he had always entertained his Friends in the most ordinary Occurrences. His Death was of a piece with his Life. There was nothing in it new, forced or affected. He did not look upon the severing of his Head from his Body as a Circumstance that ought to produce any Change in the disposition of his Mind; and as he died under a fix'd and settled hope of Immortality, he thought any unusual degree of Sorrow and Concern improper on such an occasion as had nothing in it which could deject or terrifie him. [No. 349, 3:300–1]

The passions enable that passage to account for the respect that More's life and conduct once inspired. They allow the prose to separate More's heart from his head without interrupting his habitual good humor. Nor will the executioner's grisly separation unsettle his hope, instill dejection or terror, or justify "any unusual degree of Sorrow and Concern" in his friends. Throughout the passage the established vocabulary imparts clarity, dignity, and the sense of continuance that humanists have always sought. More understood his passions completely and controlled them absolutely. The author of this passage shared the understanding and the control and was thus able to depict the passions of this heroic soul passing into a better company. The prose is schooled in the workings of the passions, internal and external, and remains alert to their numerous possibilities. It deserves, I suggest, readers similarly disciplined.

5

PHILOSOPHICAL DETACHMENT:

SUPPOSITION, TRANSITION, AND

SYMPATHY IN HUME

ECAUSE DAVID HUME CAME VERY NEAR THE end of the long tradition of the passions, that tradition was more important to him than he was to it. Accepting it as established, he inspected it with his shrewd eye for causes and connections and contributed to it a few shifts in emphasis, several systems of classification to which even he paid little attention, and his own ideas of transition and sympathy. He continued to analyze, attribute, and discuss passions in his later works but not often in ways that reflect their treatment in the *Treatise*. Nevertheless, the reliance on a tradition by a writer as thoughtful and provocative as Hume (and one so determined to resist traditions) constitutes in itself a contribution to that tradition. This contribution was amply recompensed: the passions figure centrally in his analysis of belief, they complicate and make possible his concept of the self, and they inform his morality, underlie his aesthetics, and enliven his style.

Hume's own nature was so dispassionate as to infuriate Rousseau (though he accused himself of a passion for literature and love of fame).[1] The nature he supposed for the rest of us was a passionate one, replete with traditional passions that formed the basis of his new human science. Hume drew so freely and generally from that tradition that it is not often possible, or wise, to ascribe specific sources for specific points.[2] My inspection of Hume's treatment of the passions in the *Treatise* will show that that treatment is far more traditional than most commentators suggest and that Hume is his own best interpreter of his views.[3] Thus the first half of this chapter will seem to continue, or review, chapters 2 and 3. The second half demonstrates that the passions figure in Hume's Essays and *Dialogues* in ways that have received insufficient attention. They underlie his reconstruction of the four schools of philosophy and impart intricacy to several other essays; they undermine the *Natural History of Religion;* and they modify the *Dialogues* in several slight but surprising ways.

I do not include Hume's *History of England,* even though a contemporary called it the "History of English Passions, by Human Reason."[4] The reason is that I devote a later chapter to the treatment of the passions by a historian and concentrate here on the opportunities and difficulties they offered a philosopher—an empirical philosopher who acknowledged their force and a sceptical one who exploited their clarity.

Hume's widely quoted assertion that "Reason is, and ought only to be the slave of the passions, and can never pretend to any other office than to serve and obey them" is a contribution to polemics rather than to theory.[5] As such it is far less significant than the long analysis of pride and humility, the transitions between passions, the psychologically and socially intricate principle of sympathy, the roles of probability and property in passion, and, especially, the double relationship between self and object that inform the *Treatise of Human Nature.* My discussion of that work will concentrate on Hume's obligations to the tradition, the changes in his treatment of the self that the passions forced on him, and the aesthetic and social implications of some of his ideas. Hume's control of the passions, in his prose as well as in his person, has always been either impressive or exasperating, depending, I suppose, on the disposition of one's own passions. I include several long quotations to illustrate that control.

The argument of the *Treatise,* like most of Hume's arguments, is conducted largely by means of analogy, supposition, and historical observation—a method that promotes clarity and coherence without disturbing the tradition or violating Hume's fixed aversion to metaphysics. Accepting the passions as a central, standard, and essential element of human nature, he employs them in numerous clarifying and convincing suppositions, the experiments of his "experimental method." In the following passage he offers several such suppositions to show how sympathy and comparison function in various episodes of passion. While this is a lengthy passage, it is one which the passions make both lively and clear. It also exhibits several of the intricate considerations that are crucial to Hume's treatment of them:

Since then those principles of sympathy, and a comparison with ourselves, are directly contrary, it may be worth while to consider, what general rules can be form'd. . . . Suppose I am now in safety at land, and wou'd willingly reap some pleasure from this consideration: I must think on the miserable condition of those who are at sea in a storm, and must endeavour to render this idea as strong and lively as possible, in order to make me more sensible of my own happiness. But whatever pains I may take, the comparison will never have an equal efficacy, as if I were really on the shore, and saw a ship at a distance, tost by a tempest, and in danger every minute of perishing on a rock or sand-bank. But suppose this idea to become still more lively. Suppose the ship to be driven so near me, that I can perceive distinctly the horror, painted on the countenance of the seamen and passengers, hear their lamentable cries, see the dearest friends give their last adieu, or embrace with a resolution to perish in each others arms: No man has so savage a heart as to reap any pleasure from such a spectacle, or withstand the motions of the tenderest compassion and sympathy.[6]

These suppositions (much more central to Hume's method than most commentators notice) ask readers to look into their own minds, confident that they will find the traditional passions in operation there and will know what they are called and how they work. They depend on the most salient of all assumptions about the passions: that they are the same in all of us and that our responses to the same objects are very nearly identical. Every time we enter into one of these suppositions we confirm within ourselves the uniformity and consistency with which these episodes occur—a well-established consistency that Richard Kuhns has called the "traditional dogmatism" of the passions.[7] Such suppositions are empirical in that they ask us to consult our own experience and sceptical in that they are detached from the stimulation of real objects and the distortion of actual beliefs, so that we can test their accuracy without feeling their disturbance.

Hume takes the existence of these uniform passions for granted, without doubting or inquiring into it. They have been established by so long a tradition that they can be attributed to "nature" and invoked in the most precise demonstrations: "Now 'tis obvious, that nature has preserv'd a great resemblance among all human creatures, and that we never remark any passion or principle in others, of which, in some degree or other, we may not find a parallel in ourselves." This uniformity, the passage continues, makes possible, indeed inevitable, the suppositions, transitions, and sympathy at work in that imagined shipwreck: "and this resemblance must very much contribute to make us enter into the sentiments of others, and embrace them with facility and pleasure. . . . The stronger the relation is betwixt ourselves and any object, the more easily does the imagination make the transition, and convey to the related idea the vivacity of conception, with which we always form the idea of our own person."[8]

The passions that are so prevalent and so uniform and that make such sympathetic transitions possible dominate the *Treatise* from its opening paragraph, where they are treated as impressions: "Those perceptions, which enter with most force and violence . . . all our sensations, passions, and emotions, as they make their first appearance in the soul" (1). Indeed, much of the analysis of ideas in book 1 seems designed to forge links with passion, as ideas are repeatedly dealt with in the language and systems of passion. Thus it is the animal spirits that account for most of the "mistakes" the mind makes with its ideas: "for this reason the animal spirits, falling into the contiguous traces, present other related ideas in lieu of that which the mind desir'd at first to survey. This change we are not always sensible of."[9] The brain is accorded a little control over the spirits which course through it, but for the most part they circulate in accordance with the physiology and the dynamics of Thomas Willis or, for that matter, Aquinas.

Hume does not often, it must be added, mention these spirits, or even seem to have them in mind. Thus his dissection is insistently imaginary, ignoring the actual investigations of physiology available to him. The *Treatise* is marked, and perhaps a little debilitated, by this indifference to physiology.[10] Such physiology as he does incorporate occurs in figurative Newtonianisms, for which he later apologized: "And this different feeling [in the mind—of an idea assented to rather than one known to be a fiction} I endeavour to explain by calling it a superior *force,* or *vivacity,* or *solidity,* or *firmness,* or *steadiness.* This variety of terms, which may seem so unphilosophical, is intended only to express that act of the mind, which renders realities more present to us than fictions, causes them to weigh more in the thought, and gives them a superior influence on the passions and imagination" (629). The feelings of the mind that are so essential to all of Hume's philosophy are consistently depicted as the feelings of *force.* That force produces belief, and it does so by means of the animal spirits.

In a most intriguing passage, one that makes the mind sound like a billiard table, the colliding particles, shapes, and motions that convey belief are directly, but sceptically and ironically, connected with pleasure and pain: "'Tis absurd to imagine, that . . . the shocking of two globular particles shou'd become a sensation of pain, and that the meeting of two triangular ones shou'd afford a pleasure."[11] The ideas with which Hume deals in book 1 are always both distinguished from and subject to the passions by means of pleasure and pain, the traditional component of the passions Hume takes most for granted throughout the *Treatise:* "There is implanted in the human mind a perception of pain and pleasure, as the chief spring and moving principle of all its actions" (118). Hume treats this traditional susceptibility as a received and established fact—one for which he uses the image, or at least the word, "spring" repeatedly, often in conjunction, as here and in the letter to Hutcheson cited in note 10, with "principle." These springs constitute another one of the uniform elements of human nature on which so much of his system depends.[12]

For Hume, as for Aquinas, the will is supposed to be actuated by estimations of good and evil and by careful estimations of the relative force of impressions, to keep the mind from being moved by every idle conception (119–20). In this context Hume makes his connection between passion and belief—a connection that is, in fact, a disconnection of belief from ideas. "When any affecting object is presented, it gives the alarm, and excites immediately a degree of its proper passion; especially in persons who are naturally inclined to that passion. This emotion passes by an easy transition to the imagination; and diffusing itself over our idea of the affecting object, makes us form that idea with greater force and vivacity, and consequently assent to it, according to the precedent system" (120).

The concern with tranquillity and ease evident in the preceding paragraph is characteristic of Hume's treatment and temperament. As we shall see, Fielding and Johnson shared the concern, but Fielding treats it physically, dramatically, and satirically, while Johnson treats it morally and sympathetically. Hume simply takes it for granted. Belief, which he never took for granted, is a function of easy and customary transitions between passions and ideas, transitions that ought to be governed by the will and subjected to attentive scrutiny.

The aesthetic implications of belief are implicit in the passions of the witness of that shipwreck. Hume refines the traditional aesthetic considerations of Aristotle and Addison, suggesting that the pleasure in dramatic representations of fear and terror depends on their existence in the mind as ideas on which "the imagination imposes itself indolently" (115). The corresponding passion is "softened" because we do not believe in the subject:

> There is no passion of the human mind but what may arise from poetry; tho' at the same time the *feelings* of the passions are very different when excited by poetical fictions, from what they are when they arise from belief and reality. A passion, which is disagreeable in real life, may afford the highest entertainment in a tragedy, or epic poem. In the latter case it lies not with that weight upon us: It feels less firm and solid: And has no other than the agreeable effect of exciting the spirits, and rouzing the attention. [630–31; note, again, the weight of Newtonianism here.]

In the light of that passage we can see that the episodes of horror we were invited to suppose as we watched that storm-tossed ship differ from those *The Spectator* viewed on the stage only in the greater degree of detachment available to the supposer outside the theater. The supposer, the reader, and the theatergoer know and feel the identical passions but with different force. (The viewer of a painting, one assumes, stands somewhere between the latter two in this respect.) The same detachment that assists philosophy in its supposings abets art by "exciting the spirits, and rouzing the attention."

Book 1 concludes with a crucial and disturbing discussion of identity, in the course of which the self is deconstructed into a bundle of impressions and a series of passions, or, more precisely, episodes of passion: "Pain and pleasure, grief and joy, passions and sensations succeed each other, and never all exist at the same time" (251–52). Hume is careful to "distinguish betwixt personal identity, as it regards our thought or imagination, and as it regards our passions or the concern we take in ourselves" (253), the same distinction that separates book 1 from book 2. While the disconnecting of ideas has disturbed the sense of the self, that self will have to be restored in order to respond to and figure in the passions to which the mind is and ought only to be the slave.[13] The universal springs become essential points of continuity and reassurance in what Richetti depicts as "an epistemological and moral world of turbulent uncertainty where the common sense and humanist continuities supporting the republic of letters are canceled or at best rendered arbitrary and imperiled" (190). Uniform, shared, and well-understood episodes of passion allowed, even obliged, Hume to reconstitute the self, if only to enable him to ask other selves to "suppose" and to provide a self to participate in double relationships. The long tradition they brought with them into his system both strengthened that system and forced some modifications to it.

The secondary, or reflective, impressions to which book 2 is devoted proceed from either an original impression or an idea of that impression. They have more immediacy than the ideas dealt with in book 1 but less force than the "primary" passions which emanate directly from the senses and bodily pains and pleasures (and are of little interest to Hume; 275–76). Hume's divisions of the passions into categories are not notably more successful than those of his predecessors. Some of his categories overlap, not all of them are reconcilable, and none of them is of great use or significance.[14] Even his basic division between "calm" and "violent" passions is, he himself admits, far from being exact; passions regularly rise or fall from one category into the other. The calm passions, fraught with aesthetic implications, arise in response to "the sense of beauty and deformity in action, composition, and external objects." The violent ones, love and hate, grief and joy, pride and humility, are further, or alternatively, divided into indirect ("pride, humility, ambition, vanity, love, hatred, envy, pity, malice, generosity, with their dependants") and direct ("desire, aversion, grief, joy, hope, fear, despair, and security," 276–77; see Kemp Smith, 168–69). Hume does nothing with the lists and little with the divisions. It ought, nevertheless, to be mentioned that the violence depicted by art is somehow transformed into calm episodes in the mind. This transformation, unexplained and undeveloped, seems to be at the heart of Hume's aesthetics.

Hume devotes most of his analysis to the first pair of violent indirect passions, pride and humility. In order to do so he is obliged to reconstruct, indeed to strengthen, the sense of self, if not of identity: " 'Tis evident, that pride and humility, tho' directly contrary, have yet the same OBJECT. This object is self, or that succession of related ideas and impressions, of which we have an intimate memory and consciousness. Here the view always fixes when we are actuated by either of these passions. According as our idea of ourself is more or less advantageous, we feel either of those opposite affections" (277). In earlier accounts, the passions belong or are accountable to, or are on loan from, the universe, God, the church, a school of philosophers, or the blood. But for Hume they belong unmistakably to the self; in fact, they reconstitute that self, taking account of its social possibilities and obligations but never threatening it with eternal consequences. For Hume the self is not just the slave of the passions; it is their construct.

Thus reconstructed, the self figures centrally in the "double relation" which, had this idea taken hold or the tradition survived, would certainly have been Hume's major contribution to the analysis of the passions: "Any thing, that gives a pleasant sensation, and is related to self, excites the passion of pride, which is also agreeable, and has self for its object" (288). This central concept combines Hume's customary emphasis on transition with his acute analyses of cause and requires him, again, to posit a traditional, pre-Humean self. In the case of pride and humility the transaction is a closed one; all the connections between impressions reinforce one another because they operate with the self as their object: " 'Tis after this manner, that the particular causes of pride and humility are determin'd. The quality, which operates on the passion, produces separately an impression resembling it; the subject, to which the quality adheres, is related to self, the object of the passion: No wonder the whole cause, consisting of a quality and of a subject, does so unavoidably give rise to the passion" (289).

Hume calculates this double relation for every passion. Its central tenet is: "that all agreeable objects, related to ourselves, by an association of ideas and of impressions, produce pride, and disagreeable ones, humility" (290). He considers the closeness, conspicuousness, exclusiveness, and duration of the relation of the cause to the self in a series of telling and clarifying illustrations, some of which reflect Hume's doctrines of sympathy and self while suggesting his own sociability. Thus all those who attend a great feast may feel joy at it, but, properly, only the "master of the feast" may add pride to that joy. Similarly, while health gives joy, it is so widely shared that it cannot bring pride.[15] These illustrations suggest both how supple the tradition remained and that it could still dictate to, and profit from, the scrutiny of yet another philosopher.

At this point, and without much indication, Hume switches back to the calm passions to consider taste, a concern to which he reverted repeatedly in his system, his works, and his life. He treats it as an element inherent in human nature, something between a faculty and a passion, constituted and recognized as a sensation of pleasure or unease. He makes the tenuous connections between taste and pride or humility both strong and central: "The power of bestowing these opposite sensations [pleasure and uneasiness] is, therefore, the very essence of true and false wit; and consequently the cause of that pride or humility, which arises from them" (297). This is a psychological explanation of a connection that Addison had suggested without investigating. In the process of confirming the presence or absence of wit these sensations confirm the existence and refine the nature of the self—solely on the strength of the passions available to it. Sensations of pleasure and pain, similarly isolated and emphasized, account for our similarly isolated and emphasized sense of beauty (p. 299). That taste can be *cultivated* is perhaps the most significant revision of the notion of self that the passions impose on Hume's epistemology; the idea of cultivation presupposes an entity much more continuous than a disconnected sequence or a bundle of impressions.

Hume's special emphasis on the sense of self obliged him to develop one component of the passions that had been largely implicit in previous schemes, the element of comparison. Comparison emerges with force and inevitability when the self begins to acknowledge and consider the selves of others, as above in the example of the supposer of a shipwreck. In fact that passage was supplied to illustrate the point that "no comparison is more obvious than that with ourselves; and hence it is that on all occasions it takes place, and mixes with most of our passions" (593). Comparison figures most noticeably and effectively in the pride with which we possess or desire any object: "Comparison is in every case a sure method of augmenting our esteem of any thing" (315–16).

Conversely, the exclusion of others, and thus the removal of comparison, underlies the pride attached to property, another consideration implicit in earlier schemes but enlarged upon by Hume. Property, Hume says, "may be look'd upon as a particular species of *causation*" (310), and the idea of property becomes a potent device for handling the transitions of the passions and for controlling the sense of the self in book 3. Here (book 2, in the definition of property) the implicit emphasis on a "proprietor" incorporates the component of self, without which, as we have seen, there can be no pride, and that of comparison, the exclusion of the selves of others: "such a relation betwixt a person and an object as permits him, but forbids any other, the free use and possession of it, without violating the laws of justice and moral equity" (310; compare *Essays* I, 151n).

If our own episodes of pride and the love of fame presuppose the participation of "others," so also do those others make sympathy possible. Hume goes well beyond traditional accounts of sympathy, bringing to bear the uniformity and continuity of human passion and corroborating the general idea of eighteenth-century social life as well as the specific idea of "le bon David."[16] His discussion of sympathy provides one of the few occasions for an allusion to the exterior manifestations of the passions and one of the few places in the *Treatise* where he replaces supposition with introspection, taking a rare look into his own springs:

A chearful countenance infuses a sensible complacency and serenity into my mind; as an angry or sorrowful one throws a sudden damp upon me. Hatred, resentment, esteem, love, courage, mirth and melancholy; all these passions I feel more from communication than from my own natural temper and disposition. . . .

When any affection is infus'd by sympathy, it is at first known only by its effects, and by those external signs in the countenance and conversation, which convey an idea of it. This idea is presently converted into an impression, and acquires such a degree of force and vivacity, as to become the very passion itself, and produce an equal emotion, as any original affection. [317]

Even here Hume moves quickly past the appearances of passion to their names and their effects in the mind. So determined is he to detach the passions from their sources and to concentrate on their causes that he seldom lingers over their external effects. Hume would not, I think, have stayed long in front of West's painting.[17] The reciprocity between body and mind is taken for granted and overshadowed by internal transitions and the social component of *sym*pathy, which operates at one remove from the external signs that express it. These transitions, though diffuse, are reciprocal. There are intramental correspondences between ideas and impressions within the same mind and, simultaneously, social correspondences between the passions of one member of a company and the ideas of another. Episodes of passion may have complicated the mental life of the eighteenth century, but they also provided repeated evidence that that life was, in fact, going on and, more important, was subject to informed and articulate inspection.

As the *Treatise* progresses, the principle, to use Hume's term, of sympathy takes on an air of intense conviviality, one in which the mind "naturally seeks after foreign objects, which may produce a lively sensation, and agitate the spirits. On the appearance of such an object it awakes, as it were, from a dream: The blood flows with a new tide: The heart is elevated" (353). The self becomes absolutely dependent upon other selves to stimulate, verify, and resonate its own passions:

We can form no wish, which has not a reference to society. A perfect solitude is, perhaps, the greatest punishment we can suffer. Every pleasure languishes when enjoy'd a-part from company, and every pain becomes more cruel and intolerable.

Whatever other passions we may be actuated by; pride, ambition, avarice, curiosity, revenge or lust; the soul or animating principle of them all is sympathy; nor wou'd they have any force, were we to abstract entirely from the thoughts and sentiments of others. [363]

To illustrate the reciprocal transitions and resonances of sympathy, Hume constructs a chamber of mirrors in which the pleasure of possessions reverberates from the owner to the beholder and back, through three successive rebounds: "Here then is a third rebound of the original pleasure; after which 'tis difficult to distinguish the images and reflexions, by reason of their faintness and confusion."[18] The mirrors belong to Locke and the optics to Newton, but the strong sense of property and self is Hume's own contribution to this reflective chamber.

Having dealt at such great length with pride and humility, Hume moves more briefly and conventionally to an analysis of love and hatred, passions which lack the occasion for Hume's special emphases on self and sympathy. They have others rather than the self for their objects, and the effects of those others are immediate and circumscribed. He does note that the objects of these passions must be "thinking beings" (330–31). Otherwise, the arguments and observations already made on pride and contempt are directly convertible to love and hatred—so much so that Hume predicates a "square" of passions from which he generates eight "experiments," a series of suppositions that confirms the stability, consistency, and possibilities of the system of the passions he has generated from the tradition he acquired (332–47; compare Richetti, 232–35). The square is a working example of the "controlled dogmatism" of the passions, governed by traditional sensations and objects and producing the customary episodes. It is also governed by a sense of self, traversed by principled transitions, and illuminated by the distinction between impressions and ideas. It confirms the double relation necessary to every passion and charts the ways in which a strong sense of self can disturb its symmetry. These Humean additions explain, for example, why pride and humility transform more readily into love and hate than the other way around: once a passion has fixed the attention upon the self, it resists transition elsewhere (340).

The transition between passions is governed by the principle of descent in another vaguely Newtonian analogy: "This transition is made with greater facility, where the more considerable object is first presented, and the lesser follows it. . . . Thus 'tis more natural for us to love the son upon account of the father, than the father upon account of the son; the servant for the master. . . . In short, our passions, like other objects, descend with greater facility than they ascend" (341–42). No actual spirits follow actual paths here, yet the strength of observation and the power of expression have enabled Hume to explain, with both exactness and originality, and without resorting to the subconscious, why, among other things, he thought it more disturbing for a mother to remarry than for a father to do so.[19]

Hume is ultimately more interested in the transition from one emotion to another than in isolated or blended passions, so he moves on to consider the effects of a *succession* of objects and then the itch of the mind to compare, which gives rise to malice and envy (372–80). The sense of self participates strongly in these comparative transitions—indeed they seem to be conducted, though Hume does not quite make this point, primarily to strengthen that sense: "This reasoning will account for the origin of *envy* as well as of malice. The only difference betwixt these passions lies in this, that envy is excited by some present enjoyment of another, which by comparison diminishes our idea of our own: Whereas malice is the unprovok'd desire of producing evil to another, in order to reap a pleasure from the comparison" (377). Envy, he adds, depends on proximity, in both species and degree, an insight one might usefully bring to any depiction or discussion of envy, before or after Hume.

These analyses give rise to some passages of surpassing, perhaps excessive, intricacy, showing how the "principle of parallel direction" governs benevolence and how the various combinations of the invigorating passions of pride and hatred and the enfeebling ones of love and humility may be calculated (381–93).

In considering the direct passions (desire and aversion, grief and joy, hope and fear) which arise immediately from good/evil or pleasure/pain, Hume returns to the will, which he now defines as "nothing but *the internal impression we feel and are conscious of, when we knowingly give rise to any new motion of our body, or new perception of our mind.*"[20] He dismisses all the sophistications of the Scholiasts and concludes that liberty is imaginary and necessity ("intelligible necessity") a fact, however unpleasant the consequences of that doctrine: "All actions of the will have particular causes" (412). These causes are passions, and in this context he makes the pronouncement about the slavery of the mind to the passions. His solution to the traditional dilemma is anything but traditional: "Since a passion can never, in any sense, be call'd unreasonable, but when founded on a false supposition, or when it chuses means insufficient for the design'd end, 'tis impossible, that reason and passion can ever oppose each other, or dispute for the government of the will and actions" (416).

Somewhat unexpectedly, Hume emphasizes the element of self in "surprize" and thus connects it, too, to pride: "As surprize is nothing but a pleasure arising from novelty, it is not, properly speaking, a quality in any object, but merely a passion or impression in the soul. It must, therefore, be from that impression, that pride by a natural transition arises. And it arises so naturally, that there is nothing *in us or belonging to us,* which produces surprize, that does not at the same time excite that other passion [pride]" (301). He goes on, with continued ingenuity, to connect the human capacity for lying to the eagerness for surprise—a connection he will develop in his essays on religion. The component of self is too prominent, and the physiology too vague, to permit a direct connection to Descartes who, it will be recalled, gave pride of place to "astonishment."

The following passage, which will contain few surprises for anyone who has read this far, suggests the effectiveness with which Hume was able to blend his own ideas and predilections with established components and systems. In it the perceptions and motivations of the soul are conducted by the usual means of faculties and spirits. The custom on which Hume turned his detaching eye is familiar from Bacon and the motion from Hobbes (above, 104, 108–12), among others. The convertibility evident in this passage grew naturally out of the new physiology and led into the peculiarly empirical grounds on which the passions were now to be distrusted. The tranquillity which is eventually restored seems to be Hume's special consideration:

When the soul applies itself to the performance of any action, or the conception of any object, to which it is not accustom'd, there is a certain unpliableness in the faculties, and a difficulty of the spirit's moving in their new direction. As this difficulty excites the spirits, 'tis the source of wonder, surprize, and of all the emotions, which arise from novelty; and is in itself very agreeable, like every thing, which inlivens the mind to a moderate degree. But tho' surprize be agreeable in itself, yet as it puts the spirits in agitation, it not only augments our agreeable affections, but also our painful, according to the foregoing principle, *that every emotion, which precedes or attends a passion, is easily converted into it.* Hence every thing, that is new, is most affecting, and gives us either more pleasure or pain, than what, strictly speaking, naturally belongs to it. When it often returns upon us, the novelty wears off; the passions subside; the hurry of the spirits is over; and we survey the objects with greater tranquillity. [422–23]

Hume distrusted these accustomed responses and found philosophical and rhetorical ways to discredit them. But before he did so, he wanted to be sure that he and his reader could understand them.

Hume's discussion of the effects of the imagination on the passions is brief and conventional in its details but reveals Hume's awareness of the force of particulars and of eloquence (425–27). His explanation of why objects remote in time have less influence on the passions than those remote in space and of why those in the future are more forcible than those the same distance in the past once again combines traditional components and new ideas: "The mind, elevated by the vastness of its object, is still farther elevated by the difficulty of the conception; and being oblig'd every moment to renew its efforts in the transition from one part of time to another, feels a more vigorous and sublime disposition, than in a transition thro' the parts of space, where the ideas flow along with easiness and facility."[21] Aquinas's "irascible" passions, "arduous of attainment," are now exerting themselves somewhat more strenuously through Newtonian space but are paying little attention to Willis's channels.

Of the direct passions, only hope and fear interest Hume, and his discussion of them concentrates on the probability that distinguishes them from joy and grief, which are more certain, and from desire and aversion, which are less. The mixtures in which these are likely to be found oblige Hume to turn once more to a series of suppositions: "Throw in a superior degree of probability to the side of grief, you immediately see that passion diffuse itself over the composition, and tincture it into fear" (443).

In book 3, "Of Morals," the passions figure as the causes of action and thus the basis of morality. They develop regular transitions and stability and give rise to virtues. The stability is imparted by property, and the regularity by sympathy and abstraction. Based on our own sentiments of pleasure and uneasiness, Hume's moral system becomes very like his aesthetic one, with the moral sense performing the task of taste. The difference is that virtue and vice "must necessarily be plac'd either in ourselves or others, and excite either pleasure or uneasiness; and therefore must give rise to one of these four passions [pride, humility, love, hatred]; which clearly distinguishes them from the pleasure and pain arising from inanimate objects, that often bear no relation to us" (473). Sympathy and property thus combine to arrest the transitions of the passions by stabilizing possessions (489). Hume does insist that man is not as selfish as some philosophers, or as quarrelsome as others, have made him out to be (486, 539–40).

The social covenant into which man long ago entered arrests the transitions of the passions by the artifice of property. This enables the discipline of sympathy and the chemistry of abstraction to regularize the relations between selves and objects that stimulated the passions in the first place: "All the other passions, besides this of interest, are either easily restrain'd, or are not of such pernicious consequence, when indulg'd" (491). Thus the passions that in book 1 served as the basis for all ideas and came to underlie identity and reinforce the sense of self have now been adjusted to exclusively social considerations and have developed exclusively social consequences. And yet Hume did not have to add or subtract a single component from the traditional passions to enable them to participate so substantially and reliably in his system.

The rest of book 3 deals with the schooling of the passions, the artificial origins of gratitude and allegiance, the keeping of promises, and the origins of chastity and modesty (574–80). From this unlikely direction he arrives at the crucial nexus of abstraction. Their capacity for abstraction rendered the passions supremely responsive to the prose of this age, and the prose exploited and adjusted their possibilities as abstractions repeatedly. As we saw above in chapter 3, the long tradition, semantic certainty, and recent physiological validation had made every episode of a passion an occasion for passing from the particular to the general, or vice versa, asserting both wisdom and humanity in the process. Hume's special concern with self imparts a unique urgency to this special nexus between the general and the particular: "The imagination adheres to the *general* views of things, and distinguishes betwixt the feelings they produce, and those which arise from our particular and momentary situation" (587). The employment of such abstractions, especially in the analysis of the characters of others, is, for Hume, the best way to slow down the erosion of self that results from the swift transition of the passions and to replace these swift transitions with more permanent abstractions—abstractions reinforced by lively feelings not available to the ideas in book 1: "And tho' such interests and pleasures touch us more faintly than our own, yet being more constant and universal, they counter-ballance the latter even in practice, and are alone admitted in speculation as the standard of virtue and morality. They alone produce that particular feeling or sentiment, on which moral distinctions depend" (591).

For Hume, then, the uniform springs of humanity and the controlled dogmatism of the passions make both thought and society possible. They first undermine, and then reconstruct the sense of self, their transitions require and support sympathy, and they give rise to such concepts as property and chastity. Had Hume continued to develop, or even to put forward, these ideas, he might well have given the doctrine of the passions another century of certainty and liveliness. As it was, he abandoned the most promising sections of book 2, partly, I suppose, because they were so traditional, partly because they were so complex, and partly because they did not fit in as well with his system as he had first supposed they might. Not much of the doctrine of the passions found its way into either of the *Enquiries,* and the "Dissertation on the Passions" published as one of *Four Dissertations* in 1757 is a much diminished version of book 2 of the *Treatise.* The emphasis on pride and humility and their workings, the discussion of sympathy, and the moral power of the passions are all dropped.[22] More surprising and disappointing is Hume's failure to work more of these ideas into his frequent dealings with the passions in his later works.

It is not strictly necessary for the student of Hume's essays to have mastered all these intricacies of his philosophical system, to be able, for example, to find his or her way around the square of the passions or to be able to distinguish between direct and indirect passions. It may be enough to concede the assumption of their uniformity, the concern with transition and self, and the double relationship. The essays extend the aesthetic inklings of the *Treatise,* but they do little with sympathy and nothing with the schemes of classification, while the concept of property is exchanged for the stimulus of money, without much profit.

When the essays take up rhetoric, one of the traditional sources and occasions of the passions neglected by the *Treatise,* they ignore all of the refinements and considerations introduced in that work. "Of Eloquence" admires the ancient orator for inflaming "himself with anger, indignation, pity, sorrow," the better to arouse his audience (I, 169), and laments the failure of contemporary politicians and attorneys to gather and display such flowers from Parnassus. The oratory that worked in Greece and Rome would, Hume is certain, also touch the springs of his contemporaries: "The principle of every passion, and of every sentiment, is in every man; and when touched properly, they rise to life, and warm the heart, and convey that satisfaction, by which a work of genius is distinguished from the adulterate beauties of a capricious wit and fancy" (I, 172). Extemporaneous oratory is possible because "the mind naturally continues with the same *impetus* or *force,* which it has acquired by its motion; as a vessel, once impelled by the oars, carries on its course for some time, when the original impulse is suspended" (I, 174). That mind, constantly in transition, is Hume's, and the force is Newton's, but the figure is Cicero's, nicely taken over from the *Tusculan Disputations* (IV.iv).[23]

While Hume devoted no substantial essays to single passions, he regularly incorporated episodes of envy, zeal, and obstinacy into his tracts.[24] These brief episodes impart clarity but not in complex or unsuspected ways. On the other hand, several of the aesthetic ideas implicit in the *Treatise* are extended and refined in the essays. "Of Tragedy," for example, employs the insight on lying as a function of pride and the need to excite passion (I, 259). Tragedy works by adding to the pleasures of eloquence those of imitation, which is always agreeable. All poets, indeed, all artists, produce pleasure by such conversions, smoothings, and softenings of one or another pas-

sion: "The force of imagination, the energy of expression, the power
of numbers, the charms of imitation; all these are naturally, of
themselves, delightful to the mind: And when the object presented
lays also hold of some affection, the pleasure still rises upon us, by
the conversion of this subordinate movement into that which is
predominant" (I, 263–64). It is essential that the "movements" of
the imagination dominate those of the passion; if they merely combine with them, the pain and affliction will increase.

"Of the Standard of Taste" develops the considerations of taste
and secondary qualities suggested in the *Treatise:* aesthetic responses, based as they are on secondary qualities, are so slight and so
subject to distortion by external circumstances that durability becomes the most valuable indication of aesthetic value. In this connection the anecdote of the iron key on a leather thong in the
hogshead of wine is used to illustrate the resemblance between
bodily and mental taste. The analogy might be seen to impart an
important corrective to the precept of secondary qualities as residing
only in the mind, as there was, in fact, both leather and iron in the
wine: "It must be allowed, that there are certain qualities in objects, which are fitted by nature to produce those particular feelings"
(I, 273). These qualities are so slight that they require great delicacy
of taste to detect them—a delicacy it is just possible to cultivate by
practice and comparison. Reason, however, may participate in the
operations of taste by removing prejudice and acknowledging
the authority of the perfect critic, a rare and precious creature. The
Humean critic, then, depends on his passions to draw him toward
truth and on experience to adjust his progress (I, 278–79). The
authorities to which Hume defers and the selves he finds most taste-
ful are not revolutionaries or even democrats. His taste makers, like
those of Addison, were a refined and sophisticated lot.[25]

One aesthetic insight, compatible with both the *Treatise* and the
tradition, though not, so far as I can see, drawn from either one, is
Hume's suggestive assertion that "it is a certain rule, that wit and
passion are entirely incompatible" (I, 242). One implication of this
statement is that simplicity is called for in compositions depicting
action and passion, a conclusion Hume tests with an impressive list
of authors drawn from a long tradition. Hume's assumption that the
uniformity of the passions gives rise to greater similarity in political
and military affairs than in aesthetics should, one assumes, simplify

the task of the historian while complicating that of the critic: "The wars, negotiations, and politics of one age resemble more those of another, than the taste, wit, and speculative principles" (I, 164). For Hume, *Homo politicus* is "actuated by the passions of ambition, emulation, and avarice" (I, 377) and has been at least since Roman times. Hume had read his Plutarch; indeed, he had considered composing short lives in Plutarch's manner (Mossner, 398). In any case, the minds of both the historian and the essayist may move backward or abroad with some certainty because the springs and principles at work in the men and women they study are uniform and constant. This is also true, Hume will assume, in matters of religion.

The essay on avarice that Hume withdrew was not much of a loss, and his comments on that passion in "Of Commerce" are not very searching. But in working out the traditional dogmatism of avarice in the literary market place he found some surprising intellectual implications amid some conventional cultural contrasts:

> Avarice, or the desire of gain, is an universal passion, which operates at all times, in all places, and upon all persons: But curiosity, or the love of knowledge, has a very limited influence, and requires youth, leisure, education, genius, and example, to make it govern any person. You will never want booksellers, while there are buyers of books: But there may frequently be readers where there are no authors. Multitudes of people, necessity and liberty, have begotten commerce in HOLLAND: But study and application have scarcely produced any eminent writers. [I, 176]

He extends the political implications and commercial results of avarice into an insight that seems to me unusually original and perceptive: "Avarice, the spur of industry, is so obstinate a passion, and works its way through so many real dangers and difficulties, that it is not likely to be scared by an imaginary danger, which is so small, that it scarcely admits of calculation. Commerce, therefore, in my opinion, is apt to decay in absolute governments, not because it is there less *secure,* but because it is less *honourable*" (I, 160). Avarice may in itself be uninteresting, but the elucidation of its political consequences is certainly impressive.

Similarly surprising consequences emerge when there is a financial object to consider. Money is an unstable and unworthy object, so much so that mercenaries and merchants who have chosen it will develop unstable, troublesome passions. These springs depress human nature and disturb human governments (I, 325, 355). Hume's brief stint with the merchants of Bristol did not, evidently, inspire respect for their governing passion (Mossner, 88–91). Generally, however, it seems possible to maintain, and perhaps to regret, that in the *Essays* Hume gives the same attention to money that he had devoted to property in the *Treatise*.[26]

THE FOUR PHILOSOPHERS

These passages, and there are dozens like them, will serve to indicate the degree to which the essays incorporated traditional episodes of passion and ignored Hume's modifications to that tradition. I turn now to a closer inspection of three works in which the passions are so central, so significant, and so instructive that only someone unschooled in incredulity could believe that they have not previously been subjected to critical scrutiny. But they have not. Hume's four essays contrasting the classical philosophers explore and exploit the roles of the passions in each system—attesting forcefully to his familiarity with the traditions reviewed in chapter 2. For example, in speaking of the "machine" that nature has wisely framed for him, Hume's Epicurean asks: "To what purpose should I pretend to regulate, refine, or invigorate any of those springs or principles, which nature has implanted in me?"[27] In this context, the elaborate anatomical attention of the Epicurean is especially instructive. Except for the circulation, his anatomy is wholly Galenic and, with its attention to the *in*voluntary workings of the blood and the spirits, virtually Scholastic in its argument: "In vain should I strain my faculties, and endeavour to receive pleasure from an object, which is not fitted by nature to affect my organs with delight. I may give myself pain by my fruitless endeavours; but shall never reach any pleasure" (I, 198).

The point of that passage is surely to exaggerate and undermine the primitivity and selfishness of the Epicurean, who places so much emphasis on his corporeal self and hopes to isolate pleasures from pains. Other passages make clear his subjection, because of the passions to which he is too willing to remain the slave, to time and his dependence on the company of others—a dependence much less wholesome than that of sympathy. He relies on a succession of highly sensual and severely temporal objects (music, fruits, fragrances, flowers) supplied to him in isolation by "pleasure." When, inevitably, these objects produce satiety and languor, pleasure is succeeded by her much diminished sister, virtue, who brings the social and harmonious joys of "cheerful discourses" rooted in the present.

The Epicurean is convinced that, "if any governing mind preside," his enjoyment of "mutual joy and rapture" in the shades with the charming Caelia must please that mind. Other essays might well set out to discredit a divine mind that could be thus pleased; this one discredits the capacity of a human mind to remain content with such pleasures and to believe in a divinity based on such projections. Thus, while most of this essay uses the passions to discredit Epicurean philosophy, some of it uses the philosophy to confirm the analysis of the passions.

The Stoic, in contrast, exhorts man to exert his intelligence and assert his "sublime celestial spirit" in transcending nature, replacing a succession of joys with a continuous ambition to become a "true philosopher, one who governs his appetites, subdues his passions, and has learned, from reason, to set a just value on every pursuit and enjoyment" (I, 205). The Stoic, as we would expect, renders himself indifferent to time by replacing indulgence with industry, and to the instability of fortune by cultivating indifference to external objects, and thus to the passions they stimulate. But while he is supposed to have done away with passions, he may still permit himself some pride in his offspring and some of the satisfactions of friendship. At the same time, he must be careful to respond with sympathy to the (inevitable) failures and disappointments of those around him. The first condition defies logic, but not tradition, and the second offers a form of sympathy much dimmer than the brightly reflected principle of the *Treatise*. Ultimately the Stoic may be able to contemplate a glorious, virtuous "moral beauty" within himself, certain (although Hume has neglected to provide any grounds for this certainty) that a few other virtuous men will have cultivated the same sense in themselves and will have noticed it in him. He will then have elevated himself above all his passions, including the fear of death but not the desire of fame (I, 210)! It is by no means certain that Hume is recommending such levitation.

Virtue is its own reward and thus the perfect way to discipline, or frustrate, the passions, the only constituent of human nature that *needs* rewards.

Whereas the Stoic despises the sensual joys of the Epicurean and the Epicurean dismisses the glory of the Stoic, the Platonist is a visionary whose passions have only one object—the Supreme Being from which it departs further every moment. He attaches disgust, guilt, and satiety to the pleasures of the Epicurean and thinks the Stoic's virtue too much dependent on the approval of the crowd and too little on the perfect being who created him. Worshiping his own imaginary perfections and ignoring his real imperfections, the Stoic has made himself his own idol—a double relation undone by the flaws in the self at both its ends. The Platonist asks us if we cannot, going beyond the partial imitations of art and the splendors of nature, "discover an intelligence and a design in the exquisite and most stupendous contrivance of the universe" and thus "feel the warmest raptures of worship and adoration, upon the contemplation of that intelligent being, so infinitely good and wise" (I, 213). The only diminishment the Platonist can see to the resultant happiness is the narrowness of our own faculties and the shortness of our lives, both curtailments, he hopes, to be "enlarged in another state of existence." The Platonist, not much of a philosopher and certainly no empiricist, exhibits little interest in his own passions and a cosmic indifference to those of others. His essay is also the shortest, most enthusiastic, and least passionate of all. It meets its refutation not in the *Treatise* but in the biography of its author and that author's *Dialogues concerning Natural Religion* and *Natural History of Religion,* which discredit the anthropomorphism and subvert the adoration.

The Sceptic, the only one of the four philosophers who is allowed to sound as if he might have read the *Treatise,* is given a more dispassionate self to express and more pages in which to do so. He exploits the discrepancy between the narrow conception and single-minded passions of man and the vast variety of nature. He reaches a conclusion made possible by Locke and inevitable by the detachments of the *Treatise* "that there is nothing, in itself, valuable or despicable, desirable or hateful, beautiful or deformed; but that these attributes arise from the particular constitution and fabric of human sentiment and affection" (I, 216). Like secondary qualities, the passions depend on the responses of selves rather than on qualities residing in substances or objects. The Sceptic "proves" that, when objects inspire passion in the lover, the parent, the aesthetic, and the moralist, "those qualities are not really in the objects, but belong entirely to the sentiment of that mind which blames or praises" (I, 216–17). It will be "difficult to make this proposition evident . . . because nature is more uniform in the sentiments of the mind than in most feelings of the body, and produces a nearer resemblance in the inward than in the outward part of human kind" (I, 217). It is almost as if nature, desiring to make us all sceptics, "intended to make us sensible of her authority, and let us see what surprizing changes she could produce on the passions and desires of mankind, merely by the change of their inward fabric, without any alteration on the objects."[28]

Since happiness depends on the passions and not on the objects of those passions, the Sceptic prescribes passions that are "neither too violent nor too remiss" (I, 220). He adds to this Aristo-Ciceronian mediality the Humean elements of social cheerfulness and temporal durability. He recommends gaming and hunting in this context, reminding us that these social and aristocratic pastimes had been used as an analogy for philosophy in the *Treatise* (451–52) and suggesting that chance and pursuit are ultimate archetypes for passion in Hume. If so, gaming, the first of these, would embody the detachment, transitions, exchanges, and sequential reflections that are so important to him elsewhere.[29] Hunting, on the other hand, requires skill, exertion, pursuit, and companions. Between them, these two curious pursuits might well have been developed into highly representative emblems of the refined control and detached submission to chance with which Hume approached and discussed the passions.

For those not content to spend their days in the field and their nights at the gaming table, the Sceptic recommends learning as a shrewd alternative. Its object is internal, virtuous, and the best way to happiness. It "leads to action and employment, renders us sensible to the social passions, steels the heart against the assaults of fortune, reduces the affections to a just moderation, makes our own thoughts an entertainment to us, and inclines us rather to the pleasures of society and conversation, than to those of the senses" (I, 221). In short, the Sceptic is the only philosopher who can detach himself from philosophy. He does so, not by becoming a slave to his passions, but by schooling them. Unfortunately, he cannot do much to school the passions of others. The only contribution the Sceptic can make to general human happiness is to "step in, and suggest particular views, and considerations, and circumstances, which otherwise would have escaped us; and, by that means, he may either moderate or excite any particular passion" (I, 224). The natural springs are simply too prevalent, too resilient, too lively—in short, too human—to be eradicated by a mere philosopher, even a sceptical one.

Hume incorporated those passions into his sketches of the philosophers because the passions had figured so heavily, and so variously, not to say contradictorily, in their several systems. They serve to define and condemn features of each school, and they do so along lines that those schools themselves had laid out. In two of his other works, the contemporary and cognate *Natural History of Religion* and *Dialogues concerning Natural Religion,* Hume's scrutiny of the passions is more sustained and more devastating. His tendentious sifting of causes undermines the connections between passion and belief, while his wicked supposings supply plausibility and weight. These two works confirmed the prejudices of those who took Hume's sole purpose to be the discrediting of religion. The *Natural History* is especially shrewd in depicting the passions of primitive men and women in ways that discredit the polytheism and idolatry that arise from their primitive springs: "We may conclude, therefore, that, in all nations, which have embraced polytheism or idolatry, the first ideas of religion arose not from a contemplation of the works of nature, but from a concern with regard to the events of life, and from the incessant hopes and fears, which actuate the human mind."[30] These "incessant [recurrent?] hopes and fears" give rise only to primitive religions, primitive primarily because of the unrefined episodes from which they have sprung:

No passions, therefore, can be supposed to work upon such barbarians, but the ordinary affections of human life; the anxious concern for happiness, the dread of future misery, the terror of death, the thirst of revenge, the appetite for food and other necessaries. Agitated by hopes and fears of this nature, especially the latter, men scrutinize, with a trembling curiosity, the course of future causes, and examine the various and contrary events of human life. And in this disordered scene, with eyes still more disordered and astonished, they see the first obscure traces of divinity. [32]

Those first obscure traces will be turned, by men impelled by their own passions, and seeking external causes, into an anthropomorphic polytheism that imagines its gods "to be sensible, intelligent beings, like mankind; actuated by love and hatred, and flexible by gifts and entreaties, by prayers and sacrifices" (57). These projective supposings produce behavior that is not only irrational, but, what may be worse, unsocial: "Where the deity is represented as infinitely superior to mankind, this belief, tho' altogether just, is apt, when joined with superstitious terrors, to sink the human mind into the lowest submission and abasement, and to represent the monkish virtues of mortification, pennance, humility and passive suffering, as the only qualities which are acceptable to him."[31]

The philosophical error here is one that Hume specialized in detecting, the mistaken imputing of causes. The error is compounded when these causes, themselves fabrications, become the objects, equally erroneous, of passions: "These *unknown causes,* then, become the constant object of our hope and fear; and while the passions are kept in perpetual alarm by an anxious expectation of the events, the imagination is equally employed in forming ideas of those powers, on which we have so entire a dependance" (33).

The great powers they attribute to that deity combine with the human penchant for panegyric to trap the devout in a very sticky paradox, a paradox spun entirely from within themselves—or, as Hume is careful to say, ourselves: "Hence therefore is a kind of contradiction betwixt the different principles of human nature, which enter into religion. Our natural terrors present the notion of a devilish and malicious deity: Our propensity to praise leads us to acknowledge an excellent and divine [one]" (82). Men exalt the divine being they have created from their own passions and then continue to ascribe their own passions to him. But they must do so with excruciating care and a fair amount of self-deception:

> They must then be careful not to form expressly any sentiment of blame and disapprobation. All must be applause, ravishment, extacy. And while their gloomy apprehensions make

them ascribe to him measures of conduct, which, in human creatures, would be highly blamed, they must still affect to praise and admire these measures in the object of their devotional addresses. . . . The heart secretly detests such measures of cruel and implacable vengeance; but the judgment dares not but pronounce them perfect and adorable. And the additional misery of this inward struggle aggravates all the other terrors, by which these unhappy victims to superstition are for ever haunted. [83–84]

This is not a happy sequence of episodes nor one that many careful readers will want to undertake in themselves.

These terrors and this dilemma lead to a craven, and again unsocial, religiosity as the devout "seek the divine favour, not by virtue and good morals, which alone can be acceptable to a perfect being, but either by frivolous observances, by intemperate zeal, by rapturous extasies, or by the belief of mysterious and absurd opinions" (86–87). This religiosity, in turn, will be encouraged by priests who will make it their business not to scrutinize passions but to exploit them.[32] To all this superstition Hume opposes a doubly Humean contradiction: dispassionate belief in the argument from design.

The closing lines of the *Natural History* urge us to set the various species of superstition quarreling with one another, "while we ourselves, during their fury and contention, happily make our escape, into the calm, tho' obscure, regions of philosophy" (95). Those who expect to find such calm, dispassionate regions in *The Dialogues* will be in for a surprise. Even though they all think themselves philosophers, the participants in that dialogue are intricately endowed with the essential and universal springs of human nature—far more so than previous critics have taken the trouble to notice.

In the *Dialogues,* as in the essays on the schools of philosophy, the passions establish character, discredit speculations, and indict arguments. Even Pamphilus, the young narrator, has an eye for their manifestations, detecting vehemence, embarrassment, and alacrity in Philo, finesse and impatience in his host, and distaste in Demea when he leaves the company in a huff (148, 170, 178, 244). As this incident might suggest, Demea's passions are too much in evidence throughout the *Dialogues*. He is so provoked at being called a "Mystic" that he retaliates by calling Cleanthes an "Anthropomorphite" (181), and Philo comments on the "Signs of Horror" he displays at some of Cleanthes' suppositions (194). Demea exploits the "Reverence" and "Self-Diffidence" of his students (146–47), and he thinks it right that men should be brought to religion by their hopes and fears (219; evidently he has not read the *Natural History of Religion*). He insists, somewhat Platonically, that God should "stand fixt in one simple, perfect State," so that "his Love and his Hatred, his Mercy and his Justice are one individual Operation" (182).

To which Cleanthes, every bit as anthropomorphic as Demea has accused him of being, retorts: "A Mind, whose Acts and Sentiments and Ideas are not distinct and successive; one, that is wholly simple, and totally immutable; is a Mind, which has no Thought, no Reason, no Will, no Sentiment, no Love, no Hatred; or in a Word, is no Mind at all" (182–83). As that inability to conceive of or accept a mind without episodes of passion indicates, the passions play far too great a part in Cleanthes's philosophy, where they become the major tenet in his argument from design:

> The most agreeable Reflection, which it is possible for human Imagination to suggest, is that of genuine Theism, which represents us as the Workmanship of a Being perfectly good, wise, and powerful; who created us for Happiness, and who, having implanted in us immeasurable Desires of Good, will prolong our Existence to all Eternity, and will transfer us into an infinite Variety of Scenes, in order to satisfy those desires, and render our Felicity compleat and durable. [33]

That is a more drastic projecting of passions (and desires) into eternity than anything that Addison suggested. It is bad enough to pollute eternity with human passions, but Cleanthes, who has read no more of the *Natural History* than Demea, would use religion, the product of the passions, to keep men their slaves on earth, too: "The proper Office of Religion is to regulate the Heart of Men, humanize their Conduct, infuse the Spirit of Temperance, Order, and Obedience" (251). Their passions and their comments on the passions combine to discredit the arguments of Demea and Cleanthes, at the same time making the *Dialogues* more vivid, more social, and more literary. They root the philosophy in humanity by depicting the passions it provokes. But they are also subtly tendentious, as neither Philo nor Hume displays or extrapolates from his own passions.

Philo keeps his own passions infuriatingly under control while acknowledging, but refusing to appeal to, the passions of others. He disagrees with Cleanthes over the validity and efficacy of Stoicism, and he evokes the circulation of the blood, the physiology of pain, and the prevalence of evil to refute the argument from design (149–51, 163, 229, 234). The passions that Hume had analyzed so thoroughly and had invoked and controlled so often are crucial to Philo's argument at several points. He admits, indeed insists, that they are essentially human: "All the *Sentiments* of the human Mind, Gratitude, Resentment, Love, Friendship, Approbation, Blame, Pity, Emulation, Envy, have a plain Reference to the State and Situation of Man, and are calculated for preserving the Existence, and promoting the Activity of such a Being in such Circumstances. It seems therefore unreasonable to transfer such Sentiments to a supreme Existence, or to suppose him actuated by them" (179–80).

At the same time that he insists that the passions are part of the human condition but ought to be confined to it, Philo notes that they both indict and complicate that condition: "What more useful than all the Passions of the Mind, Ambition, Vanity, Love, Anger? But how oft do they break their Bounds, and cause the greatest Convulsions in Society?" (239–40). Finally, and as if to prove that *he* has read the *Natural History,* Philo laments what Demea and Cleanthes have both conceded, that the least creditable passions induce the greatest credulity: "It is true; both Fear and Hope enter into Religion; because both these Passions, at different times, agitate the human Mind, and each of them forms a Species of Divinity, suitable to itself. . . . But still it must be acknowledg'd, that, as Terror is the primary Principle of Religion, it is the Passion, which always predominates in it, and admits but of short Intervals of Pleasure" (258–59).

The argument from design, then, finds both its sources and its objects in the passions and is therefore absurd: "It is an Absurdity to believe the Deity has human Passions, and one of the lowest of human Passions, a restless Appetite for Applause. It is an Inconsistency to believe, that, since the Deity has this human Passion, he has not others also; and in particular, a Disregard to the Opinions of Creatures, so much inferior" (259). Mankind is fortunate that the deity has no passions, Philo asserts in a triumphant conclusion, for if he did, "the only Persons, intitled to his *Compassion* and *Indulgence,* wou'd be the philosophical Sceptics . . . who, from a natural Diffidence of their own Capacity, suspend, or endeavor to suspend all Judgement with regard to such Sublime and such extraordinary Subjects" (260). Philosophical sceptics, in other words, control their own passions while keeping a shrewd and informed eye on those of others.

I suggest that readers of Hume, and especially of the *Natural History of Religion* and the *Dialogues concerning Natural Religion,* need to be equally attentive to and informed about these resilient but tricky springs. Hume's works consider and exploit the passions, insisting always that they are essentially, in every sense of that word, human. He subjects them to a scrutiny that is eminently philosophical, largely traditional, and ultimately both sceptical and profound. But it must be added that Hume's scrutiny irritated more people than it influenced, and that its importance is much more centripetal than centrifugal. The passions matter far more to Hume than some of his readers seem to have suspected, but he matters far less to the tradition of the passions than he himself seems to have hoped or might have supposed.

6

JUDGING, FEELING, AND

FEIGNING: FIELDING AND THE

PHYSIOLOGY OF DECEIT

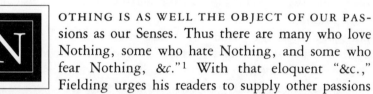OTHING IS AS WELL THE OBJECT OF OUR PAS-
sions as our Senses. Thus there are many who love
Nothing, some who hate Nothing, and some who
fear Nothing, &c."[1] With that eloquent "&c.,"
Fielding urges his readers to supply other passions
along the lines indicated by the three he has just named, confident
that his readers will be able to follow them without difficulty. That
"&c." also suggests that those lines were so familiar that few would
bother to do so. In the preface to the *Miscellanies* he posits a worthier
object, goodness, to which the soul responds with love ("of which
Passion, Goodness hath always appeared to me the only true and
proper Object"). He indicates more intricate lines in naming "greatness" "the *False Sublime*" to which the soul responds too often with
admiration. Those few objects that combine greatness and goodness
constitute the "*true Sublime* in Human Nature" and, as such, are the
only objects to which "Love, Wonder, and Delight" are the proper
responses (12).

These two passages might be adduced to prove Fielding's general
acceptance of the received tradition. He understood all the traditional definitions and components of the passions and exploited
most of them in developing his characters and generating his plots.[2]
He paid special attention to the physiology of the passions, applying that physiology to the detection of deceit—a concern central to
all his best work.

As unwilling to be imposed upon as his more sceptical contemporaries, and with an eye for deceit sharpened behind the stage and upon the bench, Fielding developed the physiology of the passions into high art. The psychological tradition in which he chose to work provided sufficient intricacy to suit his genius and integrity and to serve his artistic and moral purposes, and all his characters are well provided with highly significant episodes of passion. In some of the most crucial of these, Fielding elaborates the physiological compo-nent into great comedy, deep insight, and high art. In these epi-sodes he allows us to watch the vital spirits carry messages of satis-faction or distress throughout the body, generating either comic discomfort or the discovery of deceit as they do so. Their attendant sensations supply internal and external indications to which Field-ing's characters, readers, and critics must learn to attend.

Fielding states his faith in this internal mechanism most ex-plicitly in the preface to the *Miscellanies:* "However the Glare of Riches, and Awe of Title, may dazzle and terrify the Vulgar; nay, however Hypocrisy may deceive the more Discerning, there is still a Judge in every Man's Breast, which none can cheat nor corrupt, tho' perhaps it is the only uncorrupt Thing about him. And yet, inflexi-ble and honest as this Judge is, (however polluted the Bench be on which he sits) no Man can, in my Opinion, enjoy any Applause which is not thus adjudged to be his Due" (10). The bench is the governing figure here, and the verdicts of the judge are conveyed by, and rooted in, physiology, while the glare, dazzle, and deceit of the stage backlight the testimony and mislead the inattentive or in-judicious—for a while: "The same righteous Judge always annexes a bitter Anxiety to the Purchases of Guilt, whilst it adds a double Sweetness to the Enjoyments of Innocence and Virtue: for Fear, which all the Wise agree is the most wretched of human Evils, is, in some Degree, always attending on the former, and never can in any manner molest the Happiness of the latter" (11). Sooner or later in Fielding, the judge takes over from the actor.

Thus those bitter annexations and molestations are no mere fig-ures of speech. I shall argue that Fielding found the physiology of passion dramatic and rendered it forensic. Alert, in his earliest works, to the dramatic possibilities inherent in the changes passion induced in both voice and countenance, he made the display of passion highly, sometimes excessively, theatrical. In his later works he devised episodes of passion that began with character and ended with plot, surrounding them with comments on and allusions to their subtlety and significance.

Throughout his works those characters who can simulate or suppress manifestations of passion are to be distrusted. Characters (and readers) who wish to thrive in the world Fielding creates must learn to recognize this capacity and share this distrust. Characters like Wild and Blifil can interrupt the connections between the heart within and the face and voice without for a while, and in this way perpetrate much imposition. Eventually, however, some one passion that begins on the outside, in response to external circumstances, grows so overwhelming, so "bitter," that it restores the severed connections, and informs the bad heart of something it does not wish to know and the informed observer of something he or she ought to have seen sooner.

Thus in the bad characters the working of passion produces considerable internal discomfort, not only bitterness, but boiling, struggles, pangs, chagrin, and flame, all of which retain a trace of their physiological origins. In the good characters, on the other hand, the physiological connections are usually easy and regular and the attendant sensations pleasant. What goes on in the heart is readily and agreeably communicated to the face without distorting the voice or disturbing the body. In the following passage on the effects of grief, the violence of the physiology of a good mind is set forth with a hyperbole that in any other context would be read as comic exaggeration. Here it testifies to the significance Fielding attached to the force of feeling:

> But in a Mind of a different Cast, in one susceptible of a tender Affection, Fortune can make no other Ravage equal to such a Loss. It is tearing the Heart, the Soul from the Body; not by a momentary Operation, like that by which the most cruel Tormentors of the Body soon destroy the Subject of their Cruelty; but by a continued, tedious, though violent Agitation: the Soul having this double unfortunate Superiority to the Body; that its Agonies, as they are more exquisite, so they are more lasting.[3]

The "Anguish" of this loss is a hundredfold greater than the gout, with whose bodily torments Fielding was only too familiar.

Anyone doubting the completeness with which the traditions investigated in chapters 2 and 3 arrived in the eighteenth century need only consult this essay on affliction and the "Dialogue between Alexander and Diogenes," both of which contain many episodes of passion richly informed by traditional components. I propose, instead, to concentrate on the components of physiology, evident here, but not exploited, and of deceit, for which there was more scope in the plays and novels.

Critics have noticed that Fielding frequently lacked metaphors for action and the singleness of vision to portray it with force. More interested in repeated examinations and distorted rewordings—the reconstruction and misconstruction of action rather than the construction of it—he turned repeatedly to the passions that motivated it, and the established signs of those passions.[4] Sometimes he does so to explore character and sometimes to undermine it, but in nearly every instance episodes of passion are allowed to reach their traditional fullness. The passions participate fully in Fielding's balanced judgments of character as well as his balancing of one character against another. Commensurate as well as consistent, they work well on both sides of the balance, allowing Fielding to keep his distance and still have his say, and then to generalize beyond the character in question to those outside the book, in history and in the audience, making possible not just the stylistic, but the "moral continuities" out of which the architectonics of his novels are contrived. They were one part of the moral vocabulary that required no reexamination—just continued and attentive examination. In fact, their clarity and consistency were so well established that they made the reexamination of other terms in that vocabulary both necessary and possible. Their received usages, constantly reinforced by physiology, did not need to be called into question. They continued to give the same answers, resonant and reliable answers, they had given for centuries.

While all of Fielding's episodes of passion work centripetally, carrying ease or discomfort, and thus meaning, into the center of the character undergoing the episode, many of them also work centrifugally, conveying meanings away from a character to disturb the interpretations of the reader:

Fielding's characteristically mixed allegiance to the science of signs known as physiognomics results in a double use of physiognomic signs in his fiction. On the one hand, physiognomics provides him, as it would also Smollett, with a paradigm of the processes of judgment by which we come to know character and penetrate the meaning of events . . . ; its fallibility and inept applications, on the other hand, serve equally well to mark the fallibility, precariousness, and mediacy of our knowledge.[5]

While I think Fielding's episodes of passion are infinitely subtler and more significant than Smollett's, I do agree that he "has 'laboured to describe' the same passion differently diversified through the probable circumstances of each character, that through attention, penetration, and discrimination the reader may infer from these presented signs and circumstances back to character" (Patey, 210).

In most of Fielding's works the passions testify, first to the character through whom they course and then to the shrewd observer. Each episode works itself out along traditional lines, as the vital spirits underlying them pursue their established routes through the body. Because they occupy so prevalent and consistent a place in Fielding's prose, that testimony ought also to reach the informed reader.

PLAYS

Given the theatricality of the external manifestations of the passions, Fielding exploited them as a source of drama and humor in most of his plays. I mention several brief indications of the ways his early works might serve to alert us to the significance of episodes of passion in his later ones. In the auction scene in *The Historical Register for the Year 1736,* he goes behind the fan and the mask as instruments of imposition, suggesting that demireps who have rendered themselves unable to blush ought to employ these devices to hide that inability. Fielding never lost his belief in blushing heroines, employing them often, perhaps a little too often, as a means of proving them physiologically incapable of deceit. His frequent recourse to this manifestation of passion says something about the social and moral behavior expected of women in his age. The testimony of the blush was much facilitated by the decolletage then in style. Indeed, this fashion, which may appear immodest, must have been a response to the social demand for frequent evidence of a woman's modesty. Thus Huncamunca colors when "The burning Bridegroom" hints at his intentions toward "the blushing Bride." The dramatist has embedded the actions he is depicting in both those participles, and both his characters confirm the physiology at work within them: "O fie upon you, Sir, you make me blush." To which Tom Thumb in tiny voice replies: "It is the Virgin's sign, and suits you well——."[6]

In *The Modern Husband,* to mention one more extensive and disturbing example of Fielding's staging of the passions, the characters are so corrupted and corrosive that, while they all have passions, and most discuss them at length, few bother to dissemble them. Mrs. Modern rings the familiar changes on three primary passions when she encourages Lord Richly to "hope all, my lord, that lovers wish, or husbands fear: she will be here." He promises to return the favor with an offering to her revenge and her vanity, "the two darling passions of your sex."[7] As it happens, these characters are so corrupted that their passions can neither betray nor defend them. The only testimony they will accept from one another is that of the contrived discoveries of hidden observers: "And yet all this is true; as true as she is false. Nay, you shall have an instance; an immediate, undeniable instance. You shall see it with your own eyes, and hear it with your own ears" (IV.iii; 65; cf. V.xi–xii; 91: "These witnesses must inform you"). Only Gaywit and Emilia discuss, feel, and display passion in ways that might be regarded as wholesome. Unfortunately, the wholesome is often not very dramatic: "I have been always fearful to disclose a passion which I know not whether it be in my power to pursue. I would not even have given her the uneasiness to pity me, much less have tried to raise her love" (V.iv; 79). The absence of jealousy, perhaps the most disturbing feature of this most disturbing play, testifies, in everyone but Mrs. Bellamant, to the absence of love.

Fielding probably never set out deliberately to coerce the passions of his audience. In *The Author's Farce,* Marplay, Jr., objects to a line by Luckless because "there is nothing that touches me, nothing that is coercive to my passions," suggesting that this is not a valid critical tenet.[8] Yet when he does review the effects of actions on the stage on the passions of the audience (in the *Covent Garden Journal*), he proves how well he understood the dependence of passions upon circumstances, and the capacity of one passion to generate another. This is Fielding's equivalent of Hume's "square of passion," and his eye seems to be equally on the episodes of passion taking place on the stage and those taking place in the audience. Using "passions" and "humours" as synonyms (he has been discussing Jonson), and counting curiosity as a passion, he treats the passions explicitly as causes and regards them as both constituting and indicating character:

> By the Manner of exerting itself likewise a Humour becomes ridiculous. By this Means chiefly the Tragic Humour differs from the Comic; it is the same Ambition which raises our Horror in *Macbeth,* and our Laughter at the drunken Sailors in the *Tempest;* the same Avarice which causes the dreadful Incidents in the *Fatal Curiosity* of Lillo, and in the *Miser* of Molière; the same Jealousy which forms an Othello, or a Suspicious Husband. No Passion or Humour of the Mind is absolutely either Tragic or Comic in itself. Nero had the Art of making Vanity the Object of Horror, and Domitian, in one Instance, at least, made Cruelty ridiculous.[9]

The episodes of ambition, avarice, jealousy, vanity, and cruelty here are drawn from both history and the stage, where they have been recorded and repeated for centuries, providing frequent, clear, and stable moral exempla. These passions, in turn, become the objects of other passions in those who watch the plays or read the histories in which they figure. Every time the dramatic or historical episodes recur and reproduce the predicted response, the vocabulary, clarity, and force of the passions are reinforced—grammatically and psychologically.

His plays and essays, then, attest to Fielding's understanding of the passions. In his novels, he articulated even more episodes wherein the passions flesh out character and anchor design. The timing was most opportune: the passions reached their greatest potential to signify and complicate just as another genre that could linger over character, concoct circumstances, and challenge prose was being created.

JONATHAN WILD

Jonathan Wild was blessed by mother nature and the generic requirements of rogue biography with many attributes that qualified him for greatness—among them ingenuity, ambition, dexterity, and avarice. A passionate admirer of heroes, he had made himself a master of the passions, those of others as well as his own: "With such infinite address did this truly great man know how to play with the passions of men, to set them at variance with each other, and to work his own purposes out of those jealousies and apprehensions which he was wonderfully ready at creating."[10] His ability to manipulate the passions of others and the unnatural but essential steadiness of countenance by which he rendered his own passions impenetrable underlie all of his success—success both alarming and instructive in an age unwilling to be imposed upon.

The skillful severing of the connections between a passion within and the display without concludes Wild's fifteen maxims for the attaining of greatness: "15. That the heart was the proper seat of hatred, and the countenance of affection and friendship" (203), a confirmation of "Thus did our hero execute the greatest exploits with the utmost ease imaginable, by means of those transcendent qualities which nature had indulged him with, viz. a bold heart, a thundering voice, and a steady countenance" (56). This last phrase assumes the physiological interdependence of three parts of the body, taking each one in sequence. Of these, the heart is hidden, except from an omniscient narrator and those readers who can look under or alongside the ironic prose. The seat of the passions, it communicates their presence and nature by altering the flow of vital spirits to the voice and the face.

These physical alterations are not subject to the linguistic discrepancies exploited by the narrator. Words like "great," "admirable," "noble," "liberty," and "rapture" can float free of the actions they are meant to describe. They can even be made to take up positions over actions with which they have little to do.[11] But neither the passions themselves nor their names admit such treatment. Their nature, thanks to physiology, is too stubborn for it, and their definitions, thanks to the tradition, too well established. When, for example, Wild tries to put a face and a voice of courage over his cowardice, neither physiology nor language will let him get away with it. The steadiness of the word for courage precludes its application to an episode of bravado inspired by brandy, and eventually the vital spirits take over from the distilled one. Wild's "boldness" is, in several senses, "heroic" but also specious and may more accurately be called impudence, as Fielding shows in several incidents. Readers of "An Essay on Knowledge of Characters of Men" will know that a fierce Aspect is a sure sign not of a man of courage but only of a "Bully."[12]

The unnatural few who can prevent or simulate the manifestations of passion are wonderfully equipped to impose upon the rest of us and wonderfully equipped to act as villains in Fielding's works. Wild does so repeatedly, being "greatly superior to all mankind in the steadiness of his countenance" (108–9; cf. 69, 70). Mrs. Heartfree has no such ennobling steadiness. Her heart communicates directly with her exterior, as is evident (and alluring) when she is first introduced to Wild: "This simple woman no sooner heard her husband had been obliged to her guest than her eyes sparkled on him with a benevolence which is an emanation from the heart" (53). Her display, though free of complications of syntax or physiology, will produce several complications in the plot—such as it is. The rest of the novel is full of such signs, many of them even more awkward, of the Heartfrees' passionate inability to deceive (see Rawson, 236–46).

Fielding employs all of Wild's prowess and some of his own in a scene in which Wild discovers that his pocket has been picked by the sister of his beloved. While Wild is careful to prevent anyone watching him from making discoveries, Fielding uses musculature, expression, the stage, and "chagrin" to encourage those watching *him* to do just that: "However, as he had that perfect mastery of his temper, or rather of his muscles, which is as necessary to the forming a great character as to the personating it on the stage, he soon conveyed a smile into his countenance, and, concealing as well his misfortune as his chagrin at it, began to pay honourable addresses to Miss Letty" (63).

A later, more complex episode of bravado plays itself out in a vast but empty theater where, with no audience to stir his spirits, and no spirits to reinforce his simulated passion, Wild's courage deserts him. Set adrift in a small boat, he resorts first to blasphemy, then to a posturing defiance, and finally to what he thinks will be suicide.

The whole passage supplies an answer Wild did not intend to his own question—"What signifies fear?":

> At length, finding himself descending too much into the language of meanness and complaint, he stopped short, and soon after broke forth as follows: "D——n it, a man can die but once! what signifies it? Every man must die, and when it is over it is over. I never was afraid of anything yet, nor I won't begin now; no, d——n me, won't I. What signifies fear? I shall die whether I am afraid or no; who's afraid then, d——n me?" At which words he looked extremely fierce, but, recollecting that no one was present to see him, he relaxed a little the terror of his countenance, and, pausing a while, repeated the word, d——n! [89–90]

This highly theatrical passage depends on the absence of an audience and the presence of the vital spirits. (I pass over the theological implications of all the "damning" in the face of death and omnipotence.) Wild begins with boldness, at least in his voice. Then, as his words find no audience to convince, they succeed only in undermining the confidence of their speaker. Then his facial expression begins to fail, also for lack of an audience. Wild *needs* his facial expressions and muscle tension to help him realize within himself the passion he has simulated on the outside. As he relaxes a little the terror of his countenance, his vital spirits dissolve his spurious inner strength and imperil his soul. As his voice falters and his countenance slackens, his heart grows much less bold. The "wonderful resolution" with which he casts himself headlong into the sea is really only confusion mingled with despair.

Born to be hanged rather than drowned, Wild survives to live "under a continual alarm of frights, and fears, and jealousies" (138) until his transgressions grow too evident even for the eighteenth-century judicial system. When he is imprisoned together with one of his victims, his physiology asserts itself once again, this time producing a genuine passion rather than dissolving a counterfeit one: "But, when one of the keepers . . . repeated Heartfree's name among those of the malefactors who were to suffer within a few days, the blood forsook his countenance, and in a cold still stream moved heavily to his heart, which had scarce strength enough left to return it through his veins. In short, his body so visibly demonstrated the pangs of his mind, that to escape observation he retired to his room, where he sullenly gave vent to . . . bitter agonies" (157–58). This passage may well represent a triumph of physiology over art as well as deceit, but it would be unfortunate if we were to allow its melodramatic contrivances to obscure the deft theatrical awareness in "to escape observation." Notice also the hints of physiological discomfort in the cold, heavy blood and the bitter agonies. Fielding soon developed formal and stylistic subtleties not evident here, but he never abandoned his concern with the physiology of deceit. Nor did he revise his assumption, both moral and aesthetic, that the connections between passion and truth were strong and exploitable. We will come shortly to two comparable passages from *Tom Jones*. The first, also set in a prison, is even more theatrical; the other administers another strong dose of well-deserved and self-inflicted bitterness to a villain. Both passages, however, will immerse their episodes in a sophisticated plot and derive them from more fully developed characters, so that they can serve the elaborate purposes of a more penetrating narrator.

As Wild is drawn toward his execution, Fielding turns briefly to the passions of the crowd, genuine passions, subject to manipulation by the state and also to distrust. Fleeting and collective ones, they are given names (envy, fear, malice), a voice, gestures, and violent actions but no physiology: "When he came to the tree of glory he was welcomed with an universal shout of the people. . . . But though envy was, through fear, obliged to join the general voice in applause on this occasion, there were not wanting some who maligned this completion of glory . . . and endeavored to prevent it by knocking him on the head as he stood under the tree."[13] The physiology is saved, as so often, for the hero, who is given one last chance to die bravely, his attempt to make an early exit with the help of laudanum having failed. Once again, Wild faces "death and damnation, without any fear in his heart, or, at least, without betraying any symptoms of it in his countenance" (197). As Fielding and his sources suggest, he had fortified his vital spirits with at least one bumper full of distilled and fermented ones, enabling him to impose on the crowd but not on the judicious and informed reader.

JOSEPH ANDREWS

The straightforward passions in *Joseph Andrews* exhibit much physiology but little deceit. Lady Booby cannot control, much less dissemble, her potent passions. When she takes them to bed, as she often does, their failure to secure an object becomes all the more comic: "She then went up into her Chamber, sent for *Slipslop,* threw herself on the Bed, in the Agonies of Love, Rage, and Despair; nor could she conceal these boiling Passions longer, without bursting."[14] Given the person they inhabit and her present situation, her "Agonies," "boiling," and "bursting" do not provoke sympathy.

Joseph's passions are as innocent as the rest of his nature, so concealment of them is out of the question. When he visits "her in whom his Soul delighted" (295), the whole world knows of, and shares, that delight, at least vicariously. The blushes of his soul's delight bring out Joseph's lamentable propensity for priggishness:

An Admiration at his Silence, together with observing the fixed Position of his Eyes, produced an Idea in the lovely Maid, which brought more Blood into her Face than had flowed from *Joseph's* Nostrils. The snowy Hue of her Bosom was likewise exchanged to Vermillion at the instant when she clapped her Handkerchief round her Neck. *Joseph* saw the Uneasiness she suffered, and immediately removed his Eyes from an Object, in surveying which he had felt the greatest Delight which the Organs of Sight were capable of conveying to his Soul. [305]

Whether Fielding meant to suggest that some other organ might one day convey greater delights to Joseph's soul, one cannot say; it would not be his only innuendo. Joseph's passions would then provide the means for rescuing his nature from the paralysis of innocence, and without compromising his purity.

Parson Adams is also blessed with a pure heart and physiology in such good order that he can conceal nothing: "He felt the Ebullition, the Overflowings of a full, honest, open Heart towards the Person who had conferred a real Obligation." The openness of his heart provides an object whereon readers can test theirs: "and of which if thou can'st not conceive an Idea within, I will not vainly endeavour to assist thee" (310). Parson Adams's heart, in any case, is in such good working order, and is drawn, if not overdrawn, so well from the realm of physiology, that it conveys his goodness throughout his body and, Fielding hopes, beyond.

Only the bad characters manage, for a while, to redeploy their vital spirits. When Leonora is caught by her fiancé with a rival, she greets him with a long silence while she regains command of her voice: "At length *Leonora* collecting all the Spirits she was Mistress of, addressed herself to [Horatio], and pretended to wonder at the Reason of so late a Visit" (113). Her ability to become mistress of her spirits signals Leonora's decline. Now she can impose on those around her—but not on the narrator.

Leonora was caught by surprise, a device rather than a passion and one traceable to Fielding's apprenticeship on the stage. He employs it repeatedly in *Joseph Andrews* for comic effect, exaggerating it in the case of Parson Trulliber's astonishment at Parson Adams's purpose for visiting him (165–66, with a series of "supposes" worthy of Hume) and understating it in Mrs. Tow-wouse's unexpected entry into her bedroom (88). Its staginess is much more apparent than its physiology in the scene in Fanny's bedroom: "Then *Fanny* skreamed, *Adams* leapt out of Bed, and *Joseph* stood, as the Tragedians call it, like the *Statue of Surprize*" (334; compare 40 and n. 1). When we see Blifil taken by surprise, we will notice that his physiological response is put to judicious use.

The "roasting" Squire takes elaborate steps to gain control of his passions: "having first called his Friends about him, as Guards for the Safety of his Person, rode manfully up to the Combatants, and summoning all the Terror he was Master of, into his Countenance, [he] demanded with an authoritative Voice of *Joseph*, what he meant by assaulting his Dogs in that Manner" (242; compare 115). The preparations, the adverb, the commas, and the links with Jonathan Wild suggest that the Squire's heart is by no means bold, and perhaps also that, having insufficient spirits available for both countenance and voice, he sends what spirits he has to the former and counts on his social status to strengthen the latter.

To these scattered indications of an underlying and continuous attention to physiology and deceit I add the consideration of the subject in the preface to *Joseph Andrews*. The excessively well known passage wherein Fielding deals with affectation as the source of vanity and hypocrisy is followed by two others very much to the present purpose, as both of them incorporate the physiology underlying these two kinds of deceit. The innocence of vanity is reflected in its physiology; it "hath not that violent Repugnancy of Nature to struggle with, which that of the Hypocrite hath." Thus the affectation of liberality "sits less aukwardly on [a vain man] than on the avaricious Man, who *is* the very Reverse of what he would *seem* to be" (8). The "repugnancy" of the hypocritical liberality of the avaricious man produces physiological struggles within him. These in turn produce discomfort and eventually betray his hypocrisy. The vital spirits can be more readily summoned and more easily continued in vain persons than in hypocritical ones, making them both more easily imposed upon and more immediately transparent. The distinction is evident in the physiology, character, and depiction of Adams on the one hand and Blifil on the other.

Fielding's most extensive and penetrating discussion of this concern is in "An Essay on the Knowledge of the Characters of Men," written, as he said, to arm "the innocent and undesigning . . . against Imposition."[15] He asserts that "the Passions of Men do commonly imprint sufficient Marks on the Countenance; and it is owing chiefly to want of Skill in the Observer, that Physiognomy is of so little Use and Credit in the World" (157). But the marks that physiology imprints are so faint, and skilled observers so rare, that most of us are better advised to watch men's actions than their faces, and to watch their private actions rather than those performed in public (as, for example, in the private displays that betrayed Jonathan Wild to himself). Even then, it will never be easy to avoid imposition. As Wild well knew, and Adams and Allworthy both had to discover, the passions of the beholder can be used to help hide those of the beheld: "but while Men are blinded by Vanity and Self-Love, and while artful Hypocrisy knows how to adapt itself to their Blindsides, and to humour their Passions, it will be difficult for honest and undesigning Men to escape the Snares of Cunning and Imposition" (174).

TOM JONES

The engaging and penetrating analysis to which Fielding subjects the generous provision of human nature in *Tom Jones* incorporates and embellishes upon the judicious treatment of physiology employed in his earlier works. The confusion engendered by the deceptive display or concealment of passion generates some of the plot, while the construction of character provides hints for the alert reader and significance for the informed one. The reader who understands a little physiology will appreciate the cleverness of the words I have italicized in: "the *good* Lady [Bridget Allworthy] could not forbear giving [the foundling] a *hearty* Kiss, at the same time declaring herself *wonderfully pleased* with its Beauty and Innocence."[16] Bridget has something to hide, and Fielding allows her to hide it, except for the hints in her physiology. Throughout this novel the leisurely unfolding of character into the sophisticated leverage of plot confirms the analysis of passion as an essential, fruitful, and revealing component of humanity.

I do not propose to investigate every appearance of passion in this novel, but I suggest that most of them are, or once were, significant. I shall indicate the passions that prevail in the major characters and watch them at work in two crucial scenes. Squire Western, to begin with the least deceitful character in the novel, "had not the least Command over any of his Passions; and that which had at any Time the Ascendant in his Mind, hurried him to the wildest Excesses" (296; VI.vii). His physiology renders him wonderfully impetuous and troublesome, utterly incapable of deception and, to those who don't have to live with him, endearing. His passions displace and contradict one another with bewildering rapidity. He makes no effort to control his passions, and barely completes one episode before the next begins. His maxim, "that Anger makes a Man dry" (304; VI.ix), drawn from the nature of choler, confirms his role as the most "humourous" character in the novel.[17]

His sister Di, to whom the Squire is opposed geographically, temperamentally, and artistically, feels and exhibits only the concomitant passions of pride and contempt. She manifests these passions in her language rather than in her body, which remains, as befits "the fair Parthenissa," untouched. She gets the better of her brotherly contempt by using her digestive juices as a solvent on her vital spirits: "'Hold a Moment,' said she, 'while I digest that sovereign Contempt I have for your Sex; or else I ought to be angry too with you. There—I have made a Shift to gulp it down'" (276; VI.ii). This triumph of physiology over good manners and good sense is, it is worth noticing, Di Western's only meal in a very festive novel. And it precedes her triumphant announcement that Sophia must be in love with the unspeakable Blifil. The features of pride and contempt that Di Western displays are set forth in "An Essay on Conversation," where Fielding treats pride as folly, emphasizes its comparative element, and divides it into arrogance, insolence, contempt, and ill nature. He also sets forth the physiology of the shame provoked in those who suffer this contempt, but Squire Western feels none of this uneasiness. [18]

Compared with this pair, one with strong passions and no control and the other few passions and great control, Bridget Blifil offers a sympathetic but disturbing contrast. She is good (much better than her elder son) at simulating the passions she lacks. After her husband's funeral, she produces a sequence of episodes worthy of Garrick, each of them noticeably unconfirmed by physiology:

> Nor can the judicious Reader be at a greater Loss on Account of Mrs. *Bridget Blifil,* who, he may be assured, conducted herself through the whole Season in which Grief is to make its Appearance on the Outside of the Body, with the strictest Regard to all the Rules of Custom and Decency, suiting the Alterations of her Countenance to the several Alterations of her Habit: For as this changed from Weeds to Black, from Black to Grey, from Grey to White, so did her Countenance change from Dismal to Sorrowful, from Sorrowful to Sad, and from Sad to Serious, till the Day came in which she was allowed to return to her former Serenity. [117; III.i]

This passage provides a splendid example of the sane woman in the drawing room. The control of the passion underlying that sanity, however, goes deeper than supposed and not in the expected direction. Indeed, Bridget is able to control her passion here only because it has no depth. The manifestation is confined to the countenance, while its superficiality is reinforced by the analogy to costume. Fielding's sympathy with the widow is confined to his acknowledgment that it would be imprudent for her to manifest passions other than those prescribed ("is to make"; "with the strictest Regard to all the Rules of Custom and Decency"; "till the Day came in which she was allowed"). Finally, it ought to be noticed that the episodes are revealing, and the commentary on them addressed, to "the judicious reader."

The husband for whom Bridget appeared to grieve had provided, before he died, a strong instance of the painful, but private, alchemy of the passions. I do not suggest that his envy killed him, but Captain Blifil does become an alembic boiling over with envy, contempt, and indignation, spirits which were, in this case, much more deadly than vital: "The Doctor, however, had much the larger Share of Learning, and was by many reputed to have the better Understanding. This the Captain knew, and could not bear. For, tho' Envy is at best a very malignant Passion, yet is its Bitterness greatly heightened by mixing with Contempt towards the same Object; and very much afraid I am, that whenever an Obligation is joined to these two, Indignation, and not Gratitude, will be the Product of all three" (74; I.xiii). The writer who concocted this mixture worked in a wonderful laboratory of language and psychology.

With Lady Bellaston, Fielding invokes the physiology of passion but never of deceit, as her temperament obliges and her social position enables her to behave with indifference to the judgments of others. The convenient and controllable detachment of her heart from her body is expressed in everything that she does and everything that Fielding says about her. Her occasional "hurries of spirit" are never occasioned by love; indeed, the seat of her passions seems to be her purse. Only once is the flame in her heart conveyed into her countenance and her voice. The occasion is a passage rendered doubly theatrical in that the display occurs in front of a curtain. It is anger rather than love she displays, and she does so only because *she* has been deceived: "Lady *Bellaston* now came from behind the Curtain. How shall I describe her Rage? Her Tongue was at first incapable of Utterance; but Streams of Fire darted from her Eyes, and well indeed they might, for her Heart was all in a Flame. And now as soon as her Voice found Way . . . , she began to attack poor *Jones*" (747; XIV.ii).

Sophia's heart, in contrast, is thoroughly connected to her body and so responsive to her feelings that she blushes in nearly every appearance she makes in the novel. Perhaps the readiness with which her heart fires her blood and dispatches her vital spirits toward her lovely surfaces makes her so charming, so amiable, and sometimes so tedious? (This same hurry of spirits, doubtless inherited from her father, underlies her convenient fainting spells.) I cite but one of a dozen examples:

> He then snatched her Hand, and eagerly kissed it, which was the first Time his Lips had ever touched her. The Blood, which before had forsaken her Cheeks, now made her sufficient Amends, by rushing all over her Face and Neck with such Violence, that they became all of a scarlet Colour. She now first felt a Sensation to which she had been before a Stranger, and which, when she had Leisure to reflect on it, began to acquaint her with some Secrets, which the Reader, if he doth not already guess them, will know in due Time. [168; IV.v]

Here the physiology conveys several messages in several directions. It validates the passions and confirms and assists the work of the omniscient narrator. As it happens, the passions in this passage share the same object with those in the one above. The anti-pathetical physiologies at work in their responses to that object (Tom) figure in most of the scenes between Sophia and Lady Bellaston, underlying, explaining, and dramatizing their conflicts. [19]

Tom's own passions are as ready as his mother's but much more evident. Parson Supple quotes Juvenal (as is his wont) on Tom's excessive manifestations of passion: "A Lad of an ingenuous Countenance and of an ingenuous Modesty."[20] His ingenuousness gives Tom away in each of his (well-intended) attempts to deceive. When Lady Bellaston comes to visit him in what she expects to be a sick-bed, he forgets "to act the Part of a sick Man" and greets her with "good Humour" instead of "Disorder" in his countenance (810; XV.vii). The congenitally direct connections between Tom's mind, heart, and body are, it might be noticed, precisely those connections that Lady Bellaston has so repellently interrupted in herself.

I turn now from the reinforcement of character by the episodes of passion to which it is subject to two scenes brilliantly contrived to illuminate such episodes. They are the results of passion as well as the occasions for it. The first exploits the theatricality of the passions, while the second employs them as tools of jurisprudence. Together they evoke Fielding's apprenticeship behind the stage and his career upon the bench. Both scenes reproduce elements we encountered in *Jonathan Wild*: prison, despair, reversals of passion and fortune, and the effects of passion in voice and countenance, though the boldness, thunder, and steadiness are noticeably absent. And these scenes depend on and contribute to the plot, making more than theatrical use of those elements. Fielding has come a long but measurable artistic distance from that early work, and he has brought the passions and their physiology with him.

In the first scene Partridge reveals to Tom, already in prison for murder, an even more disturbing offense. The scene is played as a tragic one, with Terror, Fear, Horror, and Amazement on the faces, in the voices, and in the hearts of both men. It reflects the way such scenes were then played (and painted) and includes several sly references back to the scene (XVI.v) where Tom watched Partridge watch Garrick as Hamlet shying at his father's ghost. (The reference to the effect of terror on Partridge's hair recalls the contraption invented by Garrick's hairdresser to simulate his physiology.)[21] Partridge's episode of terror plays itself out quite theatrically and is succeeded, even more dramatically, by Tom's. The only deceit is in the plot and the narrator's studied attention to the theatricality of the passions. This deflected attention makes this scene bearable, even pleasurable, to read:

> While *Jones* was employed in those unpleasant Meditations . . . , *Partridge* came stumbling into the Room with his Face paler than Ashes, his Eyes fixed in his Head, his Hair standing an [*sic*] End, and every Limb trembling. In short, he looked as he would have done had he seen a Spectre. . . .
>
> *Jones,* who was little subject to Fear, could not avoid being somewhat shocked at this sudden Appearance. He did indeed himself change Colour, and his Voice a little faultered. . . .
>
> '. . . as sure as I stand here alive, you have been a-Bed with your own Mother.'
>
> Upon these Words, *Jones* became in a Moment a greater Picture of Horror than *Partridge* himself. He was indeed, for some Time, struck dumb with Amazement, and both stood staring wildly at each other. [915; XVIII.ii]

As Fielding says near the end of this scene: "The Pencil, and not the Pen, should describe the Horrors which appeared in both their Countenances" (917). And Le Brun might have held that "pencil" (that is, brush) just as well as Hogarth.

While that scene was deliberately stagey, a later scene confirms the maturity of Fielding's attention to the physiology of passion and deceit by shifting the background to that of the courtroom. In it Blifil, who has always used "the sober and prudent Reserve of his own Temper" (253; V.ix) to control the manifestations of his own all too manageable passions, is finally betrayed by his own physiology. His passions oblige him to give evidence against himself. There could be no fitter agent to undo the impositions of this selfish young man:

> There is nothing so dangerous as a Question which comes by Surprize on a Man, whose Business it is to conceal Truth, or to defend Falshood. . . . Besides, the sudden and violent Impulse on the Blood, occasioned by these Surprizes, causes frequently such an Alteration in the Countenance, that the Man is obliged to give Evidence against himself. And such indeed were the Alterations which the Countenance of *Blifil* underwent from this sudden Question, that we can scarce blame the Eagerness of Mrs. *Miller*, who immediately cry'd out, 'Guilty, upon my Honour! Guilty, upon my Soul!' [932; XVIII.v]

Whereas, earlier in the novel the passions gave rise to the plot, here in these two scenes from its conclusion, plot and passion are perfectly fused—a fusion effected by physiology, manifested in the voice and the countenance, and confirmed in the forensic "obliged to give Evidence against himself" and the judgment pronounced by Mrs. Miller. Her judgment is belated but correct, and it is based on the evidence of passion as supplied by physiology.

AMELIA

In *Amelia* the passions figure repeatedly and the physiology occasionally but without achieving the theatrical effect or judicial subtlety I detect in *Tom Jones*. The passions that prevail in this novel lend themselves a little too readily to analysis, even by a booby like Booth, who insists that the doctrine of the passions has always been his favorite study.[22] Either that or they evaporate into the ineffability of sensibility: "The cult of sensibility . . . insists on the primacy of the ineffable: the most desirable end to which a literary vehicle can convey us is to a love (or joy, or pathos) that passeth understanding and the limits of language as well" (Alter, 167). It is not edifying to see the dissolution of the clarity, or the dissipation of the force, in these episodes. In assuring Miss Matthews of his inability to articulate his passions upon taking leave of Amelia, Booth apologizes, as well he might, for a physiological figure of speech that calls attention to yet another problem in this novel: "Shall I tell you what I felt in that instant? I do assure you I am not able. So many tender ideas crowded at once into my mind, that, if I may use the expression, they almost dissolved my heart" (6.117; III.3).

Too often the physiology gives rise only to melodrama: "'There lodged in the same house—O Mrs. Booth! the blood runs cold to my heart, and should run cold to yours, when I name him'" (7.41; VII.vi). In an earlier passage, equally physiological and even more melodramatic, the spirits that desert Booth seem already to have failed his creator: "A deep melancholy seized his mind, and cold damp sweats overspread his person, so that he was scarce animated; and poor Amelia, instead of a fond warm husband, bestowed her caresses on a dull, lifeless lump of clay" (6.184; IV.iii). In passages like these the passions are no longer clear and distinct episodes, full of components and significations to be developed and interpreted. They have become mere sensations in the characters' bodies. They are confirmed into formula by physiology, without being validated by a forceful tradition or invigorated by a thoughtful pen. The narrator's loss of faith in rhetorical possibility seems to have extended even to the passions.[23]

On the few occasions when the passions produce unmanageable disturbances in *Amelia* they do so with some reference to the deceit of others, but without reference to physiology. The workings of fear in Booth evoke the traditional effects of that passion on the imagination: "Indeed, fear is never more uneasy than when it doth not certainly know its object; for on such occasions the mind is ever employed in realising a thousand bugbears and phantoms, much more dreadful than any realities, and, like children, when they tell tales of hobgoblins, seems industrious in terrifying itself" (6.296; VI.iv). When, later in the novel, Amelia is disturbed by jealousy, uncertainty, and remorse, the disturbance is only in her mind, which the narrator cuts loose and sends on a journey through a landscape that is almost gothic: "her gentle mind torn and distracted with various and contending passions, distressed with doubts, and wandering in a kind of twilight which presented her only objects of different degrees of horror, and where black despair closed at a small distance the gloomy prospect" (7.289; XI.ix; and see Golden, 88).

Amelia includes one of those passages that suggest that the traditional analysis of the passions could indicate some of the depths and complexities that we now attribute to the unconscious. When Miss Matthews thinks that James has killed Booth, her passion for the victim returns, producing hatred for the supposed murderer. Fielding is quite explicit on the workings of this defense mechanism: "It is usual for people who have rashly or inadvertently made any animate or inanimate thing the instrument of mischief to hate the innocent means by which the mischief was effected (for this is a subtle method which the mind invents to excuse ourselves, the last objects on whom we would willingly wreak our vengeance)" (6.269; V.viii). Sophia's wish, secret from her, but not from the narrator, to be "overtaken" by Tom and Western's inability to hate her as much as he hated her mother are presented in two more such passages.[24]

I conclude my review of the physiology of passion in Fielding with a passage from the posthumous *Journal of a Voyage to Lisbon*. While neither the circumstances of composition nor the topic of this work lent themselves to considerations of deceit, Fielding did not abandon his concern with either this human propensity or the means of detecting it. In the midst of his own increasing pain, he still considered the internal discomforts of imposition. Perhaps he drew some consolation from his freedom from those pains, never himself having added the bitterness of remorse to the asperity of misfortune: "Nature is seldom curious in her works within, without employing some little pains on the outside; and this more particularly in mischievous characters. . . . This observation will, I am convinced, hold most true, if applied to the most venomous individuals of human insects. A tyrant, a trickster, and a bully, generally wear the marks of their several dispositions in their countenances; so do the vixen, the shrew, the scold, and all other females of the like kind."[25] Fielding is here discussing permanent temperament instead of fleeting passions and is thus concerned with settled manifestations, but the venom that settled these marks on the countenance was distilled from the vital spirits and perverted into ill nature. It was put there by nature and, presumably, it caused discomfort and inconvenience to the character through whom it coursed as well as to those on whom it was brought to bear. Here, as elsewhere, physiology serves as a warning to villain and victim alike and as an opportunity for artistic comment.

In taking stock of his own passions on departing from England, Fielding alluded one last time to the most instructive school of the passions, the one that had taught, or had tried to teach, that pain was no evil. His illness and his passions combined to keep him from enrolling wholeheartedly: "By the light of this sun, I was, in my own opinion, last to behold and take leave of some of those creatures on whom I doated with a mother-like fondness, guided by nature and passion, and uncured and unhardened by all the doctrine of that philosophical school where I had learnt to bear pains and to despise death."[26]

From his earliest plays until his posthumous *Journal*, then, Fielding saw fit to attend to physiology and to urge his readers to do likewise. He seems to have found the vital spirits exactly that—a convenient and potent device for bringing characters and the books in which they figure to life. The passions carry out the work of an omniscient narrator, conveying into the countenance and the voice the nature and intensity of internal responses. Those who manage to interrupt or dissemble these conveyings eventually undo themselves. The inattentive and uninformed, whether character or reader, will be imposed upon. The rest of us ought to be impressed with the skillfulness and ingenuity with which Fielding articulates episodes of passion and his characters enact them.

7

THE MORAL FORCE

OF THE PASSIONS

IN *THE RAMBLER*

REVIOUS CENTURIES HAD MADE IT THE BUSI-
ness of their epics, tragedies, and odes to display the
effects of the passions of great minds, acting in high
stations. The more modest genres of the eighteenth
century, the essay and the novel, were content to
investigate the same passions in humbler circumstances. "For though
the passions of little minds, acting in low stations, do not fill the
world with bloodshed and devastations, or mark, by great events, the
periods of time, yet they torture the breast on which they seize, infect
those that are placed within the reach of their influence, destroy
private quiet and private virtue, and undermine insensibly the happiness of the world."[1] The passage just quoted names no passions, but
it mentions their internal effects ("torture the breast on which they
seize," "private,") and their external effects ("infect," "destroy," "undermine," "world"). It retains their might in its extended military
metaphor and reinforces it by strength of syntax, weight of diction,
and range of reference, which combine to accumulate considerable
moral force. That force lurks in the words "little," "low," "great,"
"virtue," and "happiness" and is generated by the deposits of social
attitude and psychological concern in these capacious semantic repositories. In this instance it emanates from the general noun that
forms the subject of the sentence and the paragraph. The periodicity
and the generality combine to unfold numerous implications from
the passions and to tell manifold truths about their long and continuing history.

Their prevalence in his essays should, in itself, entitle the passions to the attention of every careful Johnsonian.[2] Many of the *Ramblers* are given over to the analysis of a single one: hope (no. 67), fear (no. 134), grief (nos. 47, 52), greed (no. 58), anger (no. 56), and peevishness (no. 74). Other essays dwell entirely on the usual objects of the passions: fame, wealth, power, and beauty. Even in those essays not dealing with a single passion at length, the names of several will appear, and the system within which they all operate is certain to figure. I doubt that the most resolute and sceptical scrutiny could produce three consecutive paragraphs that contain no instance of the doctrine of the passions. The reader soon becomes accustomed to extended analyses, incidental sentences, and such vivid, and eminently Johnsonian, phrases as "the pungency of remorse" and "the corrosion of envy" (no. 110, 4:223; no. 17, 3:94).

Rambler no. 49 presents an extensive summary of the development of human "motives" from instinctual appetites: "The next call that rouses us from a state of inactivity, is that of our passions; we quickly begin to be sensible of hope and fear, love and hatred, desire and aversion; these arising from the power of comparison and reflexion, extend their range wider, as our reason strengthens, and our knowledge enlarges" (1:264). The six passions that Johnson enumerates here are the ordinary ones, but notice that the traditional component of comparison mingles with the Lockean process of "reflexion" to invoke both cerebral and social considerations. The component of pleasure and pain is implicit in the "sensible," while the temporal considerations produce, as so often in Johnson, intricate moral and psychological consequences: "At first we have no thought of pain, but when we actually feel it; we afterwards begin to fear it, yet not before it approaches us very nearly; but by degrees we discover it at a greater distance, and find it lurking in remote consequences."

The process continues to grow intricate and the vocabulary becomes abstract, moral, and elaborate as the pleasure and pain are transformed into good and evil: "Our terror in time improves into caution, and we learn to look round with vigilance and solicitude, to stop all the avenues at which misery can enter." Soon these natural and inevitable wants are replaced by "artificial passions," those stimulated by wishes rather than instincts:

New desires, and artificial passions are by degrees produced; and, from having wishes only in consequence of our wants, we begin to feel wants in consequence of our wishes; we persuade ourselves to set a value upon things which are of no use, but because we have agreed to value them; things which can neither satisfy hunger, nor mitigate pain, nor secure us from any real calamity, and which, therefore, we find of no esteem among those nations whose artless and barbarous manners keep them always anxious for the necessaries of life.

In the hands of a writer like Johnson, the traditional explanations account for elements of the human condition that still seem to need to be accounted for. These "artificial" passions all have established names, and Johnson uses them: avarice, vanity, ambition, envy, friendship, curiosity, and the love of fame, to the discussion of which this *Rambler* then turns. They also acquire an epithet, "adscititious," which only Johnson would have supplied. While this division is no more effective or lasting than any of the others we have encountered, the awareness, concern, and ability required to have made it is evident everywhere in Johnson's treatment of the passions.[3]

In nearly every mention of the passions Johnson demonstrates an awareness of their lexicographical possibilities, their syntactic alternatives, and their moral complexities. He treats them with scrupulosity, both lexicographical and moral. He elaborates on nearly every one he mentions and always along the lines we have seen laid out by many centuries of theory and practice. The lexicographer in him combines with the moralist to exploit those semantic distinctions that the passions have always invited: "who does not, at last, from the long habit of connecting a knife with sordid offices, feel aversion rather than terror?" (no. 168, 5:128). No distinction in the *Rambler* is more recurrent or essential than that between love and esteem: "We have all, at one time or other, been content to love those whom we could not esteem, and been persuaded to try the dangerous experiment of admitting him for a companion whom we knew to be too ignorant for a counsellor, and too treacherous for a friend."[4]

The system that established the differences between these passions encouraged opposition, both psychological and syntactic, as a tool of this discrimination. Numerous passages display direct alternatives, like the recent and thrifty widow, who was "too much an economist to feel either joy or sorrow" at her husband's death (no. 138, 4:368). This pair refers each passion to the good *or* evil inherent in its object or at least to the consequences that follow immediately upon the removal of that object. Joy and sorrow differ only in this respect. Similarly: "Every man whose knowledge, or whose virtue, can give value to his opinion, looks with scorn, or pity, neither of which can afford much gratification to pride, on him whom the pandars of luxury have drawn into the circle of their influence" (no. 53, 3:287). Everyone outside that circle is superior to the one drawn into it; the learned will look down on the recruit with scorn, the virtuous with pity. The simple opposites built into every system of the passions become considerably less simple in the hands of a lexicographer turned moralist. The binary nature of good and evil is ultimately responsible for many of the balanced sentences (and heroic couplets) of the period; Johnson built balances that supported their weight.

The same fixed idea of each passion that enabled it to be distinguished from others also made it possible for the passions to be entered into startling and just combinations. What reader cannot validate from his or her own experience the succession of passions Johnson attributes to those expectant authors whose works lie unregarded on his editorial desk, "imagining to myself the various changes of sorrow, impatience, and resentment, which the writers must have felt in this tedious interval" (no. 56, 3:303). Sorrow, impatience, and resentment: no established tradition supplied Johnson with this sequence. His own knowledge of the human heart— and of the ways of booksellers and authors—gave him that succession. But notice that it is a sequence, that sorrow, impatience, and resentment do differ from one another, might well succeed one another, and must be discriminated. Traditional psychology enabled Johnson to designate this succession and those of his readers attentive to the tradition to follow him when he had done so.

This possibility of fruitful combination sharpened Johnson's psychological insight and supplied a useful rhetorical strategy. For him, passions merge without coalescing, so that they may still be submitted to analysis: "Resentment is a union of sorrow with malignity, a combination of a passion which all endeavour to avoid, with a passion which all concur to detest" (no. 185, 5:208). In this passage Johnson divides resentment, quite Scholastically, into constituent parts: sorrow (for some evil done to the self in the past) and malignity (the desire to do evil). As the second component is, by definition, evil, it makes the others with which it has combined evil, too, and thus an object of detestation. A similar analysis of repentance begins with the Aristotelian distinction between part and adjunct: "Sorrow, and fear, and anxiety, are properly not parts, but adjuncts of repentance; yet they are too closely connected with it, to be easily separated."[5]

The scheme of the passions that Johnson inherited encouraged just such separations. Analyzing repentance into its adjuncts of sorrow, fear, and anxiety is useful only to a readership that can see distinctions among those three, and follow the lines on which those distinctions are made. Syntax and vocabulary cooperate in every *Rambler* to clarify such distinctions and to encourage the foregone conclusions provided by the inherent components, especially those of good and evil, comparison, and time.

The most consistent and recurrent element in the formula of the passions is that each passion take, or be taken by, an object. As we have seen, this requirement was retained and reinforced by the tenets of empiricism. All of this is implicit in Johnson's definition of "object": "1. That about which any power or faculty is employed. 2. Something presented to the senses to raise any affection or emotion in the mind."[6] What had been a psychological truism now became a syntactic necessity. Every passion is stimulated by some object, real or imagined, and most of Johnson's discussions of a passion will refer to its object—a thing desired, a person feared, an occasion dreaded, or an action resented. There are no passions without objects and very few sentences discussing passions which do not make some reference to the object that stimulated it. Johnson makes repeated and profound moral and rhetorical use of this psychological fact: "Change of place at first relieved his satiety, but all the novelties of situation were soon exhausted; he found his heart vacant, and his desires, for want of external objects, ravaging himself" (no. 120, 4:278). He frequently clarifies, manages, and deprecates a passion by holding its object before the reader and asking him or her to hold the object in mind. While the reader does so, Johnson pours forth his analytical solvent, and both object and passion evaporate:

> That the maxim of Epictetus is founded on just observation will easily be granted, when we reflect, how that vehemence of eagerness after the common objects of persuit is kindled in our minds. We represent to ourselves the pleasures of some future possession, and suffer our thoughts to dwell attentively upon it, till it has wholly ingrossed the imagination, and permits us not to conceive any happiness but its attainment, or any misery but its loss; every other satisfaction which the bounty of providence has scattered over life is neglected as inconsiderable, in comparison of the great object which we have placed before us, and is thrown from us as incumbering our activity, or trampled under foot as standing in our way. [No. 17, 3:93]

This paragraph keeps the fact, but not the picture, of an object constantly before the reader's mind. The imagination represents "some future possession" and its concomitant pleasures, until we are wholly engrossed, and our minds "kindled." Thus conceived, the object becomes both a distraction and an incitement to action ("vehemence of eagerness"). But whereas Fielding invented and Gibbon recovered numerous circumstances and particulars to represent the "common objects of persuit," and Abel Drugger held a very common one in front of himself on the stage (above, chapter 1), Johnson usually cites objects generally, by class—riches, power, fame, and beauty, with an occasional mention of pleasure. He seldom provides images of the objects themselves. There are many passions in *The Rambler,* or rather, a dozen or so which recur again and again. Each of these passions will be accompanied by its object, but that object will be designated without being specified. The object was an integral part of the psychological system within which Johnson worked, but its role in that system made it unnecessary, indeed unwise, to linger over the concrete details of any specific object. To do so put the emphasis on the cause of each episode, rather than on its nature and consequences, and ran the risk of producing, by the repetition of that cause, numerous subsequent episodes.

The object gains access to the passions by way of the imagination. Presenting objects to the passions had always been one of the major functions of the imagination. This function gave rise to aesthetic uses of the faculty in Addison (not to mention Coleridge), but Johnson remained ever a moralist. The discomfort that accompanies, and perhaps accounts for, the motivation that follows the presentation of an object remained an essential part of Johnson's system: "An habitual sadness seizes upon the soul, and the faculties are chained to a single object, which can never be contemplated but with hopeless uneasiness" (no. 47; 3:255).

For Johnson, then, controlling its object is, when possible, the best way to control a passion: "He who is inslaved by an amorous passion, may quit his tyrant in disgust, and absence will without the help of reason overcome by degrees the desire of returning. But those appetites to which every place affords their proper object, and which require no preparatory measures or gradual advances, are more tenaciously adhesive" (no. 155, 5:64). In no. 64, on the rarity and the psychology of friendship, the same object, Socrates, stimulates various episodes in various breasts: "Such was the opinion of this great master of human life, concerning the infrequency of such an union of minds as might deserve the name of friendship, that among the multitudes whom vanity or curiosity, civility or veneration, crouded about him, he did not expect, that very spacious apartments would be necessary to contain all that should regard him with sincere kindness, or adhere to him with steady fidelity" (no. 64, 3:340). Those who were drawn to that object by vanity expected to be thought of more highly by others for having been drawn by an object so highly regarded by them, and those drawn by curiosity thought that object new and strange. Those drawn by civility wanted to share what others were sharing, while those few drawn by veneration thought highly not of themselves or of the opinions of others but of the object in question. Their estimate of the worth of that object precluded friendship, which presupposes equality. Johnson's readers need to follow these lines, lines well established and full of possibilities, when they confront episodes of passion.

Consider the rhetorical possibilities in the following sequence, where the three objects supposed to destroy regard, friendship, and affection instead solicit these responses because of the addition of good humour: "But surely nothing can more evidently shew the value of this quality, than that it recommends those who are destitute of all other excellencies, and procures regard to the trifling, friendship to the worthless, and affection to the dull" (no. 72, 4:15–16). The differences among these kindred passions are just large enough to render the distinction instructive. The antipathies between regard and trifles, friendship and worthlessness, and affection and dullness are presupposed but not predetermined. The transformation of all three into objects worthy of regard is a triumph of Johnson's own art and nature, but these entities were operating, efficiently, originally, and intelligently, within the psychological system he inherited. In instances like this one, the liveliness of the episodes depends on the certainty of their definition, and the certainty of the definition on the sympathies of the moralist and aptitudes of the lexicographer.

The pleasure and pain that lurk beneath the good and evil in each episode appear in the by-product of discomfort. Some internal stress, hydraulic, psychological, or metaphysical, causes some form of dis-ease, so that we see, again and again, words and phrases denoting agitation, eagerness, and anxiety. This discomfort is a consequence of the stirrings of an innate propensity for good and aversion to evil. In Johnson, especially, this physiological and psychological "incitement" produces un-ease: desire for riches "would have broken out in the poet or the sage, if it had been excited by opportunity, and invigorated by the approximation of its proper object" (no. 58, 3:310). The "motion" that results from this incitement of a passion by its object finds its way into many of Johnson's metaphors, usually in the form of a fluid. Few of these are more striking in their combination of the abstract vocabulary of the passions ("remorse") with the figurative possibilities of elementary chemistry ("bitterness," "asperity") than "if we are conscious that we have not contributed to our own sufferings, . . . and we have not the bitterness of remorse to add to the asperity of misfortune."[7]

At the same time that objects inspire passions in the self, many selves become the objects of passions in others—a complicating propensity that produced considerable social disequilibrium, the plots of a good many narratives, and the occasion for many periodic sentences. Sometimes someone set out deliberately to become the object of a given passion, as did Victoria, whose mother had raised her "as an assemblage of all that could raise envy or desire."[8] She became a prosaic Anne Vane, against whose fame fondness had combined with hatred in *The Vanity of Human Wishes* (ll. 319–42). But Victoria's beauty fell victim to the pox rather than indiscretion, the object of envy became the target of insolence, and the object of desire the victim of neglect: "Though the negligence of the men was not very pleasing when compared with vows and adoration, yet it was far more supportable than the insolence of my own sex" (no. 133, 4:343). The shift from desire to neglect is obvious (and cruel) enough; the one from envy to insolence, however, needs to be referred to the comparative component of the passions, which posited envy of a superior good and insolence toward inferiority.

The role of others in the workings of the passions is the most complicating factor of all. Much of the psychological disequilibrium in *The Rambler* stems from episodes generated by changing relationships between the self and others. But whereas, for Hume, the selves of others made pride and sympathy possible, for Johnson the selfishness of others makes life difficult; perhaps this is merely a restatement of the difference between a philosopher and a moralist. More comparative, even competitive, than *The Spectator, The Rambler* is full of characters who inflict their passions on those who surpass them:

> Whoever rises above those who once pleased themselves with equality, will have many malevolent gazers at his eminence. To gain sooner than others that which all pursue with the same ardour, and to which all imagine themselves entitled, will for ever be a crime. When those who started with us in the race of life, leave us so far behind, that we have little hope to overtake them, we revenge our disappointment by remarks on the arts of supplantation by which they gained the advantage, or on the folly and arrogance with which they possess it. Of them, whose rise we could not hinder, we solace ourselves by prognosticating the fall.[9]

The comparative component dominates that passage, but it is accompanied, as always in Johnson, by several subtle temporal considerations and by an element of sympathetic understanding implicit in the plural pronouns—a sympathy that has little in common with the more philosophic sympathy generated by the passions in Hume.

This comparative component enables "others," by their own de-

meanor, to encourage certain passions to flourish. It also enables the
lexicographer to deploy his sense of definition, and the moralist his
sense of social right and wrong:

> Neither our virtues nor vices are all our own. If there were no
> cowardice, there would be little insolence; pride cannot rise to
> any great degree, but by the concurrence of blandishment or
> the sufferance of tameness. The wretch who would shrink and
> crouch before one that should dart his eyes upon him with the
> spirit of natural equality, becomes capricious and tyrannical
> when he sees himself approached with a downcast look, and
> hears the soft address of awe and servility. To those who are
> willing to purchase favour by cringes and compliance, is to be
> imputed the haughtiness that leaves nothing to be hoped by
> firmness and integrity. [No. 180, 5:186]

Some such comparative determination of relative status is inherent,
as we have seen, in the established sense of each passion. One can
love only an equal, respect only a superior, and pity only an inferior.
In order for relative status to be calculated, some evidence of status
must be manifested—here it appears in the shrinking, cringing,
flashings, and downcast looks. These make that passage as lively as
the contrasts supplied by vocabulary and syntax make it certain.
While we expect such manifestly indicative social behavior in *The
Spectator*, it is useful to be reminded that Johnson was sometimes
obliged by considerations inherent in the long tradition of the passions to cast an eye on such behavior. We may not find whole essays
on the fluttering of a fan, but we can find postures that are loaded
with significance. I return to this consideration below, in a discussion of the physiology in *The Rambler*.

Of all the traditional components of the passions, the temporal
was the one that lent itself most fully to Johnson's genius and syntax. Some temporal reference had been implicit in the definition of
each passion at least since the time of Aristotle; Johnson usually
makes it explicit: "Sorrow is properly that state of mind in which
our desires are fixed upon the past, without looking forward to the
future, an incessant wish that something were otherwise than it has
been, a tormenting and harrassing want of some enjoyment or possession which we have lost, and which no endeavours can possibly
regain" (no. 47, 3:254). Sometimes he is content with the implica-

tions: "I know not whether greater relaxation may not be indulged, and whether hope as well as gratitude may not unblameably produce a dedication" (no. 136, 4:358). Only the difference in time distinguishes hope from gratitude; one is for a good anticipated, the other for a good received; the rest of the essay develops this distinction.

The temporal element gives direction to many sentences and paragraphs in many *Ramblers,* complicating and enriching the moral philosophy of the whole work.[10] Duration, for example, determines and distorts the effects of many passions and gives rise to many others, it being the nature of the human mind to range through time in search of happiness, usually at the behest of some passion: "Thus every period of life is obliged to borrow its happiness from the time to come. In youth we have nothing past to entertain us, and in age, we derive little from retrospect but hopeless sorrow. Yet the future likewise has its limits, which the imagination dreads to approach, but which we see to be not far distant" (no. 203, 5:293–94).

Like Aristotle, Johnson associates certain passions with certain ages or professions, so that in various *Ramblers* we find rashness and insolence in youth, indignation and peevishness in age, confidence in the military, timidity in the academy, and so on. But Johnson's sympathetic understanding of the mind's temporal coursing provides a dynamic that combines the categorical fixity of Aristotle with the enriching sense of duration of Locke: "The measure or time of pronouncing may be varied so as very strongly to represent, not only the modes of external motion, but the quick or slow succession of ideas, and consequently the passions of the mind" (no. 94, 4:140–41). In the grip of fear, the mind will work (that is, will present itself with ideas) rapidly, while in that of envy, it will work more slowly. This is the most striking fusion I know of the tenets of faculty psychology with those of empiricism.[11] The empirical mind shuffles its own ideas rather than eternal ones, while the passions perturb the mind and affect its procedures by controlling the speed with which ideas pass through it. That speed, in turn, has a determining effect on the passions.

The principal effect of the passions in *The Rambler* is to turn men and women aside from the "path" (Johnson's persistent though not always developed metaphor) of virtue and truth: "It is natural to mean well, when only abstracted ideas of virtue are proposed to the mind, and no particular passion turns us aside from rectitude" (no. 76, 4:34). The passions achieve this effect most often by interfering with the process of estimation, the assessment of good and evil in the characters and actions of others and in various objects. This process, an extension of the comparative component, is perhaps the most essential, and the most difficult, of the numerous moral duties in Johnson's creed. This concern, which had occupied thoughtful writers at least since Aquinas, obliged Johnson to return to the role of "others" repeatedly and in complicating contexts in which he sets forth the capacity of the passions to interfere with our estimates: "we only discover in what estimation we are held, when we can no longer give hopes or fears" (no. 75, 4:33). And again, "Envy, curiosity, and a sense of the imperfection of our present state, inclines us to estimate the advantages which are in the possession of others above their real value."[12] The sense of the imperfection of our own state is a function and a condition of envy, a hatred of a good in the possession of others. Envy itself produces distorted assessments, and it contaminates the additional passions to which it gives rise.

All of these considerations figure intricately in the (somewhat biographical?) student of Eumathes, who had to learn to feel at home in London: "But his fear abated as he grew more familiar with its objects; and the contempt to which his rusticity exposed him . . . obliged him to dissemble his remaining terrors" (no. 195, 5:253–54). The episode of fear lasts only as long as the mistaken estimation of its objects. The self responds variously to others, and the definitions distinguish "fears" from "remaining terrors." Notice also that the dissimulation of response is much likelier in London than in the country, as rustics let all their episodes show. This brief passage is by no means the only example of one that can be construed more efficiently and fully by those attendant to the components of the passions at work in it.

In addition to these abstract and abstruse considerations, Johnson is surprisingly interested in the physiology of the passions. His mind may always have been on psychological phenomena and mental states, but his eye caught the corporeal manifestations of a good many mental states, and his pen exploited the mechanical elements in those psychological transactions. Essentially a Boerhaavian, Johnson understood very well the developments in physiology we considered in chapter 3. (He rebuked himself, though not by name, for an anachronistic reference to the circulation of the blood in *Irene*.)[13] In the following quite representative passage, the idea enters the head through the ears, and then (but whether by fluids, spirits, or whatever he does not specify) the passions of terror, sorrow, and discontent are produced in the heart, which now carries a "burden" of excessive but highly refined spirits: "for [the voice of a screech owl] will often fill their ears in the hour of dejection, terrify them with apprehensions, which their own thoughts would never have produced, and sadden, by intruded sorrows, the day which might have been passed in amusements or in business; it will burthen the heart with unnecessary discontents, and weaken for a time that love of life, which is necessary to the vigorous prosecution of any undertaking" (no. 59, 3:315).

Motion toward or from some apprehended object is induced by the passions in response to certain hydraulic and thermodynamic functions of the blood, refinements from Newtonian physics superimposed on the "fluids" of the ancients and made possible, as we have seen, by widespread but unwarranted assumptions about the hollowness of the nerves. Thus one finds numerous passages which speak of the self or the heart as "filled" or "filling" with melancholy, terror, joy, and so forth (for example, no. 54, 3:289) and more intriguing ones such as "Sorrow is a kind of rust of the soul, which every new idea contributes in its passage to scour away. It is the putrefaction of stagnant life, and is remedied by exercise and motion" (no. 47, 3:258). That passage is vaguely reminiscent of Thomas Willis in its figure but eminently Johnsonian in the suppleness and weight of its vocabulary.

Other metaphors add the notion of heat to that of flow: the mind ferments, the passions boil over (no. 74, 4:24), and metaphors of warmth and chill, more numerous than lively, abound. I do not insist that the reader pause to admire every reference to ardor or the kindling or chilling effects of one or another of the passions or even of the "frigorifick power" of bashfulness (no. 159, 5:82). I do suggest that these metaphors that seem so slight or peculiar to us had once, because of their former physiological validity, a more laudable place in Johnson's prose. That vanished physiology lurks behind nearly every word in this brief example: "Against the instillations of this frigid opiate, the heart should be secured by all the considerations which once concurred to kindle the ardour of enterprize.

Whatever motive first incited action, has still greater force to stimulate perseverance" (no. 207, 5:313). A longer, finer example captures the procedures and toys with the spirits of alchemy. Its juxtaposition of the archaic language of the laboratory with the then still valid language of the passions allows Johnson to state several truths that were once thought eternal:

> Thus one generation is always the scorn and wonder of the other, and the notions of the old and young are like liquors of different gravity and texture which never can unite. The spirits of youth, sublimed by health, and volatilised by passion, soon leave behind them the phlegmatic sediment of wariness and deliberation, and burst out in temerity and enterprise. The tenderness therefore which nature infuses, and which long habits of beneficence confirm, is necessary to reconcile such opposition; and an old man must be a father to bear with patience those follies and absurdities, which he will perpetually imagine himself to find in the schemes and expectations, the pleasures and the sorrows, of those who have not yet been hardened by time, and chilled by frustration. [No. 69, 3:365–66].

It is sometimes instructive, or at least diverting, to recover some of the physiology underlying Johnson's treatment of the passions. It is also possible, but not perhaps necessary, to descry some of the traditional philosophical concerns. The Scholastic division into concupiscent and irascible, fundamental, long-lived, and useless as it was, retained little of its force in the eighteenth century. The concupiscent passions, we recall, have as their objects simple and attainable good or avoidable evil; the irascible have remoter and more difficult objects. Johnson cited the distinction in the *Dictionary:* "The schools reduce all the passions to those two heads, the *concupiscible,* and *irascible* appetite, South's Sermons," and elaborated on it in a sermon he wrote for John Taylor. [14] Now and then he will coordinate a series or construct a parallel along lines that look as if they could, by a determined historian, be traced back: "They have shewn that most of the conditions of life, which raise the envy of the timorous, and rouse the ambition of the daring, are empty shows of felicity" (no. 66, 3:350). The connections here between timorousness and envy become somewhat clearer if one sees the connection between timorousness and concupiscence and the opposition of envy to irascibility—connections reflected in the shift from "raise" to "rouse." The distinction can be detected throughout no. 58, where those who desire riches are contrasted with those who cannot rouse themselves to the pursuit of riches. It is continued in the ironic conviction that the study of the advice of a moralist "will seldom fail to repress his ardor, and retard his violence" (no. 58, 3:313), where ardor is concupiscent and violence irascible. Johnson clearly never made much of this distinction. Other distinctions he invoked when it was convenient. That between passions and appetites is invoked without fuss in the long passage from *Rambler* no. 44 that we considered above. He thought the distinction important enough to tinker with several versions of this fragment from *Rambler* no. 77: "He, by whose writings the heart is rectified, the appetites counteracted, and the passions repressed."[15]

I am not one of those eager to enlist Johnson, on the strength of that last verb, as an early and astute pre-Freudian.[16] Those who are might cite a passage that seems to combine infantilism with empiricism, all the while hovering near the brink of determinism: "The desires that predominate in our hearts, are instilled by imperceptible communications at the time when we look upon the various scenes of the world, and the different employments of men, with the neutrality of inexperience; and we come forth from the nursery or the school, invariably destined to the pursuit of great acquisitions, or petty accomplishments" (no. 141, 4:384). Even so, the desires that are here being acquired are more traditional than libidinal. The "inexperience" is neutral, and the "imperceptible communications" come from without. Johnson is quite content to work with the established episodes, the traditional components, and the usual determinants of right and wrong: "He that, when his reason operates in its full force, can thus, by the mere prevalence of self-love, prefer himself to his fellow-beings, is very unlikely to judge equitably when his passions are agitated by a sense of wrong, and his attention wholly engrossed by pain, interest, or danger" (no. 185, 5:207).

Johnson did not, however, restrict himself to precisely those passions that he found in Aristotle, Cicero, and Burton. He was more concerned with understanding and describing states of mind than in conforming to any received system, however much that system might contribute to his understanding. He writes frequently and vividly of "interest" and "curiosity" as if they were passions, rather than dispositions of one of the faculties. As we saw in chapter 1, curiosity and attention had just begun to take on an epistemological timeliness, and interest an economic one. Curiosity is an inclination of the mind, an eagerness for it to be "taken" by any number of objects: "Curiosity is, in great and generous minds, the first passion and the last; and perhaps always predominates in proportion to the strength of the contemplative faculties" (no. 150, 5:34). I am not sure whether it was the lexicographer or the moralist who made the connection between curiosity and generosity, but as far as I know, it is an original one, and it has implications for the ruling passion of Mr. Spectator, and for the considerable appeal of that character. Attention, which the *Dictionary* defines as "the act of attending or heeding; the act of bending the mind upon any thing," is frequently at the mercy of the passions, and, like them, requires an object (no. 86, 4:87). This bending of the mind is the means through which the passions come at their objects, or vice versa, so Johnson was always alert to the quirky workings of the attention: "The mind will break, from confinement to its stated task, into sudden excursions. Severe and connected attention is preserved but for a short time" (no. 89, 4:105; note the implicit discomfort). More often than not, attention is overshadowed by an accompanying passion, as in the following example, in which Aristotle figures as both literary critic and psychologist: "As the design of tragedy is to instruct by moving the passions, it must always have a hero, a personage apparently and incontestably superior to the rest, upon whom the attention may be fixed, and the anxiety suspended" (no. 156, 5:70).

Interest is more difficult to place, if not to define: "To affect; to move; to touch with passion; to gain the affections."[17] It figures as a complicating factor and concomitant force, accompanying the engagement of every object by a passion. And like a passion, it distorts all the calculations and estimates of the mind. Whereas attention bends the mind, and curiosity changes it, interest fastens and deforms it: "Such is probably the natural state of the universe, but it is so much deformed by interest and passion, that the benefit of this adaptation of men to things is not always perceived" (no. 160, 5:85).

As his emphasis on discomfort, his awareness of physiology, and his figures such as "bending the mind" suggest, Johnson was likelier to employ than to brood over the connections between the mind and the body. And yet, as it is always at hand, the body served to illustrate the invisible, abstract, and complex episodes that took place within it. Its extremities serve, vividly and aptly, in many analogies, metaphors, and illustrations: "As any action or posture long continued, will distort and disfigure the limbs; so the mind likewise is crippled and contracted by perpetual application to the same set of ideas" (no. 173, 5:150–51). These images of the body and the mind render Johnson's humanism both vivid and articulate.

Rambler no. 124 depicts Londoners who have taken to the country for the summer, in "the Platonick penance of desire without enjoyment" and in a "state of hopeless wishes and pining recollection, where the eye of vanity will look round for admiration to no purpose, and the hand of avarice shuffle cards in a bower with ineffectual dexterity" (4:298). The reader alerted to the precepts of the passions will see that this is no mere personification. The eye is as essential to vanity as the hand is to avarice. Moreover, it is the removal of the "others" who provide the objects of both passions (admiration and wealth, respectively) that underlie the "recollections" of praise and the "wishes" for wealth. This synecdoche chooses its organs with great care, as they discredit those passions that depend on them for their gratification. In other passages passions take on tones of voice instead of limbs and features, tones appropriate, illuminating, and, again, discrediting: "But it was some satisfaction to be separated from my mother, who was incessantly ringing the knell of departed beauty, and never entered my room without the whine of condolence, or the growl of anger" (no. 133, 4:341).

I do not propose to convert the friend of Garrick and Reynolds into their rival, but Johnson occasionally creates caricatures of expressions, as, for example, when he amuses himself with speculating about how a miser might "gape with curiosity, or grin with contempt" at a wit (no. 128, 4:318). The point here depends on the lexicographical subdivision of laughter into two categories that no one with the least bit of wit wants. This turning of a smile into a gape or a grin would be enough for a comedian or a cartoonist. A moralist and an essayist must trace the facial distortions to their underlying intellectual causes, making the face expose the mind.

Such passages combine Johnson's own deep understanding of the inner workings of the passions with the elaborate system of expressing them that we saw in chapter 1.

Occasionally when Johnson's characters rely on facial manifestations, one passion is mistaken for another, and the passions contribute even more confusion and distress to the human condition. When his aunt and uncle resolved to disencumber a country boy of his "villatick bashfulness," he wrote to *The Rambler* as follows: "My indignation at familiarity thus contemptuous flushed in my face; they mistook anger for shame, and alternately exerted their eloquence upon the benefits of publick education, and the happiness of an assurance early acquired" (no. 147, 5:21). While anger and shame are quite different passions, one directed at a wrong done by another to the self, the other at a wrong done by the self and detected by another, the aunt and uncle, having assumed bashfulness, must mistake one for the other, as someone who was bashful would be unlikely to be angry, and certain to have much to be ashamed of. Only the articulations of prose can remove the confusions that have emerged from a little warm blood.

Johnson did not concern himself with the feigning of passions, but sometimes he did, like Fielding, count on physiology to set the crooked straight. Friends who have fallen into a dispute may continue to appear before one another with civility for a while, "but the poison of discord is infused, and though the countenance may preserve its smile, the heart is hardening and contracting" (no. 64, 3:343). Here the underlying physiology is so hard at work that it is doubtful that the countenance will be able to belie it for long. As the heart hardens and contracts under the weight of the vital spirits rushing back to it, it will, necessarily, produce changes in the face by acting upon the muscles that govern the smile. Johnson attended to real passions rather than feigned ones and to the inner discomforts of these very real passions. His sympathetic attention to those discomforts adds depth and vividness to his account of their external manifestations, but it is the depth and vividness of a sympathetic moralist rather than that of, say, a novelist who had learned about the passions from actors and criminals.

We have already seen that their capacity for refinement enabled the passions to play a major role in the aesthetics of Addison and Hume. Johnson's most important pronouncements of aesthetics lie outside *The Rambler,* in *Rasselas,* the *Lives of the Poets,* and his conversation. Here, for example, he runs over the Aristotelian possibilities for pity and terror, for Boswell's edification. The entire passage confirms his acceptance of the main tenets of the received system, psychological as well as aesthetic:

> "But how are the passions to be purged by terrour and pity?" (said I, with an assumed air of ignorance, to incite him to talk. . .).
>
> JOHNSON. "Why, Sir, you are to consider what is the meaning of purging in the original sense. It is to expel impurities from the human body. The mind is subject to the same imperfection. The passions are the great movers of human actions; but they are mixed with such impurities, that it is necessary they should be purged or refined by means of terrour and pity. For instance, ambition is a noble passion; but by seeing upon the stage, that a man who is so excessively ambitious as to raise himself by injustice, is punished, we are terrified at the fatal consequences of such a passion. In the same manner a certain degree of resentment is necessary; but if we see that a man carries it too far, we pity the object of it, and are taught to moderate that passion."[18]

There are, of course, aesthetic considerations of the passions all through *The Rambler,* but they are subordinated, even more thoroughly than usual, to moral considerations. Pastorals appeal to passions that Johnson thinks his readers either ought not to feel ("and suffer ourselves, without resistance, to be transported to elysian regions, where we are to meet with nothing but joy, and plenty, and contentment; where every gale whispers pleasure, and every shade promises repose"), or have never felt ("We are therefore delighted with rural pictures, because we know the original at an age when our curiosity can be very little awakened, by descriptions of courts which we never beheld, or representations of passion which we never felt"; no. 36, 3:195, 196). He distrusts the genre because he distrusts both the passions on which it depends and those it evokes. For an empiricist, the episodes of passion evoked in pastoral are simple, silly, and uninstructive:

> The state of a man confined to the employments and pleasures of the country, is so little diversified, and exposed to so few of

those accidents which produce perplexities, terrors and surprises, in more complicated transactions, that he can be shewn but seldom in such circumstances as attract curiosity. His ambition is without policy, and his love without intrigue. He has no complaints to make of his rival, but that he is richer than himself; nor any disasters to lament, but a cruel mistress, or a bad harvest. [3:198]

Johnson well knew that the human condition consisted of complicated transactions, great rivalries, and frequent disasters, so he called for, and employed, a more authentic and complex medium to articulate it.

The discussion of *Paradise Lost* in *The Rambler* (nos. 86, 88, 90, 92, 94), doubtless in acknowledgment of *The Spectator*'s thorough treatment of the passions in that poem, restricts itself to the effects of Milton's versification on the passions of the reader. The important comments, consistent with the tradition and with Johnson's own beliefs and aesthetic, on the restricted implications of passions for theology occur not in *The Rambler* but in the "Life of Milton":

As human passions did not enter the world before the Fall, there is in the *Paradise Lost* little opportunity for the pathetick; but what little there is has not been lost. That passion which is peculiar to rational nature, the anguish arising from the consciousness of transgression and the horrours attending the sense of the Divine Displeasure, are very justly described and forcibly impressed. But the passions are moved only on one occasion; sublimity is the general and prevailing quality in this poem—sublimity variously modified, sometimes descriptive, sometimes argumentative.[19]

The passions have an aesthetic place in Johnson's system, and he is determined to keep them in it: "Pleasure and terrour are indeed the genuine sources of poetry; but poetical pleasure must be such as human imagination can at least conceive, and poetical terrour such as human strength and fortitude may combat. The good and evil of Eternity are too ponderous for the wings of wit; the mind sinks under them in passive helplessness, content with calm belief and humble adoration" (*Lives*, 1.182).

Having ventured outside *The Rambler* in pursuit of aesthetic concerns, I mention *Idler* no. 81, in which an Indian orator well schooled in the traditional effects and intricacies of the passions knows what to call them, how to appeal to them, and how to predict their consequences. While his own indignation may be a little sullied with vengeance, he pronounces upon the cruelty and rapacity of the invaders with dignity and force. (As it happens, he is watching the English army march toward Quebec, and the battle at which Wolfe fell:)

> But the time perhaps is now approaching when the pride of usurpation shall be crushed, and the cruelties of invasion shall be revenged. The sons of rapacity have now drawn their swords upon each other, and referred their claims to the decision of war; let us look unconcerned upon the slaughter, and remember that the death of every European delivers the country from a tyrant and a robber. . . . Let them then continue to dispute their title to regions which they cannot people, to purchase by danger and blood the empty dignity of dominion over mountains which they will never climb, and rivers which they will never pass.[20]

Few passages in *The Rambler* illustrate more clearly the underlying control and overall effect of the passions than the following paragraph, in which Johnson describes the effects of death and the deathbed on the passions of the living:

> It seems to me remarkable that death increases our veneration for the good, and extenuates our hatred of the bad. Those virtues which once we envied, as Horace observes, because they eclipsed our own, can now no longer obstruct our reputation, and we have therefore no interest to suppress their praise. That wickedness, which we feared for its malignity, is now become impotent, and the man whose name filled us with alarm, and rage, and indignation, can at last be considered only with pity, or contempt. [No. 54, 3:292]

The list of passions dealt with here is a long one: veneration, hatred, envy, interest, fear, alarm, rage, indignation, pity, and contempt. Its length is less striking than its coherence, and this coherence is drawn from the relationships, established relationships, among these ten passions. These relationships combine with Johnson's orderly syntax to construct a paragraph that is a model of concurrence, most of it borrowed rather than imposed. The veneration and the hatred, for example, presuppose one another. They are psychological alternatives and were so long before Johnson made them syntactic ones. And here, as elsewhere, he has taken advantage of the simplicity in this alternation in the nouns to complicate the parallel in their verbs, so that while veneration and hatred are simple alternates, "increases" and "extenuates" are complex. The source of this complexity in the verbs follows in the next sentence: the superior good that is the object of veneration produces some envy as a kind of by-product. But the by-products of the potent evil that is the object of hatred are alarm, rage, and indignation. The removal of that object by death converts the hatred for it, together with its concomitant passions, into either pity or contempt, pity if the deceased is now simply inferior, contempt if he was formerly simply evil. Similarly, the accompanying envy loses its object, and we are left with pure veneration. The death of their object modifies the passions that object provoked. The paragraph bases its intricacies on those of a system external to it, a system that invites the turn from good to bad and guides the descent from veneration to pity and contempt.

There is, then, a good deal to be learned about the passions from watching them at work in *The Rambler*. I might add that the passions figure extensively and traditionally in Johnson's other works. They enrich his poetry: "O'er Love, o'er Fear, extends his wide Domain, / Unconquer'd Lord of Pleasure and of Pain"; and inform his political writings: "It may therefore not be improper to lay before the public the reflections of a man who cannot favour the opposition, for he thinks it wicked, and cannot fear it, for he thinks it weak."[21] I have already mentioned their appearance in his criticism; I include two more examples, both of which suggest that Johnson thought that, while passions belonged primarily in prose, they worked better in plays than in poetry and constituted an essential element in literature: "Dryden could not now repress these emotions, which he called indignation, and others jealousy; but wrote upon the play and the dedication such criticism as malignant impatience could pour out in haste."[22] And more complexly:

How is it that grief in Leonato and Lady Constance, produces effects directly opposite, and yet both agreeable to nature. Sorrow softens the mind while it is yet warmed by hope, but hardens it when it is congealed by despair. Distress, while there remains any prospect of relief, is weak and flexible, but when no succour remains, is fearless and stubborn; angry alike at those that injure, and at those that do not help; careless to please where nothing can be gained, and fearless to offend when there is nothing further to be dreaded. Such was this writer's knowledge of the passions. [23]

The next chapter opens with an (imagined) example of the passions at work in Johnson's conversation. I shall close this one with an actual passage from his correspondence:

There lurks, perhaps, in every human heart a desire of distinction, which inclines every man first to hope, and then to believe, that Nature has given him something peculiar to himself. This vanity makes one mind nurse aversions, and another actuate desires, till they rise by art much above their original state of power; and as affectation, in time, improves to habit, they at last tyrannise over him who at first encouraged them only for show. Every desire is a viper in the bosom, who, while he was chill, was harmless; but when warmth gave him strength, exerted it in poison. [24]

He is writing, of course, to Boswell, a man especially given to the episodes of desire set forth here with clarity, sympathy, severity, and skill. Johnson could understand and express Boswell's desires because he had made himself an expert in the language and workings of the passions. He deserves readers who have done likewise. Of all the abstractions in his prose, the passions are the most lively and, to my mind, the most convincing repositories of his wisdom and humanity.

8

THE PLACE OF THE PASSIONS IN

THE DECLINE AND FALL OF

THE ROMAN EMPIRE

 ATE IN HIS LIFE SIR JOSHUA REYNOLDS imagined a conversation in which Edward Gibbon and Samuel Johnson discuss the merits of David Garrick's portrayals of passion. For some reason, the piece is manifestly unfair to Gibbon, who is made to sound every bit as naive an observer of Garrick as Partridge (above, chapter 5):

> GIBBON. But you will allow, however, that this sensibility, those fine feelings, made him the great actor he was.
> JOHNSON. This is all cant, fit only for kitchen-wenches and chambermaids. Garrick's trade was to represent passion, not to feel it. Ask Reynolds whether he felt the distress of Count Ugolino when he drew it.
> GIBBON. But surely he feels the passion at the moment he is representing it.[1]

Gibbon would certainly not have been alone in being fooled, or at least convinced, by the displays of passion that Garrick brought from what Johnson derisively called an actor's "study" to the stage. But Gibbon was not in the least fooled by the passions he encountered in his own study, in the innumerable narratives, papers, and records over which he pored year after year in compiling *The Decline and Fall of the Roman Empire*. No one excelled Gibbon in detecting, attributing, and articulating the passions of the past and no one, not even Garrick, had encountered more episodes of passion in his work. But Gibbon dealt with them circumspectly, selectively, and often collectively. He found places for many of them, but they were strict and subtle places, never theatrical, and seldom deep.

A single central statement of their prevalence, power, and intricacy will attest to Gibbon's acknowledgment of their significance and his awareness of their established components. He views them primarily as "motives" and in this passage as the primary constituents of the laws by which humanity is governed, or rather, driven. Episodes of ardor, pride, despair, vengeance, and fear are sorted out from one another and allowed to feed the flames that provoke the mind to "tumult and civil discord." But the only trace of a rhetorical flourish in this extensive treatment lies in the bestowing of a "voice of its own" on pity. Only pity is given such a voice, and that is all it is given. And while the catalogue explains much history, Gibbon's point here is that it leaves the cruelty of Commodus unexplained:

> Of all our passions and appetites, the love of power is of the most imperious and unsociable nature, since the pride of one man requires the submission of the multitude. In the tumult of civil discord the laws of society lose their force, and their place is seldom supplied by those of humanity. The ardour of contention, the pride of victory, the despair of success, the memory of past injuries, and the fear of future dangers, all contribute to inflame the mind, and to silence the voice of pity. From such motives almost every page of history has been stained with civil blood; but these motives will not account for the unprovoked cruelties of Commodus.[2]

The traditional passions will not, however, often fail the historian. They are crucial to his purposes, well within the mastery of his technique, and regularly absorbed into larger considerations or subtler constructions.[3] Of the numerous explicit statements to this effect, I cite an early one: "Surrounded with imperfect fragments, always concise, often obscure, and sometimes contradictory, he is reduced to collect, to compare, and to conjecture: and though he ought never to place his conjectures in the rank of facts, yet the knowledge of human nature, and of the sure operation of its fierce and unrestrained passions, might, on some occasions, supply the want of historical materials" (1:237). The historian's right to conjecture depends on two assumptions: first, that the passions are continuous, consistent, and commensurate from one age to the next and from one culture to another, and second, that many centuries of analysis, philosophical, physiological, rhetorical, and critical, had clarified and crystallized each of the passions so that historian and reader alike might know their place and follow their "sure operation."

Fourteen hundred years of history did not shake Gibbon's faith in their potency or consistency, as he testified when he came to narrate the fall of Constantinople: "In the fall and the sack of great cities, an historian is condemned to repeat the tale of uniform calamity; the same effects must be produced by the same passions; and, when those passions may be indulged without control, small, alas! is the difference between civilised and savage man" (7:196).

Gibbon's sources provided him with the circumstances, objects, and occasions of the passions and often their names as well. His models, from Tacitus to Bayle and Montaigne, encouraged him to find a place for these potent terms. He eagerly acknowledged that Tacitus had given him his "knowledge of the Roman constitution and of human nature" (1:320), and the same source showed him some artful ways to manage the passions—both historically and aesthetically: "When Tacitus describes the deaths of the innocent and illustrious Romans, who were sacrificed to the cruelty of the first Caesars, the art of the historian, or the merit of the sufferers, excite in our breasts the most lively sensations of terror, of admiration, and of pity" (3:19). Gibbon follows Tacitus's example in detecting passions in his subjects but not in exhibiting his own on the page.

Given his subject, his library, and his method, Gibbon could reach into the long tradition of the passions at more points along it than any other writer: "From these institutions of peace and war, Polybius has deduced the spirit and success of a people incapable of fear and impatient of repose" (4:161). His footnotes attest repeatedly to the availability and continuity of the passions in his sources. For example, Claudian supplied the passions of Rufinus, by way of Bayle (3:229), and Racine added delicacy to the patience of the female captives in Homer (3:244). Gibbon's steady reliance on, and deference to, these sources provides additional evidence of the continuity and sustained significance of these ephemeral and since neglected episodes.

Gibbon's library and *Autobiography,* not to mention a cloud of commentators, connect him directly to most of the major contributors to the tradition dealt with in chapter 2, not only to Cicero, whom he mentions repeatedly, but even to St. Augustine, with whom he was connected by the Jansenism of Tillemont.[4] His affinities with later writers are less uniform but no less important. He shared Bayle as a source with Addison, he corresponded with and admired Hume and celebrated *Tom Jones;* he even appreciated *Irene,* though with reservations (7:171, 187).

At the great distance, both temporal and intellectual, from which Gibbon surveys the characters and actions he discusses, all the passions look rather alike, and the similarity is increased by the subordination to syntax and circumstance. Commensurate, almost in the sense in which the Stoics had urged, and all but interchangeable and equivalent in ways that enabled the Scholastics to manipulate them endlessly, they seem to balance and succeed one another effortlessly and relentlessly in Gibbon's prose. The narrator's remoteness and unwillingness to disturb this balance make the passions more often names than episodes, or episodes only for the historically informed and independently imaginative. The historian does not wish to bring the passions back to life.

The passions do not, however, lie inertly on the pages of *The Decline and Fall.* In *The Spectator* and the works of Fielding and, more surprisingly, Johnson, the reader may—I think should—look at passions as if from a seat in the theater or from a distance of a few paces in an art gallery. In Gibbon, on the other hand, they occupy a low place on a far horizon, where they are mingled with exotic names (Odoacer, Thebais, and so forth) and tendentious abstractions such as "dexterous" and "unwarlike." Often they are subsumed under more capacious substantives such as "virtue" and "policy" or are subjected to surprise or disbelief. Gibbon found a place for the passions, but it was a constricted place and a subservient one.

Those episodes that seem so lively in the prose of other writers are absorbed into larger, more impersonal causes, in ways that Gibbon learned from Montesquieu and others. The components that figure in other accounts remain undeveloped and unimplied while Gibbon pursues larger issues or smaller details. The passions retain their traditional clarity without acquiring any new force. They enter Gibbon's prose shorn of most of their usual components—the temporal considerations, estimates of relative power, enumeration of "objects," and others that might have impaired their ability to balance and compress. These consistent, controlled entities participated in, but are very much subjected to, the variety and elegance of his style, whereas, in the other writers we have considered, they seem to have been the impetus for much of that variety and elegance. Gibbon places them on his own page with care, and sometimes a smile, but he never lingers to allow episodes of passion to exfoliate. He uses the terms we have been studying to compress and explain, not to develop and enlarge: "From all the camps and garrisons of Italy, the confederates, actuated by the same resentment and the same hopes, impatiently flocked to the standard of this popular leader [Odoacer]" (4:48). There is simply no room in such a sentence to consider the futurity of hope or the physiology of resentment—considerations that might well have detained Johnson and Fielding, respectively.

The following passage, routine in content and excellence, exhibits the ways in which the passions are both secondary to and summaries of the historical context. They are subsumed, as so often, under a more capacious and significant abstraction ("virtue"), and they are subjected to the syntax and the historical sequence: "but, as soon as Maria of Antioch had given a son and heir to the empire, the presumptive rights of Bela were abolished, and he was deprived of his promised bride; but the Hungarian prince resumed his name and the kingdom of his fathers, and displayed such virtues as might excite the regret and envy of the Greeks" (5:232). The "regret" sharpens the edge of the "envy," and both yield to the "virtue" of the barbarian.

Gibbon imposes so much geographical control on his materials that his work might be said to be presided over by Terminus, the Roman god of boundaries (1:7; compare 1:xiv). On every page he relies on the "indelible characters of nature" (1:23)—rivers, mountains, and seacoasts—and, less indelibly, on cities to provide firm and vivid ground for the actions he records. Only when these features have been established does he consider the delible inhabitants or invaders, collecting the fleeting episodes of temperament, sentiment, and passion that stain their history: "The palace was soon distracted with conspiracy, the city with tumult, the provinces with insurrection; and the cruel execution of the guilty and the suspected served to irritate rather than subdue the public discontent" (5:50). In this passage, the passions are distributed throughout Constantinople and the eastern empire at the same time that they are subordinated to mental and political abstractions such as "conspiracy." Having noticed them in his sources, the historian has found places for them on his page—places that fix them in the mind of the reader.

This device of ascribing passions to places, not required by the other writers we have studied, supplies compression and force by consolidating all the episodes of a single passion in a single city into one word that encloses them in space and isolates them in a vivid historical moment—an episode expanded in the only way that this historian has allowed them to expand. Thus we read, at the very beginning of the work, of Augustus's discovery "that Rome, in her present exalted situation, had much less to hope than to fear from the chance of arms" (1:2) and later that the "aspiring genius of Rome sacrificed vanity to ambition, and deemed it more prudent, as well as honourable, to adopt virtue and merit for her own wheresoever they were found, among slaves or strangers, enemies or barbarians" (1:33). These urban collectives become a regular and effective feature of Gibbon's treatment of the passions.

As the history progresses, Rome becomes the repository of increasingly ignoble passions: "The long absence of the emperors had filled Rome with discontent and indignation." It is almost, in that passage, as if the aqueducts had carried "vital spirits" rather than water. The passions of this city continue to shrink. As his *History* nears its end, Gibbon mentions the "ignorance and credulity" of the Romans, who can no longer conduct even a survey of their own lands without provoking "a smile of contempt and indignation" (7:321).

Increasingly disdainful of the passions of its inhabitants, Gibbon was nevertheless fascinated by the passions this place inspired in subsequent beholders. Temporarily emptied of its Gothic invaders, it becomes the object of Belisarius's pity and reverence (4:405; almost all of Belisarius's passions are commendable). Later he imagines a "wandering stranger" contemplating "with horror the vacancy and solitude of the city" (5:31), and the resonant reflections of Poggius, delivered from the Capitoline Hill, introduce the final chapter, on the city's final decay (7:301–5). These are followed by the gratification and astonishment of Petrarch when he beheld her ruins and her inhabitants, respectively (7:316, 321).

Gibbon evoked the responses of his contemporaries to convey those of Constantius: "The traveller, who has contemplated the ruins of ancient Rome, may conceive some imperfect idea of the sentiments which they must have inspired when they reared their heads in the splendour of unsullied beauty" (2:261). His own uncharacteristically strong sentiments when he first entered this place are the most familiar and compelling example of this concern: "But at the distance of twenty five years I can neither forget nor express the strong emotions which agitated my mind as I first approached and entered the *eternal City.*"[5] Even here the passions are seen from a distance and are subordinated to that eloquent "neither forget nor express."

In contrast, Gibbon treats Constantinople, "the seat of Turkish jealousy and despotism" (2:149), as a city without a soul, a place that has never been the repository of substantial or heroic passions: "But it is not in the city of Constantine, nor in the declining period of an empire when the human mind was depressed by civil and religious slavery, that we should seek for the souls of Homer and of Demosthenes" (2:151). The site of prodigality, luxury, and indolence, the center of the silk trade and Arianism, and the stronghold of eunuchs, it is here that "the simplicity of Roman manners was insensibly corrupted by the stately affectation of the courts of Asia" (2:159). "By a philosophic observer [Gibbon continues], the system of the Roman government might have been mistaken for a splendid theatre, filled with players of every character and degree, who repeated the language, and imitated the passions, of their original model" (2:160). The historian evidently prefers passions that were genuinely heroic, not theatrically so.

The few corrupt passions he could find evidence of, he knew exactly how to place; Constantinople had, after all, been inhabited by humans: "The writer who should impute these tumults solely to a religious principle would betray a very imperfect knowledge of human nature; yet it must be confessed that the motive which misled the sincerity of zeal, and the pretence which disguised the licentiousness of passion, suppressed the remorse which, in another cause, would have succeeded to the rage of the Christians of Constantinople" (2:385–86). Their passions are all too human, but religion and pride have prevented them from following the humane sequence that Hume might have supposed and Johnson imagined.

Other cities and states exhibit other passions. Spain has her pride (1:48), Antioch and Alexandria their disdain (1:50), and Venice "the avarice of a trading, and the insolence of a maritime power" (6:382; "yet her ambition was prudent"). The way "maritime" anchors "insolence" is, in itself, a shining example of Gibbon's placement of the passions. This conjunction of place and spirit supplies an impressive example of continuity when, in 540 A.D., Antioch greeted Chosroes with the same passions that had annoyed Julian in 362: "The people of Antioch had inherited the vain and satirical genius of their ancestors" (4:367). The collective episode became a useful device in so extensive a history—evaluative, explanatory, and economical.

In one striking passage Gibbon manages to put the passions in places without mentioning any by name: "On that celebrated ground [Southern Italy] the first consuls deserved triumphs, their successors adorned villas, and *their* posterity have erected convents" (1:21). This passage leaves it to the discerning reader to follow the succession of passions in succeeding generations and successive structures and to reflect on the termination of the series.[6]

One group presented itself so cohesively that its passions were always felt and displayed collectively. The Praetorian Guard exhibits a shared physiology and group passions. It is always treated as a body—a body governed by passions deadly to the society that had called it into being. Gibbon endows the real villains of his work with perceptions, musculature, judgment, imagination, sensuality, substance, insight, extremities, reflections, and pleasures, in that order, and detects the passions of contempt, awe, pride (repeatedly), and, finally and most dangerously, only a "precarious faith."

> Such formidable servants are always necessary, but often fatal, to the throne of despotism. By thus introducing the Praetorian guards, as it were, into the palace and the senate, the emperors taught them to perceive their own strength, and the weakness of the civil government; to view the vices of their masters with familiar contempt, and to lay aside that reverential awe which distance only, and mystery, can preserve towards an imaginary

power. In the luxurious idleness of an opulent city, their pride
was nourished by the sense of their irresistible weight; nor was
it possible to conceal from them that the person of the sovereign, the authority of the senate, the public treasure, and the
seat of the empire, were all in their hands. To divert the Praetorian bands from these dangerous reflections the firmest and
best established princes were obliged to mix blandishments
with commands, rewards with punishments, to flatter their
pride, indulge their pleasures, connive at their irregularities,
and to purchase their precarious faith by a liberal donative.
[1:104–5]

To create this villain Gibbon has relied, not on the lurid exaggera-
tions of the melodramatist, but only on the concise vocabulary of
the humanist. He has created an inhuman menace by collecting
human passions. Having done so, he alludes repeatedly to the
Guard's collective passions: its despair when it is temporarily dissolved (1:115), its dissatisfactions with the virtues of Alexander
(1:153), and its haughty discontents and sullen countenance when it
confronts Maximus (1:187–88).

In contrast to these and other early passages in which the passions
of the Romans are precisely located and designated, Gibbon found,
or made, the barbarians difficult to situate, and governed only by
"impetuous and irregular passions" (1:11). These wandering bands
could not be brought under the abstractions of humanism with certainty, so their history remains obscure. The "unwarlike natives of
those sequestered regions" south of the tropic were saved by their
climate rather than by any passions of their own, while to the north,
the Caledonians owed their "wild independence" more "to their
poverty than to their valour" (1:5). Such unclassical and unheroic
conditions and motives required awkward syntactic recombinations
of a vocabulary established for (and by) more "civilized" subjects.
The Briton tribes were activated by "valour without conduct" and
"the love of freedom without the spirit of union" (1:4). The few
passions that the barbarians can be assigned do not take hold. The
fortitude, despair, and fanaticism imputed to Caractacus, Boadicea,
and the Druids, respectively, are all ineffectual in the face of the
disciplined might of the Roman legions.

Gibbon's reluctance to ascribe certainty to unrecorded episodes of passion among the barbarians imparts added complexity to a passage in which he contrasts those passions that MacPherson has imagined for Fingal with those that Gibbon has uncovered in the Romans. In doing so, he manages to indict both the ascriber of fanciful passions and the actual passions of those who have, or who ought to have, cultivated them in their language, their culture, and themselves:

> The parallel would be little to the advantage of the more civilized people, if we compared the unrelenting revenge of Severus with the generous clemency of Fingal; the timid and brutal cruelty of Caracalla, with the bravery, the tenderness, the elegant genius of Ossian; the mercenary chiefs who, from motives of fear or interest, served under the Imperial standard, with the freeborn warriors who started to arms at the voice of the King of Morven; if, in a word, we contemplated the untutored Caledonians, glowing with the warm virtues of nature, and the degenerate Romans, polluted with the mean vices of wealth and slavery.[7]

I do not detect any envy of the fabricator of "the warm virtues of nature" on the part of the historian.

Generally, the barbarians are permitted only such passions as despair (the Germans) and contempt of life (the Dacians). The eastern barbarians are generally more warlike, ferocious, and savage, while the Cantabrians and Asturians derive obstinacy from their mountain strongholds (1:21–27). They wander over a landscape as featureless as their character: "A sandy desert, alike destitute of wood and water, skirts along the doubtful confine of Syria, from the Euphrates to the Red Sea. The wandering life of the Arabs was inseparably connected with their independence, and wherever, on some spots less barren than the rest, they ventured to form any settled habitations, they soon became subjects to the Roman empire" (1:24–25).

The indistinct passions of the barbarians, a reflection of their wanderings and the landscape over which they wandered, became a repeated source of annoyance to the historian: "In this interval, therefore, of about seventy years, we must place the second migration of the Goths from the Baltic to the Euxine; but the cause that produced it lies concealed among the various motives which actuate the conduct of unsettled barbarians" (1:242–43). This vagueness and instability in the place and passions complicated the historian's task repeatedly: "The Barbarians, who had been restrained by his [Fritigern] authority, abandoned themselves to the dictates of their passions; and their passions were seldom uniform or consistent" (3:125; but compare 3:71).

In the later volumes, the barbarians acquire a few passions of their own, or more precisely, the established passions are invoked to account for their actions, but often they do so under an evident strain. The clash between Alboin and Turisund and the marriage of Alboin and Rosamund (5:4–6, 12–14) produce great strain on the traditional vocabulary as an explanation of motive and an evocation of action. One can scarcely picture, much less comprehend, the actions of these figures from Gibbon's account. Doubtless the incomprehensibility is part of his point.

For some of the later barbarians, however, it is the same old story, calling for the same old passions: "By the fatal vicissitude of human affairs, the same scenes were renewed at Ctesiphon, which had been exhibited in Rome after the death of Marcus Antoninus" (5:43). Michael the Third offers another striking instance of the extension of the classical passions beyond the limits of the empire, in his case, the passions of Nero (5:199–201).

Those barbarians who dealt regularly with a language and culture that provided an established repertoire of passions eventually acquired recognizable passions of their own. Thus the barbarians who frequented the Roman or the Byzantine court soon became given to episodes identical to those that they found displayed there. This was not always an improvement. For example, the fury of the barbarians, their only consistent passion, was intensified and complicated by their exclusion from Christianity: "By these arts, the faith of the Barbarians was preserved, and their zeal was inflamed; they discharged, with devout fury, the office of spies, informers, or executioners; and, whenever their cavalry took the field, it was the favourite amusement of the march to defile the churches and to insult the clergy of the adverse faction" (4:86). The epithet that "fury" is assigned here is justified, or at least prepared for, throughout the paragraph. It may stand as a splendid example of the "reflective insinuation" in what Carnochan has called "Antonine irony" and as a reminder of Gibbon's great admiration for Hume.[8]

If those on the fringes of the empire could sometimes be taught to feel the passions, they could never learn to write forcibly for or about them: "But the provincials of Rome, trained by a uniform artificial foreign education, were engaged in a very unequal competition with those bold ancients, who, by expressing their genuine feelings in their native tongue, had already occupied every place of honor" (1:57). Centuries later the refusal of the Saracens to study the language and read the literature of Greece and Rome denied them, among other things, "the just delineation of character and passion" (6:33).

II

Locative or collective passions abound, and Gibbon's deft treatment of the passions of the barbarians is intriguing, but these are not by any means the most important places of the passions in *The Decline and Fall of the Roman Empire*. The "strong and various picture of human nature" exhibited by the annals of the emperors required frequent recourse to the palette of the passions, especially the darker hues: "Their unparalleled vices, and the splendid theatre on which they were acted, have saved them from oblivion. The dark unrelenting Tiberius, the furious Caligula, the stupid Claudius, the profligate and cruel Nero, the beastly Vitellius, and the timid inhuman Domitian, are condemned to everlasting infamy" (1:79). This passage mingles the passions of fury, cruelty, and timidity with more comprehensive and severe terms. It also neglects to develop any of the implications of these passions, turning them into neither episodes nor syntactic opportunities. They serve to summarize rather than to generate. They need only be named to inform, convince, and indict, and Gibbon is obliged, well able, and content to name them repeatedly.

As this passage implies, the distribution of "infamy" is one of the historian's major responsibilities (it had been one for Tacitus). The indulgence of excessive or evil passions entitles several emperors to heroic portions of infamy, and throughout the work it is the fate, or rather the punishment, of evil: Elagabulus's "memory was branded with eternal infamy by the senate, the justice of whose decree has been ratified by posterity" (1:148). The failure to distribute fame properly is a corollary consideration. Theodoric "was audaciously praised in his own presence by sacred and profane orators, but history . . . has not left any just representation of the events which displayed, or of the defects which clouded" his virtues (4:180–81).

In the course of his own "just delineation of character and passions," Gibbon renders history intelligible by the intelligent imputing of a few passions justly but sparely delineated. He reads the passions *back into* the heroic age from which they emerged in a reading that is always compressed, self-conscious, and retroactive. From a distance of many centuries and with deliberation and precision, he replaced the passions in those breasts in which, as he saw it, they had occurred. For example, their passions help to establish the hypocrisy of Augustus and the ambition of Diocletian, the latter of whom is made to sound like a more polished, indeed a more Roman, Jonathan Wild:

> His abilities were useful rather than splendid; a vigorous mind, improved by the experience and study of mankind, dexterity and application in business; a judicious mixture of liberality and economy, of mildness and rigour; profound dissimulation under the disguise of military frankness; steadiness to pursue his ends; flexibility to vary his means; and above all the great art of submitting his own passions, as well as those of others, to the interest of his ambition, and of colouring his ambition with the most specious pretences of justice and public utility. [1:351]

While neither enumerated nor developed, implicit passions inhabit the vigorous mind of Diocletian. They will be found in its mildness and rigor, if not in its liberality and economy. Without the "great art" of submitting them, Gibbon's and Diocletian's, there could be neither steadiness nor flexibility. As the passage escalates toward the secret strength of this character, the passions are subordinated to a larger state of mind (ambition), a state open to the historian, who refrains, or seems to refrain, from passing judgment upon it.

Other characters are constructed with similar materials and efficiency. The "ruling passions of [Hadrian's] soul were curiosity and vanity" (1:75; I will return to that participle below), and Marcus Aurelius was imposed upon by "[a]rtful men, who study the passions of princes and conceal their own" (1:83). That the most eminent disciple of the Stoics became the husband and the father of two of the most passionate characters in history is an irony Gibbon manages with silent juxtaposition (1:83–87). Passions govern the account of the sensuality, cruelty, hatred, and terrors of Commodus, who, having tasted human blood, "became incapable of pity or remorse" (1:87). His remaining passions were exploited by the "artful courtier" Cleander (whose own ruling passion was avarice; 1:90), so that Commodus became an omen as well as an ogre, "every sentiment of virtue and humanity was extinct in the mind of Commodus" (1:92). He became, in a word—perhaps the ugliest word in the vocabulary of a humanist—ineducable.

I offer one more perfectly representative passage in which the passions are employed as a routine but effective tool in establishing brief characters. Without the name of Gratian to which these episodes could be tied, the character here constructed would be scarcely distinguishable from any of several dozen others in the work, though no other character offers quite this combination or subsumes any combination under so much generosity: "Whatever resentment the rash and jealous vanity of his uncle might deserve, the resentment of a generous mind is easily subdued by the softer emotions of grief and compassion: and even the sense of pity was soon lost in the serious and alarming consideration of the state of the republic" (3:118).

The passions are so routine a part of the character of every emperor that when Gibbon came to Honorius, a man virtually without them, he paused to consider, and then to exploit, that lack: "His subjects, who attentively studied the character of their young sovereign, discovered that Honorius was without passions, and consequently without talents; and that his feeble and languid disposition was alike incapable of discharging the duties of his rank or of enjoying the pleasures of his age" (3:238). Afraid that he might forget to mention the death of so languid and inconsequential a figure, Gibbon does so in advance, and in passing (3:339). Had there been more characters like Honorius, both the Roman empire and the history of its decline would have been over sooner. The passions take place in the construction of every character, however brief or obscure. They inform the account of the ambitions of Artaxerxes, the success of Athanasius, the pride of Cyprian, and so on, through the centuries and the alphabet.

Consider the following passage, in which Gibbon builds his narrative by contrasting the passions of Constantine to those of several others, Galerius (1:400), Licinius (1:432–33), and, here, Maxentius: "A stranger to the exercises of war, he trembled at the apprehension of so dangerous a contest; and, as fear is commonly superstitious, he listened with melancholy attention to the rumours of omens and presages which seemed to menace his life and empire. Shame at length supplied the place of courage, and forced him to take the field" (1:420–21; compare 403 and 412). The routineness of that "at length" seems to me wholly expected and utterly representative of much of Gibbon's reliance on the passions. The fear has the usual source and takes the usual manifestation; the result, produced by a shift in the expected remedy, is surprising only to those who do not know history or human nature.

The passions thin out noticeably in the rapid summaries of the final volumes. All we hear of the abhorrent Nicephorus, for example, is the list of "his vices of hypocrisy, ingratitude, and avarice," while not even the reputed incest or the evident ambition of Charlemagne detain the historian as he pushes on toward the fall of Constantinople (5:192, 284). They return, rather nicely, with the account of books and cities: "In every city the productions of Arabic literature were copied and collected by the curiosity of the studious and the vanity of the rich. . . . The royal library of the Fatimites consisted of one hundred thousand manuscripts, elegantly transcribed and splendidly bound, which were lent, with jealousy or avarice, to the students of Cairo" (6:28). The dispassionate historian had a keen eye for the passions provoked by these familiar but valuable objects.

Elsewhere, he combines the library and the concubines of Gordianus in a passage devastating in its implications and its plausibility. The balance and the exactness sharpen the innuendo at the same time that they stretch our sense of character: "from the productions which he left behind him, it appears that both the one and the other were designed for use rather than for ostentation" (1:176). Faustina, Origen, and the Priscillianists (3:154), among others, provided irresistible opportunities for this device. With the passions of the empress Theodora, the wife of Justinian, however, Gibbon does not take shelter in innuendo. Her passions had achieved the indelibility of landmarks: "But the reproach of cruelty, so repugnant even to her softer vices, has left an indelible stain on the memory of Theodora" (4:216). The simple sequence of episodes, reflected in the simplicity of the syntax, unfolds in accordance with the temporal considerations that have always helped to distinguish the passions. In this instance, that sequence imparts both judiciousness and narrative shape to the history, thus distributing infamy to those who have earned it by the episodes of passion they indulged.

III

Occasionally Gibbon devises a construction that looks like oxymoron or paradox—until the full circumstances and context are thought through. Thus "obstinate modesty" makes perfect sense (and good prose) in the context of the refusals of both senate and army to name a successor to Aurelian (1:318). That "the Stoic might blush when he was hired to preach the contempt of money" (4:263) seems a paradox only to those who do not understand Stoics, physiology, and human nature. Elsewhere he distills a phrase with the linguistic alchemy that one expects from Samuel Johnson. When the Goths "gazed with hopeless desire on the inaccessible beauties of Constantinople" (3:115), for example, the desire is rendered lively and significant first by the "hopeless," in this case a historical epithet rather than a moral or psychological one. The inaccessibility of the object at which they gaze confirms and expands the episode. Or consider, as evidence of Gibbon's ability to produce concise moral constructions from the materials of the passions, this comment on Mahmud the Gaznevide, whose only defect was avarice: "His behaviour, in the last days of his life, evinces the vanity of these possessions, so laboriously won, so dangerously held, and so inevitably lost" (6:228).

Gibbon perfected several other stylistic devices to exploit the settled definitions and established certainties of the passions without allowing their traditional complexities to disturb the smooth surface of his exposition. His syntax kept the passions in their place. The cunning "or rathers" with which he seems to correct himself offer one prevalent and typical example. Antoninus Pius promoted Marcus Aurelius "with a noble disdain, or rather ignorance, of jealousy" (1:76)—an adjustment that mitigates its acquittal considerably. Sometimes the offering of an alternative passion seems to hesitate out of reluctance or scrupulosity: "The resentment, or the fears, of Diocletian at length transported him beyond the bounds of moderation" (2:127).

A more subtle and suggestive pair of alternatives is informed by a sense of the Scottish landscape and Gibbon's command, or at least awareness, of Gaelic: "The eastern coast of Caledonia may be considered as a level and fertile country, which, even in a rude state of tillage, was capable of producing a considerable quantity of corn; and the epithet of *cruitnich*, or wheat-eaters, expressed the contempt, or envy, of the carnivorous highlander" (3:41). In instances like these, Gibbon exploits the acquired precision of the passions for his own ends. The passions have been so clarified and refined by previous writers that he can shift them about in his balance with great exactness and to good effect. These tendentious adjustments are intermingled with more routine but no less essential distinctions, most of which we have seen before: "The excessive demonstrations of grief, or at least of mourning" (of Constantine; 2:220) is one such example.

Sometimes instead of providing tendentious alternatives, Gibbon refuses to decide among, or even to suggest, motives: "We are too imperfectly acquainted with the court of Constantine to form any judgment of the real motives which influenced the leaders of the conspiracy; unless we should suppose that they were actuated by a spirit of jealousy and revenge against the praefect Ablavius" (2:221). Such passages manage to suggest both that this ascription is probably right and that all the others in which Gibbon does not express such caution are very nearly certainly so! Conversely, the scrupulous reluctance to ascribe unseemly passions to Belisarius becomes very nearly a tribute: "I desire to believe, but I dare not affirm, that Belisarius sincerely rejoiced in the triumph of Narses. Yet the consciousness of his own exploits might teach him to esteem without jealousy the merit of a rival" (4:425). Bond notes a number of passages in which passions, virtues, and vices are cast as the agent without actual personification: "It is characteristic of Gibbon that in his efforts to eliminate vagueness from his writing he should go so far as to atomize the human personality in the same fashion that he dissects the totality of events to emphasize significant features" (Bond, 78).

Usually motives are simply named, then dropped into place: "the motives of his conversion, as they may variously be deduced from benevolence, from policy, from conviction, or from remorse" (2:129). Sometimes Gibbon adds or subtracts a passion until the balance quivers perfectly. Only the most compressed episodes will work in such a device; Gibbon actually invokes the balance in an instance that would not seem to invite compression—the last judgment of Islam: "The good and evil of each Musulman will be accurately weighed in a real or allegorical balance" (5:350). It was still theoretically possible to divide the passions into their constituent parts, but Gibbon seldom chose to do so. That passage is strikingly *un*resonant in its spare reference to the procedures of eternity. The analysis seems to diminish the ramifications, whereas other writers had almost always divided the passions into constituent parts in order to embellish or extend them.

Such examples prove that Gibbon was not as dubious about his ability to get the passions right as has been suggested: "But the rhetorical balance and tense certainty of Hume are gone because Gibbon is basically sceptical about the historian's ability to express the precise relations of motives and actions. Circumstances always play an overpowering role in his descriptions of human actions. . . . Events force actions that were never contemplated" (Braudy, 231–32). The balance we have seen in so much of Gibbon's handling of the passions would appear to be a special, tendentious variant of what Braudy calls "epistemological doublets" (216). These nudge us to summon and to consider the application of our own assumptions about human nature. These assumptions depend upon the established definitions and manifestations of the passions, while the placing of passions in so delicate a balance suggests not scepticism but a rhetorical scrupulosity and a humanistic certainty, both based on a long tradition.

Time and temperament obliged Gibbon to keep his distance from those whose history he recorded, but the doctrine of the passions enabled him both to keep that distance and to transcend it. He did not have to enter the hearts of his characters because the passions he knew he would find there came to meet him, in their actions and in his sources. When they had done so, he found the right places for them, partly because he was able to exert a mastery over the names of the passions that he never attempted to apply to the passions themselves. While he could work with signs, controlling, balancing, and placing them, he seems never to have gone near the potent episodes they stood for: "There are also in the *Decline and Fall* many suggestions of a valorization of the sign precisely because it is not the thing itself and lacks its overwhelming authority, its annihilating presence."9

The frequency with which Gibbon weighs and enumerates the motives of his subjects was, as I see it, made possible by the clarity of the passions and was much more a stylistic device prompted by humanism and scepticism than an elaborate defense mechanism: "It is not unlikely that he wished at one and the same time to unmask his heroes and to undo his unmasking, to discover their secret and to preserve it by imparting to the reader a sense of the impossibility of ever fixing the meaning of the signs the historian has to decipher" (Gossman, 29). With the passions, at least, it is not the impossibility of these signs, but the likelihood, that strikes me. Perhaps this is also why, with them, he concentrates so much on their names and their consequences, and so little on their manifestations. Distrusting his own passions, and everyone else's, he nevertheless encountered them so often in his subjects and his sources that he had to find a place, or rather, many many places, for them in his history. His solution confirmed his own dispassionate temperament and style, without distorting or ignoring the abundant passions of the (long dead) characters with whom he was obliged to deal.10

One of the simplest of Gibbon's devices is his cunning attribution of "surprise." This is not a passionate or a dramatic surprise, like Fielding's, but a cerebral and a rhetorical one. Of the innumerable examples, I cite only two, the wickedly parenthetic disclaimer in "Yet all these sages (it is no less an object of surprise than of concern) overlooked or rejected the perfection of the Christian system" (2:68) and the conclusion to Eunapius's account of the glorification of the martyrs: "Without approving the malice, it is natural enough to share the surprise, of the Sophist, the spectator of a revolution which raised those obscure victims of the laws of Rome to the rank of celestial and invisible protectors of the Roman empire" (3:208). The historian expresses his own surprise only once, at the literary treasures that have survived, rather than the losses occasioned by, "the lapse of ages, the waste of ignorance, and the calamities of war" (5:455). Otherwise he is content to descry or impute the surprise of others—always for his own rhetorical purposes.

Gibbon, then, devised or adapted his own means for sharpening points on the passions, compressing or omitting most of their components, so that they would not disturb the balance of his prose. In addition, he shared some of the concerns we have encountered in previous chapters, among them the role of oratory, the usefulness of blushing, the distrust of the court, and the role of passions in religion. He treats the gifts and methods of the orator more circumspectly than Hume, referring to "the sublime Longinus" (1:58) but distrusting Augustus's manipulation of the senate (whose dignity he had restored, while destroying its independence): "Before an assembly thus modelled and prepared, Augustus pronounced a studied oration, which displayed his patriotism, and disguised his ambition" (1:60). He alerts the reader to the passions that this address evoked with innuendo and acknowledgment: "It would require the pen of Tacitus . . . to describe the various emotions of the senate; those that were suppressed, and those that were affected" (1:61).

Two of the three would-be successors to Didius Julianus, Clodius Albinus and Septimus Severus, also prove the effectiveness, but not the authenticity, of oratory (1:109–15). The third, Niger, was too dull and indolent to wield this weapon. The peroration of Septimus Severus, it must be added, took the form of a substantial donative, a form of eloquence that became formulaic: "As soon as the praefect was silent, the emperor [Tacitus] addressed himself to the soldiers with elegance and propriety. He gratified their avarice by a liberal distribution of treasure, under the names of pay and donative. He engaged their esteem by a spirited declaration."[11]

The historian's distrust of the orator is a principled one, based on distortions of language, material, and passion: "The voluminous writings of Libanius still exist: for the most part, they are the vain and idle compositions of an orator, who cultivated the science of words; the productions of a recluse student, whose mind, regardless of his contemporaries, was incessantly fixed on the Trojan war and the Athenian commonwealth" (2:487). The Crusades, he suggests, were precipitated by the specious eloquence of Peter the Hermit and encouraged by the "pathetic vehemence" of St. Bernard (6:259–60, 332–34). Yet, for all this distrust, Gibbon repeatedly avails himself of the observations, and sometimes the prejudices and witticisms, of rhetoricians. His skillful wielding of Libanius, "the sophist of Antioch," against Valens (3:113–14) is an excellent example of his ability to appropriate rhetoricians for his own ends. Gibbon's own work has been studied as an epideictic oration, "a commemorative address on the fate of the Roman empire" (Bond, 57ff.).

Mahomet, though illiterate, or so Gibbon insisted, was a powerful orator, one who predisposed his audience in his favor by his presence and then manipulated its passions: "Before he spoke, the orator engaged on his side the affections of a public or private audience. They applauded his commanding presence, his majestic aspect, his piercing eye, his gracious smile, his flowing beard, his countenance that painted every sensation of the soul, and his gestures that enforced each expression of the tongue" (5:335). This picture of an orator at work, though eminently conventional, is not at all characteristic of Gibbon. The beards, gestures, and countenances of all the other orators in his pages go unmentioned.

Gibbon occasionally alludes to "the nice and secret springs of action which impel, in the same uniform direction, the blind and capricious passions of a multitude of individuals" (3:186). He regards the capacity to discover them as both rare and essential to the historian. [12] He also, as several of my examples have shown, uses the phrase, and perhaps the concept, "ruling passion" more frequently than any other of the writers we have discussed: "Cruelty and superstition were the ruling passions of the soul of Maximin" (2:134). I do not see that it retains or acquires any resonance when he does so. It is usually a mere phrase ("Of [Mahomet's] last years, ambition was the ruling passion," 5:377). Frequently, as in the Empire itself, the scepter was shared: "The hatred of the Christians, the love of spoil, and the contempt of danger were the ruling passions of the audacious Saracen" (5:421). [13] Gibbon also retained the Scholastic division between concupiscent and irascible, to good rhetorical effect. He employs it to distinguish the love of pleasure from the love of action and then to separate the Christians from the former (2:34–35).

The passions of Gibbon's readers, or rather, of a suspect subset of contemporaries of his readers, are sometimes implied in order to discredit. Here they are indicated and indicted in a passage which attributes the blushing in which his age specialized to emperors in whom it does not seem to belong: "Their family, however numerous or splendid, was composed entirely of their domestic slaves and freedmen. Augustus or Trajan would have blushed at employing the meanest of the Romans in those menial offices which, in the household and bedchamber of a limited monarch, are so eagerly solicited by the proudest nobles of Britain" (1:68). In this instance the emperors had no occasion to blush, while those of Gibbon's contemporaries who fill, or seek, positions at court ought to but do not. While one does not readily associate the blush with the toga, Gibbon employs the figure frequently. It serves as testimony to provocation (1:170, 174), and Claudius, who was celebrated for his virtues, gives an honest blush (1:287). Often those who are said not to have blushed are condemned for not having done so. Thus the senate under Augustulus repeated the name "republic" without blushing (4:51), while the unblushing decline of the Romans moved even the barbarians to do so: "The king of the Goths, who blushed for the baseness of his enemies, pursued with rapid steps the path of honour and victory" (4.395–96). Conversely, the modest blush that tempers the sparkle in Julian's eyes on his first appearance in public reassures his audience and, evidently, his historian (2:257). Perhaps of more significance than I am willing to make them are the blushes to which Gibbon confesses in his *Autobiography,* once in conjunction with Suzanne and again at the death of Deyverdun.[14] The blush descends into the footnotes at least once, when Gibbon is pleased to observe one on the cheek of Baronius (5:110).

Usually, however, Gibbon treats the passions so historically and abstractly that he does not trouble to incorporate them. Caracalla "ran towards the Pretorian camp" with "hasty steps and horror in his countenance" after having had his brother assassinated (1:132), but then, the features of Caracalla were fixed in the minds of his soldiers and his historian, doubtless, by coins and busts: "The demeanour of Caracalla was haughty and full of pride" (1:137; compare 142). The only truly plastic countenance among the emperors belonged to Justinian's successor: "After composing his countenance to surprise, sorrow, and decent modesty, Justin, by the advice of his wife Sophia, submitted to the authority of the senate" (5:2).

Gibbon shares and exhibits every humanist's distrust of the affectations and excesses of the court. The dissimulation, language, flattery, luxury, and general indulgence all disturbed him, and all are mentioned repeatedly and in nearly every reign. The Byzantine court seems to have been especially offensive, and Gibbon especially deplores the flabby and inflated language of the court of Chosroes (4:382). Gordian, to cite one example from the western court, escaped from the "venal tribe of courtiers" with the help and praise of the rhetorician Misitheus (1:190), while Julian's wizard, Maximus, "was insensibly corrupted by the temptations of a court" (2:450). Julian's attitude toward the court at Milan and the courtiers at Antioch (below) is another instance and just what we would expect from someone of whose character Gibbon most nearly approved. The account of the "empty pageantry" wherein the court of Constantine continued, passionlessly, to approach the *corpse* "of their sovereign with bended knees and a composed countenance" (2:221) deserves to be set alongside the passages on the death of More from *Spectator* no. 349 and the deathbed in *Rambler* no. 54. In that context the witholding of all passions and the naming of only two (hope and dread) demonstrate that Gibbon thoroughly understood their possibilities, both courtly and stylistic, and found a tight place for them in his work.

While Gibbon found an infuriatingly prominent place for the passions in his treatment of religion, the routineness with which he imputes them makes them effective. His early treatment of the workings of fear, gratitude, and curiosity in the "republic" of polytheism is drawn from Herodotus and is sharpened by Hume's *Natural History of Religion,* which he acknowledges with enthusiasm (1:29, n.3). The passions most often imputed here are inward contempt and external reverence.

Of the best-known and most studied chapters, those on the rise and persecution of Christianity (25 and 26), I mention only that the passions abound in them, especially the unclassical "zeal" and the unchristian "contempt." They abound for reasons both human and divine. First, "the wisdom of Providence frequently condescends to use the passions of the human heart, and the general circumstances of mankind, as instruments to execute its purpose" (2:2). Gibbon was only too willing to turn those instruments against those who regarded themselves as the custodians of that wisdom. Furthermore, the melancholy duty of the historian obliged him to deal with the human character as he found it, and he found it full of discrediting passions: "But the human character, however it may be exalted or depressed by a temporary enthusiasm, will return, by degrees, to its proper and natural level, and will resume those passions that seem the most adapted to its present condition" (2:39). Or at greater length and with more passions:

In the church as well as in the world the persons who were placed in any public station rendered themselves considerable by their eloquence and firmness, by their knowledge of mankind, and by their dexterity in business; and, while they concealed from others, and perhaps, from themselves, the secret motives of their conduct, they too frequently relapsed into all the turbulent passions of active life, which were tinctured with an additional degree of bitterness and obstinacy from the infusion of spiritual zeal. [2:40]

They have not been concealed from Gibbon, who reaps all of the benefits of that abundance, detecting "relapses" and ascribing passions with a plausibility and detachment that has infuriated many devout readers.

The account of miracles in the early church (3:212–13) also depends on Hume's definition and analysis. Later Gibbon locates monasteries in places that suggest the nature and bleakness of the passions within them. They spread out from "Egypt, the fruitful parent of superstition," and soon "the prolific colonies of monks multiplied with rapid increase on the sands of Libya, upon the rocks of Thebais, and in the cities of the Nile" (4:59). The passions that underlay this proliferation were seldom the right ones: "These unhappy exiles from social life were impelled by the dark and implacable genius of superstition" (4:62). That epithet "unhappy," for which we were prepared in the preceding pages, is richly justified in the succeeding ones and is contrasted with the "eternal happiness" that those under discussion are supposed to have been seeking. The epithet "social," loaded by both Addison and Hume, tips the balance. The unsociable passions retained in the monasteries are feeble and selfish, and religious attempts to mortify or deny humanity would inevitably fail, so that pride, licentiousness, and luxury would eventually find their way into these institutions, however remote or severe: "Their natural descent from such painful and dangerous virtue to the common vices of humanity will not, perhaps, excite much grief or indignation in the mind of a philosopher" (4:70). This was merely a descent, not a decline or a fall.

The passions at work in the religion of Islam are the familiar ones, but their combination is unique and unremarked upon: "The intrepid souls of the Arabs were fired with enthusiasm; the picture of the invisible world was strongly painted on their imagination; and the death which they had always despised became an object of hope and desire" (5:361). The "fearless confidence" (5:361) that this religion produced changed the face of the world, but Gibbon treats the rise of Islam, like that of Christianity, as a part of human history, and its prophet as just another human being, although he regards Islam as a religion "less inconsistent with reason than the creed of mystery and superstition which, in the seventh century, disgraced the simplicity of the gospel."[15]

The passions assume an equally important and discrediting place in Gibbon's account of the Crusades. He mentions episodes of zeal, credulity, jealousy, ambition, fear, avarice (repeatedly), and courage (occasionally). The Crusades were conducted, after all, by the Franks, whom Gibbon described in what might well be called an outburst of passions: "But the firmest title of these adventurers was the right of conquest: they neither loved nor trusted; they were neither trusted nor beloved; the contempt of the princes was mixed with fear, and the fear of the natives was mingled with hatred and resentment. Every object of desire, an horse, a woman, a garden, tempted and gratified the rapaciousness of the strangers; and the avarice of their chiefs was only coloured by the more specious names of ambition and glory" (6:180). Only the motives and actions of Godfrey of Bouillon and the virtues of Saladin remain unsullied. One of the most vivid passages describes first the "bloody sacrifice" of the defenders and then the "joy and penitence" of the victors. "This union of the fiercest and most tender passions has been variously considered by two philosophers [Hume and Voltaire]: by the one, as easy and natural; by the other, as absurd and incredible" (6:311–12).

A few passages suggest depths of the sort we saw lurking under the bereaved father in *Spectator* no. 520 and the hatred in Amelia. The analysis of the repentance of Caracalla, replete with a disordered vision of his father and brother and menaces to his grieving mother (1:133–34) is one of these, as is the account of the cruelty of carnivores (3:72) and the psychological appeal of gladiators (3:258–59). For all its manifest rationality, the discussion of Christian symbols and the dreams of Constantine (2:299–303) suggests some depths to the minds in which these work, though Gibbon refuses to look into them. Every reader will be able to suggest several angles from which the long discussion of paternal power in early and republican Rome might be viewed to reveal depths (4:472–76), though these depths would have been unsuspected by, and probably inimical to, Gibbon. Occasionally the refusal to acknowledge the possibility of such depths is one of Gibbon's most effective techniques. Thus, with regard to the infidelities and cruelty of Antonina (4:334–39), the philosopher's pity and forgiveness fall well and truly short.

IV

I turn, in conclusion, to Gibbon's reconstruction of the character of Julian, in whose humane and philosophical temper most of the right passions found an eloquent and significant place. [16] I do so as a last indication and reminder of how certainly and variously the passions could be called upon to articulate meanings we have all but lost the means of summoning. Early in his career, for example, Julian is on his way, most reluctantly, to receive the title of Caesar—a title just vacated, in disgrace, by his brother Gallus: "He approached with horror the palace of Milan; nor could the ingenuous youth conceal his indignation, when he found himself accosted with false and servile respect by the assassins of his family" (2:257). Julian clearly does not belong in a court if he cannot conceal his passions; he would never learn to do so. Nor could he ever accept the elaborately displayed respect of courtiers. He had been sufficiently schooled in the passions to identify the ones at work here, and thus to become an object of genuine respect for Gibbon. And Gibbon was sufficiently schooled to set all this before us with clarity and efficiency.

Julian derived his passions, including his capacity for indignation, from classical sources and on classical ground: "Yet even this speculative philosophy [Plato's] . . . had filled the mind of Julian with the noblest precepts and the most shining examples; had animated him with the love of virtue, the desire of fame, and the contempt of death" (2:274). While it would have been better had he absorbed some of the lessons of Plato's less speculative successor ("Such indeed was the temper of Julian, who seldom recollected the fundamental maxim of Aristotle that true virtue is placed at an equal distance between the opposite vices," 2:421), Julian's temper and career provided his admirer with frequent opportunities to employ, indeed almost to redeem, the vocabulary of the passions. In Julian, almost alone in *The Decline and Fall of the Roman Empire,* they acquire a sense of purpose and grandeur.

His studies at Athens complicated Julian's task as emperor: "As he had discovered from his earliest youth a propensity, or rather passion, for the language, the manners, the learning, and the religion of the Greeks, . . . Julian inviolably preserved for Athens that tender regard which seldom fails to arise in a liberal mind from the recollection of the place where it has discovered and exercised its growing powers" (2:255; notice the sense of place at work here). His affinities with Athens estranged him from Rome, and even more so from Antioch, where his passions clashed vividly, repeatedly, and illuminatingly with those of the natives (2:482–83).

The education that made him a philosopher combined with a temperament that made him a hero—a combination that Gibbon did not encounter elsewhere in his history: "Julian was slow in his suspicions and gentle in his punishments; and his contempt of treason was the result of judgement, of vanity, and of courage. . . . The philosopher could excuse the hasty sallies of discontent; and the hero could despise the ambitious projects which surpassed the fortune or the abilities of the rash conspirators" (2:425). It is certainly true that the passions do not do all the work in that passage, though there are many of them, and it is difficult to see what terms they could be replaced with. But whereas in Fielding and Johnson the passions imparted force and direction to other terms, here they receive it from the adjectives (slow, gentle, hasty, and rash) and from the nouns they accompany (hero, philosopher, sallies, projects, and conspirators). Occasionally, however, the sequence of passions is in itself forceful, original, and impressive: "He affected to pity the unhappy Christians, who were mistaken in the most important object of their lives; but his pity was degraded by contempt, his contempt was embittered by hatred; and the sentiments of Julian were expressed in a style of sarcastic wit" (2:460). I trust that I do not, at this point, have to lead the reader through the complex sequence whereby Julian's pity is distilled into sarcasm or call attention to Gibbon's manipulation of the "object." On the evidence of that passage alone, it is clear that Gibbon and Julian were kindred spirits.

His temperament and his education enabled Julian, more than any other figure in the *Decline and Fall,* to discern the passions of others and to express and enforce his own. Thus his serious piety was offended by the sacrifices of Batnae when "he too clearly discerned that the smoke which arose from their altars was the incense of flattery rather than of devotion" (2:488). What he could discern he could express; Gibbon is much impressed with the examination of the heart and the springs of action in Julian's philosophical fable, the *Caesars,* and its rendering of the modest silence of the Imperial Stoic (2:480). Whether he chose to express his own passions in person or in prose, Julian did so to good effect: "We may enjoy the pleasure of reading the sentiments of Julian, as he expresses them with warmth and freedom in a letter to one of his most intimate friends."[17] Gibbon took equal pleasure in Julian's severe reply to a haughty letter from Constantius, where he "expressed, in a strain of the most vehement eloquence, the sentiments of contempt, of hatred, and of resentment, which had been suppressed and embittered by the dissimulation of twenty years" (2:408).

Julian was no less effective as an orator than as a correspondent (in this respect he differed from his historian). He controlled the passions of his army in the best rhetorical tradition: "Their zeal was insensibly turned into impatience, and their impatience into rage" (2:402). Later he had occasion to rebuke their avarice, and his "just indignation was expressed in the grave, and manly language of a Roman."[18] Even the barbarians were impressed: "The Barbarians withdrew from his presence, impressed with the warmest sentiments of gratitude and admiration" (2:282).

While he can dissemble when he must, he does so without hypocrisy (2:280), and Julian is the only character in the *Decline and Fall* to feel the physiological checks so hard at work in Fielding: "But, as every act of dissimulation must be painful to an ingenuous spirit, the profession of Christianity increased the aversion of Julian for a religion which oppressed the freedom of his mind and compelled him to hold a conduct repugnant to the noblest attributes of human nature, sincerity and courage."[19]

In expressing the best passions so effectively, and in proclaiming his own glory to the world "in the simple and concise narrative of his exploits" (2:273), Julian ought to have done the historian's job for him. But "the triumph of the party which he deserted and opposed ha[d] fixed a stain of infamy on the name of Julian" (2:433), and so Gibbon undertook to erase that stain, by reading, as far as he was able, the fine mind behind those expressions and actions. The characters of that mind were eminently legible to the clear-sighted, but they take that sight only so far, and the historian is never more eloquent, more satisfied, or more successful, than when he knows where to stop. The minds of most of the emperors, especially Constantine and Constantius, and of characters such as John of Cappadocia (4:240–42) were open books to Gibbon, quickly read and quickly closed. Julian had more complex passions and required more complex analysis:

> The grief of Julian could proceed only from his innocence; but his innocence must appear extremely doubtful in the eyes of those who have learned to suspect the motives and professions of princes. His lively and active mind was susceptible of the various impressions of hope and fear, of gratitude and revenge, of duty and of ambition, of the love of fame and of the fear of reproach. But it is impossible for us to calculate the respective weight and operation of these sentiments; or to ascertain the principles of action, which might escape the observation, while they guided or rather impelled the steps, of Julian himself. [2:402–3]

I know of no better example of the place of passions in the reconstruction of character. But even here, they are subordinated to another abstraction, innocence, and their refusal to submit to calculation is exploited for the historian's own rhetorical purposes.

As he had done with Constantine, Gibbon propels this part of the narrative by opposing to the passions of Julian the more troublesome passions of his contemporaries, especially Constantius (2:397; there are numerous other examples). At several points the passions become the hinges on which this narrative turns rather than episodes of character in their own right: "The Christians, who beheld with horror and indignation the apostasy of Julian, had much more to fear from his power than from his arguments." In fact, the emperor's "prudent humanity" provides an unexpected turn even to this sequence (2:444; compare 510).

Julian might have simplified the historian's task had he settled on a single ruling passion. As it is, he has several, among them, "a

devout and sincere attachment for the gods of Athens and Rome"
(2:432), "superstition and vanity" (2:451), "love of fame" (2:502),
and "love of virtue and of fame" (2:516–17). This multiplicity did
not trouble Gibbon, who found a good place even for the bad passions of this character: "Julian beheld with envy the wise and humane regulations of the church; and he very frankly confesses his
intention to deprive the Christians of the applause, as well as advantage, which they had acquired by the exclusive practice of charity
and beneficence" (2:448–49). It was not his passions that undid
Julian, but his credulity, which ruined his magnanimity and
prompted him to listen to the traitorous tale of a Persian noble and
destroy his navy (2:508).

At one point in this narrative of the life that comes closest of any
in the work to being heroic, Gibbon describes a tableau in which
the wives and infants of his soldiers cry out to Julian "in the mixed
language of grief, of tenderness, and of indignation" (2:400). The
scene is reminiscent of Le Brun, and the humanity of Julian is as
touched as was that of Alexander in *The Tent of Darius*. That scene
ought to remind us that Gibbon had looked at art carefully. When
he did so he looked to see how well the expressions in it were suited
to the actions depicted, though he seems to have distrusted the
capacity of images to convey character.[20]

When he came to narrate the death of this hero, Gibbon did so in
a passage worthy of the brush of West, and in a scene that brings
together, as if contrived for my purposes, the contemplation of passions by philosophers and the witnessing of them by spectators: "He
employed the awful moments with the firm temper of a hero and a
sage; the philosophers who had accompanied him in this fatal expe-
dition compared the tent of Julian with the prison of Socrates; and
the spectators, whom duty, or friendship, or curiosity, had as-
sembled around his couch, listened with respectful grief to the funeral oration of their dying emperor" (2:515). The episodes of passion in that scene and in that account of that scene are as eloquent,
as intricate, and as certain as any of the many others we have looked
into. As in the death of Wolfe, the death of More (*Spectator* no. 349),
or the death of Socrates (*Rambler* no. 64), the passions of the hero are
there for the informed reader to contemplate and admire.[21] They
were put there by a historian who understood them. Presumably he
hoped for readers who shared that understanding.

CONCLUSION

OR A BRIEF INTERVAL OF LESS THAN A CEN-
tury, when philosophy had codified the passions and
physiology had, as it thought, found the ways
through which they worked, writers employed these
complex, certain, and resonant elements to set forth
and explore new problems. The increasingly unstable self, the rapid
changes in the old relationships between the new selves, and intense
scrutiny of ordinary behavior combined to summon the passions into
sentence after sentence. They were named, sorted, and depicted.
Their manifestations were staged and painted, their physiology was
sketched and invoked, and their nature was extended. Traditional
components were seized upon and reworked. The prop that Abel
Drugger turned so comically before himself and his audience had
systematic affinities with the supposed objects of pity in Hume's
shipwreck and the city of Rome. The taxonomies were repeatedly
invoked and reinforced, so that readers of *The Spectator* were asked to
distinguish between resentment and anger, readers of *The Rambler*
between aversion and terror, readers of *The Decline and Fall* between
contempt and envy, and so on. When they dealt with the same
component—Addison and Johnson on comparison, for example, or
Hume and Gibbon on surprise—they did so in different and revealing ways. The passions were sturdy enough, and complex enough, to
accommodate several kinds of genius and to serve the purposes of a
varied excellence.

In addition to these and other shared concerns, each of the writers
dealt with here developed different components—Addison and

Steele assessed stratification, Hume deposited the self in the center of every episode, Fielding staged physiology, Johnson invoked the essential propensity of each passion to define and exert itself over time, and Gibbon found places for them in the characters and regions of history.

These writers found it reassuring that the envy of Captain Blifil and that of the neighbors of Mr. Spectator and the readers of the *Rambler* were comparable, certain, and wrong. They agreed that impudence was bad in whatever company it was found and that blushing was something to watch. They distrusted excessive display of passions as well as preternatural control of them, and they took their physiology seriously but never solemnly. They were willing to invoke them as components of character and determined to see them as elements of human nature. Episodes of passion illuminated one another and in doing so reinforced the humanity of the character in whom they occurred and the meaning of the sentence in which they operated.

These writers agreed that the mental and emotional lives of men and women were subject to inspection, to generalization, and to judgment. Whether one wanted to look into the courage of Jonathan Wild or that of Thomas More, the passions would allow it. Every episode mediated between the abstract and the particular, the present and the past, and the self and others—precisely the mediations that the writers and readers of this period had in mind. They knew what envy felt like, what contempt looked like, what pride acted like, in short, what every episode of passion *meant*. We need to share that knowledge in order to continue to read their writings.

Viewers of West's *Death of General Wolfe,* readers of Addison on the death of More, of *Rambler* no. 54 on the passions surrounding a deathbed, or of Gibbon on the passions of the survivors of Julian, will always, one hopes, be moved. But one may also hope for a more informed and articulate response, certain of the meaning and alert to the liveliness, of these and countless other episodes.

NOTES

1. READING THE PASSIONS ON PAGE, STAGE, AND CANVAS

1. The account of Garrick's performance is from *La Belle Assemblée; or, Bell's Court and Fashionable Magazine*, 2 (April 1807):148; and William T. Whitley, *Artists and Their Friends in England, 1700–1799*, vol. 1 (London: Medici Society, 1928), 282.

2. Robert A. Bromley, *A Philosophical and Critical History of the Fine Arts* (London: T. Cadell, 1793; repr. New York: Garland, 1971), 60; the reading subsequently pays particular attention to the "erected hair of the soldier behind" (61), a manifestation of terror we will encounter again; see also Ann Uhry Abrams, *The Valiant Hero: Benjamin West and Grand-Style History Painting* (Washington, D.C.: Smithsonian Institution Press, 1985), 180–81, 229 n.5.

3. For these, see, in addition to Abrams, 161–84; Robert C. Alberts, *Benjamin West: A Biography* (Boston: Houghton Mifflin, 1978), 103–11; and Charles

Mitchell, "Benjamin West's 'Death of General Wolfe' and the Popular History Piece," *JWCI,* 7 (1944):20–33.

4. For Plutarch, see Abrams, 55, 133; and John Galt, *The Life, Studies, and Works of Benjamin West,* 2 vols. (London: Cadell and Davies, 1816–20), 36–37. One performance of a West painting that must very nearly have rivaled Garrick's was Lady Hamilton's tableau vivant of *Agrippina Bearing the Ashes of Germanicus* at Fonthill Abbey! See Alberts, 255–57.

5. Denis Diderot, *The Paradox of Acting,* trans. W. H. Pollock, in *"The Paradox of Acting" and "Masks or Faces?"* intro. Lee Strasberg (New York: Hill and Wang, 1957), 32–33. The *Paradox* was written in 1773 but was not published until 1830. It has been dealt with fully and suggestively by Joseph R. Roach, *The Player's Passion: Studies in the Science of Acting* (Newark: University of Delaware Press, 1985), 116–59.

6. Leonardo is quoted by Rensselaer W. Lee, *"Ut Pictura Poesis:* The Humanistic Theory of Painting," *Art Bulletin,* 22 (1940):219; see also 217–26, 265–68. See also E. H. Gombrich, *Art and Illusion: A Study in the Psychology of Pictorial Representation,* Bollingen Series 35.5 (New York: Pantheon Books, 1960), 330–89; Dean Tolle Mace, "Transformation in Classical Art Theory: From 'Poetic Composition' to 'Picturesque Composition,'" *Word & Image: A Journal of Verbal/Visual Enquiry,* 1 (1985):59–86; David Piper, *The English Face* (London: Thames and Hudson, 1957); and John Pope-Hennessy, *The Portrait in the Renaissance,* Bollingen Series 35.12 (New York: Pantheon Books, 1966), 101–54.

7. For Le Brun, see Anthony Blunt, *Art and Architecture in France, 1500–1700* (Baltimore: Penguin Books, 1954), 225–82; Norman Bryson, *Word and Image: French Painting of the Ancien Régime* (Cambridge: Cambridge University Press, 1981), 29–57; Henry Jouin, *Charles Le Brun et les arts sous Louis XIV* (Paris: Henri Laurens, 1889); Pierre Marçel, *Charles Le Brun* (Paris: Plon, 1909); the catalogue *Charles Le Brun, 1619–1690, peintre et dessinateur* (Versailles; Chateau de Versailles, 1963), especially the introduction by Jennifer Montagu; Joseph R. Roach, *The Player's Passion,* 66–73; and my introduction to *A Method to Learn to Design the Passions,* trans. John Williams (London, 1734), Augustan Reprint Society, nos. 200–201 (Los Angeles: William Andrews Clark Memorial Library, 1980), iii–xii. John Montgomery Wilson, *The Painting of the Passions in Theory, Practice, and Criticism in Later Eighteenth Century France* (New York: Garland, 1981), surveys the continued influence of Le Brun in France. Thomas E. Crow, *Painters and Public Life in Eighteenth-Century Paris* (New Haven: Yale University Press, 1985), discusses the struggles of French painters and critics to convey the repertoire of signs to the Salon-goer.

8. Hubert Gillot, *La querelle des anciens et des modernes en France* (Nancy: Champion, 1914), 454.

9. *The Tent of Darius Explain'd; or, The Queens of Persia at the Feet of Alexander,* trans. Collonel [*sic*] Parsons (London, 1703), 15–16. Paintings in France were frequently accompanied by very elaborate prose *livrets*—see Bryson, 32, and Crow, 81–82.

10. *Conférence de M. Le Brun sur l'expression générale et particulière* (Paris: E. Picard, 1698); see also the ARS reprint cited above in n. 7.

11. See the 1963 Le Brun catalogue, no. 31 (above, n. 7); Bryson has some provocative remarks on this image—in this case on Le Brun's sadism (37–43).

12. Mitchell, 31–32; Alberts, 110; John Tinney, who had done his own set of engravings of the *Conférence,* was William Woollett's teacher; Woollett made a fortune for himself, his publisher, Boydell, and West with his engraving of *The Death of General Wolfe.*

13. *The School of Raphael; or, The Student's Guide to Expression in Historical Painting* (London: John Boydell, 1769), 2; cf. Jonathan Richardson, *An Essay on the Theory of Painting* (London, 1715), 84–114.

14. *The Poems of Samuel Johnson,* ed. David Nichol Smith and Edward L. McAdam, 2d ed. (Oxford: Clarendon Press, 1974), 181–82; Horace Walpole, *Anecdotes of Painting in England* (London, 1827), 4, 126.

15. William Hogarth, *The Analysis of Beauty,* ed. Joseph Burke (Oxford: Clarendon Press, 1955), 25 (cf. 209); I have relied on Burke's introduction as well as on Ronald Paulson, *Hogarth: His Life, Art and Times,* 2 vols. (New Haven: Yale University Press, 1971).

16. F. Antal, "Hogarth and His Borrowings," *Art Bulletin,* 29 (1947):43, n. 25; Robert L. S. Cowley, *Hogarth's "Marriage-à-la-Mode"* (Ithaca: Cornell University Press, 1983), 22, 36–38, 46, 103, 124; and Paulson, *Hogarth,* 1:264–65, 473–75, 2:29.

17. *The Art of Painting of Charles Alphonse Du Fresnoy,* trans. William Mason, with annotations by Sir Joshua Reynolds (York, 1783), 92–93; and F. W. Hilles, *The Literary Career of Sir Joshua Reynolds* (Cambridge: Cambridge University Press, 1936), 232, n. 2. For *Mrs. Siddons,* see Robert R. Wark, *Ten British Pictures, 1740–1840* (San Marino: Huntington Library, 1971), 49–52.

18. Studies of the staging of the passions include, in addition to Roach, cited above in n. 7: Alan S. Downer, "Nature to Advantage Dressed: Eighteenth-Century Acting," *PMLA,* 58 (1943):1002–37; George Taylor, "'The Just Delineation of the Passions': Theories of Acting in the Age of Garrick," in *Essays on the Eighteenth-Century English Stage,* ed. Kenneth Richards and Peter Thomson (London: Methuen, 1972), 55–72; Brewster Rogerson, "The Art of Painting the Passions," *JHI,* 14 (1953):68–94; Alastair Smart, "Dramatic Gesture and Expression in the Age of Hogarth and Reynolds," *Apollo,* 82 (1965):90–97; and Leigh Woods, *Garrick Claims the Stage: Acting as Social Emblem in Eighteenth-Century England,* Contributions in Drama and Theatre Studies, 10 (Westport, Conn.: Greenwood Press, 1984).

19. Angelica Goodden, *Action and Persuasion: Dramatic Performance in Eighteenth Century France* (Oxford: Oxford University Press, 1986); Goodden emphasizes the influence of Du Bos as well as Diderot.

20. Aaron Hill, *An Essay on the Art of Acting* (London, 1779), 5–6; Hill's system is studied in some detail in Roach, 78–86.

21. Samuel Foote, *A Treatise on the Passions, So Far As They Regard the Stage* (London: C. Corbet, n.d.), 23; Foote likes to see one passion blend into

another rather than the "turns" with which Garrick trapped so much applause.

22. For Lichtenberg, see Roach, 86–89, and J. P. Stern, *Lichtenberg: A Doctrine of Scattered Occasions Reconstructed from His Aphorisms and Reflections* (Bloomington: Indiana University Press, 1959), 22–36; for Garrick and footlights, see Kalman A. Burnim, *David Garrick, Director* (Pittsburgh: University of Pittsburgh Press, 1961), 78–83, and "Looking upon His Like Again: Garrick and the Artist," in *British Theatre and the Other Arts, 1660–1800*, ed. Shirley Strum Kenny (Washington, D.C.: Folger Shakespeare Library, 1984), 182–218. See also Lance Bertelsen, "David Garrick and English Painting," *ECS*, 11 (1978):308–24; and George Winchester Stone, Jr., and George M. Kahrl, *David Garrick: A Critical Biography* (Carbondale: Southern Illinois University Press, 1979), 30–51, 544–48. The wig is discussed by Burnim, *David Garrick, Director*, 160–61, and Roach, 58–59.

23. David Garrick, *An Essay on Acting* (London, 1744), 7–8; Roach, 89–92.

24. For Pope, see Rebecca Ferguson, *The Unbalanced Mind: Pope and the Rule of Passion* (Philadelphia: University of Pennsylvania Press, 1986); Bertrand A. Goldgar, "Pope's Theory of the Passions: The Background of Epistle II of the *Essay on Man*," *PQ*, 41 (1962):730–43; and Steven Shankman, *Pope's Iliad: Homer in the Age of Passion* (Princeton: Princeton University Press, 1983).

25. John Sitter, *Literary Loneliness in Mid-eighteenth-Century England* (Ithaca: Cornell University Press, 1982), 152. Sitter is one of a number of scholars and critics who treat the passions in poetry well, if sometimes only in passing. See, for example, Fredric V. Bogel, *Literature and Insubstantiality in Later Eighteenth-Century England* (Princeton: Princeton University Press, 1984); Ralph Cohen, *The Unfolding of "The Seasons"* (London: Routledge and Kegan Paul, 1970); Jean H. Hagstrum, *Sex and Sensibility: Ideal and Erotic Love from Milton to Mozart* (Chicago: University of Chicago Press, 1980); Wallace Jackson, *The Probable and the Marvelous: Blake, Wordsworth, and the Eighteenth-Century Critical Tradition* (Athens: University of Georgia Press, 1978); Janet Todd, *Sensibility: An Introduction* (London: Methuen, 1986); and Richard Wendorf, *William Collins and Eighteenth-Century English Poetry* (Minneapolis: University of Minnesota Press, 1981). P. W. K. Stone, *The Art of Poetry, 1750–1820* (New York: Barnes and Noble, 1967), 64–76, reviews the adoption of the rhetorical theory of the passions into poetic theory. The passions are mentioned frequently in *Psychology and Literature in the Eighteenth Century*, ed. Christopher Fox (New York: AMS Press, 1987).

26. For Burke, see Barbara C. Oliver, "Edmund Burke's Enquiry and the Baroque Theory of the Passions," *SBHT*, 12 (1970):1661–76.

27. For the Scots, see Harvey Mitchell, "'The Mysterious Veil of Self-Delusion' in Adam Smith's Theory of Moral Sentiments," *ECS*, 20 (1987):405–21.

28. For the distinctions, see Gilbert Ryle, *The Concept of Mind* (London: Hutchinson, 1949), 81–95; for the causes and the pronouncement, see Anthony Kenny, *Action, Emotion, and Will* (London: Routledge and Kegan Paul, 1963), 73, 62. For the philosophical implications of modern physiological discov-

eries, see Georges Rey, "Functionalism and the Emotions," in *Explaining Emotions*, ed. Amélie Oksenberg Rorty (Berkeley: University of California Press, 1980), 163–95.

29. Kenny, 53; Ryle, 94; Robert M. Gordon, *The Structure of Emotions: Investigations in Cognitive Philosophy* (Cambridge: Cambridge University Press, 1987), 48.

30. Albert O. Hirschman, *The Passions and the Interests: Political Arguments for Capitalism before Its Triumph* (Princeton: Princeton University Press, 1977); the links between passion and commerce have been set forth, together with the humanist recuperation of virtue, in J. G. A. Pocock, *The Machiavellian Moment: Florentine Political Thought and the Atlantic Republican Tradition* (Princeton: Princeton University Press, 1975), 467–98.

31. For Hume's "Of Avarice," see chapter 5, n. 24; Edward Gibbon, *The History of the Decline and Fall of the Roman Empire*, ed. J. B. Bury, vol. 3 (London: Methuen, 1901), 221.

32. Richard Sennett, *The Fall of Public Man* (New York: Vintage Books, 1978), 108. As for "roles," notice the differences in Reynolds's paintings of actors and others, for which see Ronald Paulson, *Emblem and Expression: Meaning in English Art of the Eighteenth Century* (Cambridge, Mass.: Harvard University Press, 1975), 80–94. See also the devastating comments on "roles" and the study of "character" in Alasdair MacIntyre, *After Virtue: A Study in Moral Theory*, 2d ed. (Notre Dame: University of Notre Dame Press, 1984), 27–32. Douglas Lane Patey, *Probability and Literary Form: Philosophic Theory and Literary Practice in the Augustan Age* (Cambridge: Cambridge University Press, 1984), 84–125, discusses probability and character, as does Paul J. Korshin, "Probability and Character in the Eighteenth Century," in *Probability, Time, and Space in Eighteenth-Century Literature*, ed. Paula R. Backscheider (New York: AMS Press, 1979), 63–77; and George L. Dillon, "Complexity and Change of Character in Neo-Classical Criticism," *JHI*, 35 (1974):51–61. It was Hume, of course, who brought the question to the foreground. John Barrell has suggested that the fragmentation of society in the face of specialization and the division of labor made it increasingly difficult, especially for history painters, to represent the heroic passions convincingly—"The Functions of Art in a Commercial Society: The Writings of James Barry," *ECent* 25 (1984):117–40.

33. Those who have explored the period's preoccupation with the self include: Stephen Cox, *"The Stranger within Thee": Concepts of the Self in Late-Eighteenth-Century Literature* (Pittsburgh: University of Pittsburgh Press, 1980); Morris Golden, *The Self Observed: Swift, Johnson, Wordsworth* (Baltimore: Johns Hopkins University Press, 1972); and Patricia Meyer Spacks, *Imagining a Self: Autobiography and Novel in Eighteenth-Century England* (Cambridge, Mass.: Harvard University Press, 1976).

34. E. P. Thompson, "Patrician Society, Plebeian Culture," *Journal of Social History*, 7 (1973–74):389.

35. Rey, "Functionalism and the Emotions," in Rorty, 188; it is tempting to

bring to bear some of the innovations from these sources. MacLean's concept of the "triune brain" (Rorty, 9–36), for example, has implications for the Scholastic faculties, and the Gururumba "wild pig" syndrome (Rorty, 44–48) offers an astonishing analogue to the "Infirmary" in *Spectator* nos. 424, 429, and 440; see below, chapter 4.

36. Paul Ekman, "Biological and Cultural Contributions to Body and Facial Movement in the Expression of Emotions," in Rorty, 87.

37. Robert C. Solomon, "Emotions and Choice," in Rorty, 277; see also his *The Passions* (Garden City: Anchor Press, 1977).

38. For the James-Lange theory, see William James and C. G. Lange, *The Emotions* (Baltimore: Williams and Wilkins, 1885); for a cogent modern objection to the theory, see Gordon, *The Structure of Emotions,* 86–109.

39. John J. Richetti, *Philosophical Writing: Locke, Berkeley, Hume* (Cambridge, Mass.: Harvard University Press, 1983), 29.

40. MacIntyre, 27–32; Martha C. Nussbaum, *The Fragility of Goodness: Luck and Ethics in Greek Tragedy and Philosophy* (Cambridge, Mass.: Cambridge University Press, 1986). MacIntyre, Nussbaum, Patey, and Richetti, all of whom mine the territory between literature and philosophy to very good effect, crystallized my ideas on eighteenth-century humanism, ideas I owe originally to Walter Jackson Bate, *From Classic to Romantic: Premises of Taste in Eighteenth-Century England* (Cambridge, Mass.: Harvard University Press, 1946; repr. New York: Harper and Row, 1961); and Paul Fussell, *The Rhetorical World of Augustan Humanism: Ethics and Imagery from Swift to Burke* (Oxford: Oxford University Press, 1965).

41. For sophrosyne, see MacIntyre, 136; for Hume, see below, chapter 5.

2. CLASSICAL ANALYSES OF THE PASSIONS

1. For general intellectual and psychological history I have relied on: Herschel Baker, *The Dignity of Man: Studies in the Persistence of an Idea* (Cambridge, Mass.: Harvard University Press, 1947); G. S. Brett, *Brett's History of Psychology,* ed. R. S. Peters, rev. ed. (London: George Allen and Unwin, 1962); H. M. Gardiner, Ruth Clark Metcalf, and John G. Beebe-Center, *Feeling and Emotion: A History of Theories* (New York: American Book, 1937); Thomas S. Hall, *History of General Physiology, 600 B.C. to A.D. 1900: Vol. 1. From Pre-Socratic Times to the Enlightenment* (Chicago: University of Chicago Press, 1975); E. Ruth Harvey, *The Inward Wits: Psychological Theory in the Middle Ages and the Renaissance,* Warburg Institute Surveys, 6 (London: Warburg Institute, 1975); Anthony Levi, S. J., *French Moralists: The Theory of the Passions 1585–1649* (Oxford: Clarendon Press, 1964); Alasdair MacIntyre, *After Virtue: A Study in Moral Theory,* 2d ed. (Notre Dame: University of Notre Dame Press, 1984); Martha C. Nussbaum, *The Fragility of Goodness: Luck and Ethics in Greek Tragedy and Philosophy* (Cambridge: Cambridge University Press, 1986); Joan Wynn Reeves, *Body and Mind in Western Thought: An Introduction to Some Origins of Modern Psychology* (Harmondsworth: Penguin Books,

1958); Daniel N. Robinson, *An Intellectual History of Psychology* (New York: Macmillan, 1976); Bertrand Russell, *History of Western Philosophy and Its Connection with Political and Social Circumstances from the Earliest Times to the Present Day,* 2d ed. (London: George Allen and Unwin, 1961); and Robert I. Watson, *The Great Psychologists from Aristotle to Freud* (Philadelphia: J. B. Lippincott, 1963).

2. In addition to Nussbaum, *The Fragility of Goodness,* see Jacqueline de Romilly, *L'évolution du pathétique d'Eschyle à Euripide,* 2d ed. (Paris: Société d'Édition "Les Belles Lettres," 1980). Greek art was remarkably expressive. The Alexander mosaic from Pompeii, a second-century B.C. copy of a fourth-century painting, is full of passionate faces, especially those of Alexander and Darius. This is an intriguing analogue for both Le Brun and West; see Roger Ling, "Hellenistic and Graeco-Roman Art," in *The Oxford History of the Classical World,* ed. John Boardman, Jasper Griffin, and Oswyn Murray (Oxford: Oxford University Press, 1986), 511–15 and the plate facing p. 438.

3. For Hippocrates, see Arthur J. Brock, *Greek Medicine* (London: J. M. Dent and Sons, 1929), 8–12, 35–96; Brett, 54–59; Gardiner, 4–9; and Watson, 12–16.

4. *The Sacred Disease,* xvii, in *Hippocrates,* trans. W. H. S. Jones, Loeb Classical Library, vol. 2 (Cambridge, Mass.: Harvard University Press, 1923), 175.

5. Samuel Johnson, "The Life of Dr Sydenham," from Swan's *Entire Works of Sydenham,* 2d ed., 1749, quoted from *Early Biographical Writings of Dr Johnson,* intro. J. D. Fleeman (Westmead, Farnborough: Gregg International, 1973), 191.

6. For Empedocles et al., see Brett, 42–45, and Hall, 45–58. For Plato I have relied on T. M. Robinson, *Plato's Psychology* (Toronto: University of Toronto Press, 1970); Brett, 69–93; and Gardiner, 10–25.

7. *Phaedo,* trans. Hugh Tredennick, in *The Collected Dialogues of Plato,* ed. Edith Hamilton and Huntington Cairns, Bollingen Series 71 (Princeton: Princeton University Press, 1963), 49.

8. *Timaeus,* 42–43, trans. Benjamin Jowett, *Collected Dialogues,* pp. 1171–72. See also Robinson, 59–110.

9. *Timaeus,* 70–71, pp. 1193–94; see also Gardiner, 4–5, 23–24.

10. For Aristotle, I have relied on W. W. Fortenbaugh, *Aristotle on Emotion* (London: Duckworth, 1975); Hall, 104–19; MacIntyre, 146–64; Nussbaum, *The Fragility of Goodness,* 235–394; and Sir David Ross, *Aristotle,* 5th ed. (London: Methuen, 1949); see also J. O. Urmson, "Aristotle's Doctrine of the Mean," in *Essays on Aristotle's Ethics,* ed. A. O. Rorty (Berkeley: University of California Press, 1980), 157–87.

11. *Analytica Posteriora,* trans. G. R. G. Mure, in *The Works of Aristotle Translated into English,* ed. W. D. Ross, vol. 1 (Oxford: Oxford University Press, 1928), 94b; see also Fortenbaugh, 11–16.

12. *Ethica Nicomachea,* trans. W. D. Ross, in *The Works of Aristotle Translated into English,* ed. W. D. Ross, vol. 9 (Oxford: Oxford University Press, 1915), 1095a, 1098a; see also Gardiner, 42–45.

13. Ross, 195–208; the problem is apparent in the table in book 2 of the

Eudamean Ethics (1221a), where Aristotle tries to chart an excess, a deficiency, and a mean for each of fourteen passions. It does not seem to me that the place of each passion on the list is either certain or illuminating, even as compared with the other two passions in its own "set." Few of those listed here would find their way back into place once removed, nor does any principle govern the order in which the sets are arranged. The list is only a list and not a systematic arrangement full of possibilities of exploitation and extension. There is no room, for example, to consider circumstance, comparison with others, or even the careful assessment of the nature of the object. Aristotle's ethics and logic supplied him with a potent system for generating order and ideas, and he was content to incorporate the passions into that system rather than devise a systematic arrangement of the passions themselves.

Furthermore, anger, which, as we have seen, greatly concerned Aristotle, is inexplicably missing from this list, while in the *Nicomachean Ethics* (1108a) he posits an excess, "irascibility," a deficiency, "inirascibility" (!), and a mean, "good temper." The vocabulary of his predecessors and contemporaries had failed to supply names for all the spots on the matrix his system obliged him to construct. The vocabulary improved somewhat, but the improvements required the introduction of closely related passions and of principles of arranging and distinguishing them subtler than the principle of the mean.

14. *Rhetorica*, trans. W. Rhys Roberts, in *The Works of Aristotle Translated into English*, ed. W. D. Ross, vol. 11 (Oxford: Clarendon Press, 1946), 1356a.
15. For duration, see *Nicomachean Ethics* 1174a and Gardiner, 27–28. For the "unmoved mover," see Watson, 60–62.
16. For the classical rhetoricians, see Charles Sears Baldwin, *Ancient Rhetoric and Poetic* (New York: Macmillan, 1924); M. L. Clarke, *Rhetoric at Rome: A Historical Survey* (New York: Barnes and Noble, 1966); George Kennedy, *The Art of Persuasion in Greece* (Princeton: Princeton University Press, 1963) and *The Art of Rhetoric in the Roman World, 300 B.C.–A.D. 300* (Princeton: Princeton University Press, 1972).
17. There is a good account of the Aristotelian soul in Watson, 48–63, and of the pneuma, which Aristotle added to the animal spirits, in Brett, 113–14. The best composite view of the Aristotelian soul appears in Ross, 129–53.
18. For the Stoics I have relied on Michael Frede, "The Stoic Doctrine of the Affections of the Soul," in *The Norms of Nature: Studies in Hellenistic Ethics*, ed. Malcolm Schofield and Gisela Striker (Cambridge: Cambridge University Press, 1987), 93–110; A. C. Lloyd, "Emotion and Decision in Stoic Psychology," in *The Stoics*, ed. J. M. Rist (Berkeley: University of California Press, 1978), 233–46; J. M. Rist, *Stoic Philosophy* (Cambridge: Cambridge University Press, 1969); and especially F. H. Sandbach, *The Stoics* (London: Chatto and Windus, 1975).
19. Rist 92; and chapter 4 below.
20. H. A. K. Hunt, *The Humanism of Cicero* (Melbourne: Melbourne University Press, 1954), 7, 41, 101.
21. Rist, 19; for the sage, see Baker, 74–77.
22. Gardiner, 77; Rist, 263–67; Galen objected to the vagueness of this phys-

iology when Chrysippus tried to use the supposed eventual relaxation of the soul in the face of evil to explain changes in the intensity of passions—a change not otherwise explicable in the Stoic system but not even taken into account in earlier ones.

23. The best summary of the sources, intentions, and limitations of the *Tusculan Disputations* is H. A. K. Hunt, *The Humanism of Cicero;* Sandbach, 62–67, 123–25, treats Cicero with the other Stoics. For Diodotus, see Sandbach, 142, and *Tusculan Disputations* V.38.113. Levi, 13–14, writes that Cicero's clarity and consistency imparted much of the Stoic doctrine directly to the seventeenth-century French moralists. Peter Jones establishes the links between Cicero and Hume in *Hume's Sentiments: Their Ciceronian and French Context* (Edinburgh: Edinburgh University Press, 1982).

24. Cicero, *Tusculan Disputations,* trans. J. E. King, Loeb Classical Library (Cambridge, Mass.: Harvard University Press, 1960), 3.11.25, p. 255.

25. For Galen I have relied on Brock, 20–33; Ross, 137–63; George Sarton, *Galen of Pergamon* (Lawrence: University of Kansas Press, 1954), and *Galen on the Passions and Errors of the Soul,* ed. Walther Riese, trans. Paul W. Harkins (Columbus: Ohio State University Press, 1963), as well as on Brett, 197–204, and Watson, 78–81. Hall, 137–62, sets forth the details of the Galenic system with exceptional clarity. See also Friedrich Solmsen, "Tissues and the Soul: Philosophical Contributions to Physiology," *Philosophical Review,* 59 (1950):435–68, and John D. Spillane, *The Doctrine of the Nerves: Chapters in the History of Neurology* (Oxford: Oxford University Press, 1981), 7–34.

26. The clearest account of this physiology and of that of the Middle Ages is in Harvey.

27. Samuel Johnson, *A Dictionary of the English Language* (London, 1755; repr. New York: AMS Press, 1967).

28. Baker, 124–31, 166–67. Levi, 16–17, offers a concise account of the difficulties attendant upon those who ascribed passions to the soul of Christ.

29. Watson, 95, proclaims Augustine's paternity. Baker, 172–75, 275–92, treats the other matters in this paragraph.

30. Saint Augustine, *The City of God against the Pagans,* vol. 3, trans. David S. Wiesen, Loeb Classical Library (Cambridge, Mass.: Harvard University Press, 1968), 167; 9.5; Aquinas returns to this point, citing Augustine (*Summa theologiae,* Ia.2ae.22,3 and 24,3).

Augustine's *De cura pro mortuis* 5.7 includes a fascinating passage on the connections between the motions of the body and those of the heart and mind in prayer. This passage is quoted and analyzed by Gareth Matthews, "Ritual and the Religious Feelings," in *Explaining Emotions,* ed. Amélie Oksenberg Rorty (Berkeley: University of California Press, 1980), 339–53.

31. For Nemesius, see Harvey, 2; for Gerson, see Gardiner, 104; for Peter, see Watson, 124.

32. Harvey, 16–17, 19; Hirschman, *The Passions and the Interests,* regards the treatment of one passion by another as an essential and original feature of the seventeenth-century psychological and social theorists' thought. See above, chapter 1. For Avicenna, see Harvey, 26–27.

33. Brett, 247–49; Harvey, 24, 41.
34. For Aquinas I have relied on F. C. Copleston, *Aquinas* (London: Penguin Books, 1955); Harvey, 53–60; and the introductions and notes to the *Summa theologiae*, vols. 19–20, by Eric D'Arcy (London: Blackfriars, 1975), and vol. 21, by John Patrick Reid (London: Blackfriars, 1965). The "De passionibus animae" occurs in the "Prima secundae" (1a.2ae) of the *Summa*, which I cite by question and article number.
35. Harvey, 54 (see also 58); cf. Copleston, 125–26.
36. *Summa* 23.4; see 23.2 and Harvey, 46–47, for the roots of the distinction in Aristotle. There are unelaborated hints of the division in Plato and Galen (Riese, 46–48). Ficino's use of these terms to translate Plato was also enormously influential (Levi, 8n).
37. *Summa* 25.1; cf. 23.2, which cites Avicenna and Aristotle as the authorities for this essential component of the movement toward good and away from evil.
38. Gardiner, 108–12, sets forth some of the variations of the scheme and traces its continuation, largely in Catholic writers, into the eighteenth century. Levi, 142–65, follows the fortunes of the *Prima secundae* among the French Scholastics of the seventeenth century and enumerates their confusions and adaptations with his customary thoroughness and lucidity.
39. Copleston, 64–65, 79–80, 81–85.
40. *Summa*, 84.6.2; 78.4; 83.1; Harvey, 55–56, 72, n.146; Levi, 21, 31–35.

3. QUICKENING FORCES

1. G. S. Brett, *Brett's History of Psychology*, ed. R. S. Peters, rev. ed. (London: George Allen and Unwin, 1962), 311–12.
2. Anthony Levi, S. J., *French Moralists: The Theory of the Passions, 1585–1649* (Oxford: Clarendon Press, 1964), 31; see also 50–51. Levi summarizes most of the French theories of the passions thoroughly.
3. Levi, 23, 74–95. Du Vair's *La sainte philosophie* was written before 1585.
4. "Un mouvement de l'appetit sensitif, causé de l'apprehension, ou de l'imagination du bien ou du mal, qui est suivy d'un changement qui arrive au corps, contre les loix de la nature" (Levi, 144).
5. Norman Bryson, *Word and Image: French Painting of the Ancien Régime* (Cambridge: Cambridge University Press, 1981), 40.
6. Bryson, 38 (citing Starobinski); see also Levi, 177–94, 299–328.
7. Levi, 251; the other information in this paragraph is drawn from 250–55.
8. See "The Reception of Harvey's Doctrine during his Lifetime, 1628–1657," in Geoffrey Keynes, *The Life of William Harvey* (Oxford: Clarendon Press, 1966), 447–55; Richard Toellner, "The Controversy between Descartes and Harvey regarding the Nature of Cardiac Motions," in *Medicine, Science, and Culture: Historical Essays in Honor of Owsei Temkin*, ed. Lloyd G. Stevenson and Robert P. Multhauf (Baltimore: Johns Hopkins University Press, 1972), 73–90.

9. *The Passions of the Soul,* in *The Philosophical Works of Descartes,* trans. Elizabeth S. Haldane and G. R. T. Ross (Cambridge: Cambridge University Press, 1968), 1:331; all quotations, cited by article number, are from this translation. For the background, sources, and influence of this work, see the introduction to the edition of Geneviève Rodis-Lewis (Paris: Librairie Philosophique J. Vrin, 1955), 5–39. For Descartes's obligations to Plato and Epicurus as interpreted by Seneca and his distrust of Aristotelian motion and scholastic interpretations, see Levi, 258–64, Brett, 359–70, Hall, 250–64, and Watson, 127–63.

10. For Malebranche and Leibniz, see Brett, 388–94, 406–16; Gardiner et al., 171–82; and Charles J. McCracken, *Malebranche and British Philosophy* (Oxford: Clarendon Press, 1983).

11. The passions have been well and frequently studied in conjunction with Renaissance literature: Lawrence Babb, *The Elizabethan Malady: A Study of Melancholia in English Literature from 1580 to 1642* (East Lansing: Michigan State College Press, 1951); Herschel Baker, *The Dignity of Man: Studies in the Persistence of an Idea* (Cambridge, Mass.: Harvard University Press, 1947); J. B. Bamborough, *The Little World of Man* (London: Longmans, Green, 1952); David Bevington, *Action Is Eloquence: Shakespeare's Language of Gesture* (Cambridge, Mass.: Harvard University Press, 1984); James W. Broaddus, "Renaissance Psychology and Britomart's Adventures in Faerie Queene III," *English Literary Renaissance,* 17 (1987):186–206; Geoffrey Bullough, *Mirror of Minds: Changing Psychological Beliefs in English Poetry* (London: Athlone Press, 1962); Patrick Cruttwell, "Physiology and Psychology in Shakespeare's Age," *JHI,* 12 (1951):75–89; H. James Jensen, *The Muses' Concord: Literature, Music, and the Visual Arts in the Baroque Age* (Bloomington: Indiana University Press, 1976); Theodore Spencer, *Shakespeare and the Nature of Man,* 2d ed., (New York: Macmillan, 1961); Basil Willey, *The English Moralists* (London: Chatto and Windus, 1965; L. C. T. Forest, "A Caveat for Critics against Invoking Elizabethan Psychology," *PMLA,* 61 (1946):651–72. Baker, 275–92, offers a convenient and brief summary of the faculty psychology of the English Renaissance. The section on the sensitive soul (282–88) is especially cogent. Gerard G. LeCoat, "Comparative Aspects of the Theory of Expression in the Baroque Age," *ECS,* 5 (1971–72):207–23, surveys the passions in other artists, media, and countries.

12. Primaudaye, Coeffeteau, and Huarte were translated in 1618 (by Bowes), in 1621 (by Grimestone), and in 1594 (by Carew). Du Vair was translated by Thomas James as *The Moral Philosophy of the Stoicks* in 1598 and by Charles Cotton in 1664. Native works such as Timothy Bright, *A Treatise of Melancholy* (1586), and Thomas Wright, *The Passions of the Mind in Generall* (1604), were primarily compilations of classical theory.

13. Paolo Giovanni Lomazzo, *A Tracte Containing the Artes of Curious Paintinge* (1598), English Experience, no. 171 (Amsterdam: Da Capo Press, 1969), 11.

14. Bamborough, 119–44, provides a good summary of the connections between the soul and the body and numerous examples of the concern. See also W. Lee

Ustick, "Changing Ideals of Aristocratic Character and Conduct in Seventeenth-Century England," *MP*, 30 (1932–33):147–66. For the ethics of gentility, see Baker, 296.

15. Robert Burton, *The Anatomy of Melancholy*, ed. Holbrook Jackson (New York: Vintage Books, 1977), 252; pt.1, sec.2, mem.3, subs.1. However many sources Burton cites, this passage leans very heavily on Wright's *The Passions of the Mind in Generall* (quoted by Bamborough, 88–89). The quotations from Eccles, Piso, and Montanus are Burton's contribution.

16. *Of the Dignity and Advancement of Learning*, book 7, in *The Works of Francis Bacon*, ed. James Spedding, Robert L. Ellis, and Douglas D. Heath (London: Longmans, 1857–74; repr. New York: Garrett Press, 1968), 5:23–24. Brett, 330–32, makes the connection with Vives. See Willey, *The English Moralists*, 124–47, for the practicality and moral context of Bacon's insights into human nature. See also Lisa Jardine, *Francis Bacon: Discovery and the Art of Discourse* (Cambridge: Cambridge University Press, 1974), 76–108, and D. P. Walker, "Francis Bacon and *Spiritus*," in Stevenson and Multhauf, *Medicine, Science, and Culture*, 121–30.

17. For Bacon's dualism, see Hall, 1:231–32.

18. *Faerie Queene* II.9.33–34; *Hamlet* II.2.554–610. See Bamborough, 86, 133, 16, and, for Spenser, Harry Berger, Jr., *The Allegorical Temper: Vision and Reality in Book II of Spenser's Faerie Queene*, Yale Studies in English, 137 (New Haven: Yale University Press, 1957), 65–88, 211–40.

19. From *Certain Sonnets;* see *The Poems of Sir Philip Sidney*, ed. William A. Ringler, Jr. (Oxford: Clarendon Press, 1962), 149–51, and Bullough, 34.

20. For Hobbes I have relied on D. G. James, *The Life of Reason: Hobbes, Locke, Bolingbroke* (London: Longmans, Green, 1949); Michael Oakeshott, "Introduction" to *Leviathan* (Oxford: Basil Blackwell, n.d.); Clarence DeWitt Thorpe, *The Aesthetic Theory of Thomas Hobbes, With Special Reference to His Contribution to the Psychological Approach in English Literary Criticism*, Publications in Language and Literature, 18 (Ann Arbor: University of Michigan Press, 1940); and Willey, *The English Moralists*, 148–71.

21. *Leviathan; or, The Matter, Form, and Power of a Commonwealth Ecclesiastical and Civil*, 1.8, in *The English Works of Thomas Hobbes of Malmesbury*, ed. Sir William Molesworth (London: John Bohn, 1839), 3:61–62.

22. *Human Nature; or, The Fundamental Elements of Policy. Being a Discovery of the Faculties, Acts, and Passions, of the Soul of Man, From Their Original Causes; According to Such Philosophical Principles, As Are Not Commonly Known or Asserted*, in *The English Works of Thomas Hobbes of Malmesbury*, ed. Sir William Molesworth (London: John Bohn, 1840), 4:31.

23. *Leviathan* 1.6, 3:47–48. Elsewhere in *Leviathan* Hobbes mentions the effectiveness of the passions in determining the quickness and direction of imagined connections, their susceptibility to habit, and the usefulness of the fear of death. He also dwells on the social implications of the passions that emerge from the constant competition for honor and dignity.

24. Edward Reynolds, *A Treatise of the Passions and Faculties of the Soule of Man*

(1640), reprinted with an introduction by Margaret Lee Wiley (Gainesville: Scholars' Facsimiles and Reprints, 1971), 317.

25. Walter Charleton, *Enquiries into Human Nature, in VI. Anatomic Praelections in the New Theatre of the Royal Colledge of Physicians in London* (London, 1680), C2r.

26. *An Essay concerning Human Understanding*, ed. Peter H. Nidditch (Oxford: Clarendon Press, 1975), 129. For Locke I have relied on James, *The Life of Reason*; Kenneth MacLean, *John Locke and English Literature of the Eighteenth Century* (New Haven: Yale University Press, 1936; repr. New York: Garland, 1984); Willey, *The English Moralists*; and especially John W. Yolton, *Thinking Matter: Materialism in Eighteenth-Century Britain* (Minneapolis: University of Minnesota Press, 1983). For the vital spirits, see *Essay*, 2.10, 2.33, and Yolton, 157–60.

27. MacLean, 20, 45, 91–95.

28. Isaac Watts, *The Doctrine of the Passions Explain'd and Improv'd*, 2d ed. (London, 1732), 5, 84.

29. The rhetorical tradition has been well studied and set forth in: Wilbur Samuel Howell, *Logic and Rhetoric in England, 1500–1700* (Princeton: Princeton University Press, 1956) and *Eighteenth-Century British Logic and Rhetoric* (Princeton: Princeton University Press, 1971). The application of rhetoric to several art forms is set forth in Jensen, *The Muses' Concord*, 47–108.

30. John Ward, *A System of Oratory, Delivered in a Course of Lectures Publicly read at Gresham College, London* (London, 1759), I, 31–32; quoted by Howell, *Eighteenth-Century British Logic and Rhetoric*, 74.

31. Howell, *Eighteenth-Century British Logic and Rhetoric*, 98.

32. Douglas Lane Patey, *Probability and Literary Form: Philosophic Theory and Literary Practice in the Augustan Age* (Cambridge: Cambridge University Press, 1984), 50–62, emphasizes the possibilities of "circumstance."

33. John W. Yolton, *Perceptual Acquaintance from Descartes to Reid* (Minneapolis: University of Minnesota Press, 1984), 105–8.

34. *The Usefulnesse of Experimental Naturall Philosophy* (1663), pt. 2, 3, quoted by G. S. Rousseau in "Psychology," in *The Ferment of Knowledge: Studies in the Historiography of Eighteenth-Century Science*, ed. G. S. Rousseau and Roy Porter (Cambridge: Cambridge University Press, 1980), 155n. For the physiology of this age I have relied on the sources cited in chapter 2, n.1 (especially Hall), and on: Theodore M. Brown, "From Mechanism to Vitalism in Eighteenth-Century English Physiology," *Journal of the History of Biology*, 7 (1974):179–216; Edwin Clarke, "The Doctrine of the Hollow Nerve in the Seventeenth and Eighteenth Centuries," in *Science, Medicine, and Society in the Renaissance: Essays to Honor Walter Pagel*, ed. Allen G. Debus (New York: Science History Publications, 1972), 2:123–42; Sir Michael Foster, *Lectures on the History of Physiology during the Sixteenth, Seventeenth, and Eighteenth Centuries* (Cambridge: Cambridge University Press, 1901); Lester S. King, *The Medical World of the Eighteenth Century* (Chicago: University of Chicago Press, 1958; Karl E. Rothschuh, *History of Physiology*, trans. and ed. Guenter B.

Risse (Huntington, N.Y.: Robert E. Krieger, [1953], 1973); G. S. Rousseau, "Nerves, Spirits, and Fibres: Towards Defining the Origins of Sensibility," in *Studies in the Eighteenth Century, III: Papers presented at the Third David Nichol Smith Memorial Seminar, Canberra 1973*, ed. R. F. Brissenden and J. C. Eade (Toronto: University of Toronto Press, 1976), 137–57; and Robert E. Schofield, *Mechanism and Materialism: British Natural Philosophy in an Age of Reason* (Princeton: Princeton University Press, 1970). For an illuminating account of some of the difficulties to be encountered in wandering these paths, see Joseph F. Musser, "The Perils of Relying on Thomas Kuhn," *ECS*, 18 (1984–85):215–26.

35. R. K. French, *Robert Whytt, the Soul, and Medicine* (London: Wellcome Institute, 1969), 109–16.

36. Bernard Mandeville, *A Treatise of the Hypochondriack and Hysterick Diseases* (London, 1711, 1730; repr. Delmar, N.Y.: Scholars' Facsimiles and Reprints, 1976), 137–38. For Cheyne, see Yolton, *Thinking Matter*, 179; Brown, "From Mechanism to Vitalism," 198–99; and Schofield, *Mechanism and Materialism*, 57–62. Cheyne's eclectic and influential *An Essay of Health and Long Life* (London, 1724), 152–72, makes a useful distinction between "Acute" and "Chronical" passions that considers, with Boerhaavian reciprocity, the effects of various passions on the "Nervous System" and vice versa.

37. Sir Michael Foster, "Harvey and the Circulation of the Blood: The Lacteals and Lymphatics," in Foster, *Lectures on the History of Physiology*, 47. For Harvey, I have also relied on Keynes, cited above in n.8, and on Kenneth D. Keele, *William Harvey: The Man, the Physician, and the Scientist* (London: Thomas Nelson, 1965).

38. William Harvey, *An Anatomical Disquisition On the Motion of the Heart and Blood in Animals*, in *The Works of William Harvey, M.D.*, trans. Robert Willis (London: Sydenham Society, 1847; repr. New York: Johnson Reprint, 1965), 12; Harvey returns to the connections between the spirits and the blood in the *Second Disquisition to John Riolan*, 115–18, 129–30, and *On Animal Generation*, 379–91, 501–12.

39. See Yolton, *Thinking Matter*, 153–89; Thomas S. Hall, *History of General Physiology, 600 B.C. to A.D. 1900*: vol. 2, *From the Enlightenment to the End of the Nineteenth Century* (Chicago: University of Chicago Press, 1969), 5–106; and Frederick Cummings, "Charles Bell and *The Anatomy of Expression*," *Art Bulletin*, 46 (1964):191–203.

40. Richard S. Westfall, *Science and Religion in Seventeenth-Century England* (New Haven: Yale University Press, 1958), 51.

41. The teakettle comparison is from Richard S. Westfall, *The Construction of Modern Science: Mechanisms and Mechanics*, Cambridge History of Science Series (Cambridge: Cambridge University Press, 1971, 1977), 94.

42. Foster, *Lectures on the History of Physiology*, 55–120; Hall, 1:342–48.

43. The connections between the court and the passions continued in this period when Charles I retreated to Oxford to avoid the Puritans and the plague. He placed the deer herd at Windsor Great Park at the disposal of Harvey's knife—a gesture equivalent to giving Galen access to wounded gladiators,

oxen, and apes and about as misleading in the comparative anatomy to which it gave rise.

44. *Thomas Willis's Oxford Lectures,* ed. and trans. Kenneth Dewhurst (Oxford: Sandford Publications, 1980). In addition to Dewhurst's introduction, see that of William Feindel in his edition of Samuel Pordage's translation of *Cerebri anatome, Thomas Willis: The Anatomy of the Brain and Nerves* (Montreal: McGill University Press, 1965), which I cite as "Feindel"; I cite Willis's text, which is paginated separately, as "Willis, *Anatomy.*" I have also relied on Foster, *Lectures on the History of Physiology,* 270–79; Hall, 1:312–25; Hansruedi Isler, *Thomas Willis, 1621–1675, Doctor and Scientist* (New York: Hafner Publishing, 1968); Rousseau, "Nerves, Spirits and Fibres"; and John D. Spillane, *The Doctrine of the Nerves: Chapters in the History of Neurology* (Oxford: Oxford University Press, 1981), 53–107.

45. This point is made by Michael V. DePorte, *Nightmares and Hobby Horses: Swift, Sterne, and Augustan Ideas of Madness* (San Marino: Huntington Library, 1974), 62–64, which also considers Willis's potent spirits as a cause of mental disorder and discusses the mechanistic emphasis of the psychiatry of the age in connection with insanity (8–12). The most speculative account of the connections of physiology and madness is the chapter "Passion and Delirium" in Michel Foucault, *Madness and Civilization: A History of Insanity in the Age of Reason,* trans. Richard Howard (New York: Vintage Books, 1973), 85–116.

46. For the cerebral circulation, see Feindel, 53–56; for the cerebrum and cerebellum, Dewhurst, 14, 138–49, and Willis, *Anatomy,* 110–21; for the explosions, Isler, 67–68, 103, 120–23.

47. Dewhurst, 69, 122–23. Dewhurst calls attention to the farmhouse component of Willis's analogies in his introduction (11–12) and in many of his footnotes. The passage on p. 66 employs the term "tabula rasa" and the image of a "storehouse" for the animal spirits. Cf. Willis, *Anatomy,* 113. Dewhurst discusses Locke's desertion of Willis for Sydenham in an appendix, 159–60; see also Isler, 174–79.

48. Dewhurst, 142; see the equivalent passage in Willis, *Anatomy,* 110, which extends the discussion to include the vivid appearance of the animal spirits, and thus the passions, in the eyes; see also 129–30.

49. Rousseau, "Nerves, Spirits, and Fibres." The exquisite refinement of the nervous system that Mrs. Donnellan found in Richardson but not in Fielding, which Rousseau sees as the essential and causal connection between Willis and the age of sensibility (151–52), was mentioned by as early a writer as Aquinas and assumed considerable importance in the concern with taste in *The Spectator.*

50. *Early Biographical Writings of Dr Johnson,* ed. J. D. Fleeman, 25–35; Johnson's account relies very heavily on the funeral oration by Schultens, Boerhaave's colleague. For Boerhaave, see G. A. Lindeboom, *Herman Boerhaave: The Man and His Work* (London: Methuen, 1968); King, *The Medical World of the Eighteenth Century,* 59–121; Schofield, *Mechanism and Materialism,* 146–56, 193–94; and Hall, 1:367–90.

51. Book 3 of Spinoza's *Ethics* supplied a most influential study of the egoism of

the passions; see Jerome Neu, *Emotion, Thought, and Therapy* (Berkeley: University of California Press, 1977), which compares Spinoza and Hume.

52. Lindeboom, *Herman Boerhaave*, 201–6; 223n; 356; 368–73. Nearly one-third (659) of Boerhaave's students in the years between 1701 and 1738 were British. The *Gentleman's Magazine* estimated that he brought in £20,000 a year from his British students alone. The newly founded and much admired medical school at Edinburgh University was almost completely in the hands of Boerhaavians.

53. Lindeboom, *Herman Boerhaave*, 70–71; see also G. A. Lindeboom, *Bibliographia Boerhaaviana* (Leiden: E. J. Brill, 1959), 27–40.

54. For Von Haller, see Hall, 1:391–408; for Malebranche, see Yolton, *Thinking Matter*, 128–31, 160–84; and for Maupertuis, see Hall, 2:18–28. These issues are dealt with at great length but with different emphases, in French, *Robert Whytt*, and Schofield, *Mechanism and Materialism*. Lindeboom, *Herman Boerhaave*, discusses the influence of Descartes on Boerhaave and of Boerhaave on La Mettrie, 266–69.

55. Brown, "From Mechanism to Vitalism"; Schofield, *Mechanism and Materialism*, 54–55.

56. James Parsons, *Human Physiognomy Explain'd* (London, 1747). Schofield, *Mechanism and Materialism*, 194–96, describes some of the confusion in Parsons's Croom Lectures, concluding that he was not, after all, a mechanist.

57. Sir John Hill, *The Actor; or, A Treatise on the Art of Playing* (London, 1755), quoted by Joseph R. Roach, *The Player's Passion: Studies in the Science of Acting* (Newark: University of Delaware Press, 1985), 108 (italics added).

58. Foucault, 129–39; see also John Mullan, *Sentiment and Sociability: The Language of Feeling in the Eighteenth Century* (Oxford: Clarendon Press, 1988); and Rousseau, "Nerves, Spirits, and Fibres."

59. George Henry Lewes, *On Actors and the Art of Acting* (Leipzig: Bernhard Tauchnitz, 1875); quoted by Roach, 181–94; also Cummings, "Charles Bell and *The Anatomy of Expression*"; and Graeme Tytler, *Physiognomy in the European Novel: Faces and Fortunes* (Princeton: Princeton University Press, 1982), 87–97.

60. For Richardson, see Raymond Stephanson, "Richardson's 'Nerves': The Physiology of Sensibility in *Clarissa*," *JHI*, 49 (1980):267–85. Smollett's application of the passions is relentless and formulaic; see Albrecht B. Strauss, "On Smollett's Language: A Paragraph in *Ferdinand Count Fathom*," in *Style in Prose Fiction*, English Institute Essays, 1958, ed. H. L. Martin (New York: Columbia University Press, 1958), 25–54; Thomas R. Preston, "The 'Stage Passions' and Smollett's Characterization," *SP*, 71 (1974):105–25; and Patey, 179–97. For Sterne, see Henri Fluchère, *Laurence Sterne: From Tristram to Yorick: An Interpretation of Tristram Shandy*, trans. Barbara Bray (London: Oxford University Press, 1965), 282–354; and Valerie Grosvenor Myer, "Tristram and the Animal Spirits," and Roy Porter, "Against the Spleen," both in *Laurence Sterne: Riddles and Mysteries*, ed. Valerie Grosvenor Myer (London: Vision Press, 1984), 99–112, 84–98.

61. Wittgenstein's figure of "idling" is from *Philosophical Investigations*, 132; I

encountered it in Peter Jones, *Hume's Sentiments: Their Ciceronian and French Context* (Edinburgh: Edinburgh University Press, 1982), 180.

4. INTO COMPANY AND BEYOND

1. *The Spectator,* ed. Donald F. Bond, 5 vols. (Oxford: Clarendon Press, 1965), no. 10, 1:44. Cicero said that Socrates brought Philosophy down from heaven (*Tusculan Disputations,* 5.4.10). Having chosen this text partly because it indicates that the passions were well recognized and generally available, I have not attempted to establish differences between Addison and Steele in their application. I doubt very much that such a distinction could be made. We might guess that Steele is likelier to discuss the passions in association with marriage, occasionally using his own marriage, even his own love letters, to do so, and we may be certain that Addison makes more of their aesthetic connections and theological implications, but on the whole an understanding of the passions is one of many things the two writers had in common. Thus Steele knew the contemporary theater better and commented on it more often, but as we shall see, Addison was equally able to discuss and employ the staging of the passions. As inevitably happens in connection with this text, Addison is disproportionately represented in this chapter.

    Other contributors found no difficulty in merging their understanding of the passions with Addison's and Steele's. Thomas Amory, whose isolated eccentricity exaggerated some of Mr. Spectator's own peculiarities, praised the Reverend Henry Grove for his four papers in terms that suggest that expertise with the passions was expected of anyone who picked up Mr. Spectator's pen (and the papers that emerged from under it): "By these papers Mr. *Grove* showed himself well acquainted with the lovely and generous affections of the human soul, as well as its surprizing dignity and large capacities for happiness." Quoted by Bond, 1,lxxx; Grove wrote nos. 588, 601, 626, 635. For another example, one of many, see Parnell's "Grotto of Grief" in no. 501.

2. Bond, 1,lxxxviii–xcvi; for a more complicated view of Addison's class consciousness, see Lee Andrew Elioseff, "Joseph Addison's Political Animal: Middle-Class Idealism in Crisis," *ECS,* 6 (1973):372–81. I have also relied on Edward A. Bloom and Lillian D. Bloom, *Joseph Addison's Sociable Animal in the Market Place, on the Hustings, in the Pulpit* (Providence: Brown University Press, 1971); Lee Andrew Elioseff, *The Cultural Milieu of Addison's Literary Criticism* (Austin: University of Texas Press, 1963), hereafter cited as "Elioseff"; and Michael G. Ketcham, *Transparent Designs: Reading, Performance, and Form in the "Spectator" Papers* (Athens: University of Georgia Press, 1985).

3. No. 2, 1:9; no. 600, 5:53—probably written somewhat earlier.

4. No. 41; 1,174. See also no. 86, which denounces *Prosopolepsia* on the authority of Cicero, and no. 95, in which a correspondent expresses a witty distrust of the connections between weeping and grief.

5. No. 1, 1:2–3. Mr. Spectator's passionate curiosity, established in the first paper, is mentioned repeatedly; see, for example, nos. 37, 85, 156, and

244 : Notes to Chapter 4

especially 266, in which curiosity is the only passion he was tempted to indulge with a pert young prostitute.

6. No. 114, 1:469; Irus takes his name, proverbial for a beggar, from the troublesome one in the *Odyssey* (book 18), which may mean that the extravagant Laertes is named after Odysseus's father. Both king and beggar have been transported into the urban society and agrarian economy of Augustan England, where they are neighbors, displayers of equipage, growers of "corn," and employers of laborers. Their "motives" are about to invert their ranks.

7. No. 471, 4:165; Ketcham, 82–104, and William H. Youngren, "Addison and the Birth of Eighteenth-Century Aesthetics," *MP*, 79 (1982):267–83, consider some other complexities in *The Spectator*'s treatment of time.

8. No. 111, 1:458, 459; no. 447 repeats the expected continuation of passions, using them to define notions of Heaven and Hell. See also nos. 574, 575, and especially 580. This consideration also adds irony to the passage cited above from no. 185, on the passions of a zealous atheist. For a discussion of the nature and sources of Addison's theological beliefs, especially the eclectic Latitudinarianism of his conception of the soul, see Bloom and Bloom, 173–202.

9. The proportions of pain and pleasure in this soul are notably more Augustan than Platonic: "The truth of it is, they generally found upon Search, that in the most vicious Man Pleasure might lay a claim to an hundredth part, and that in the most virtuous Man Pain might come in for at least two thirds" (no. 183, 2:223—the original is entirely in italics). Even more remarkable than these proportions are the theological implications of the arrangements whereby the dead are dispatched to Infernal or Celestial regions, according to their *proportions* of good and evil.

10. Elioseff, 13, Youngren, 277. For accounts of the aesthetics of *The Spectator*, see Leopold Damrosch, Jr., "The Significance of Addison's Criticism," *SEL*, 19 (1979):421–30; and Wallace Jackson, "Addison: Empiricist of the Moral Consciousness," *PQ*, 45 (1966):455–59. No. 339 offers a careful distinction of the pathetic from the sublime—the former produces tumult and agitation. No. 409 discusses taste at length but without recourse to the passions. It remained for Hume to develop their implications for that faculty.

11. Elioseff, 103, 179–82; see also Martin Kallich, "The Association of Ideas and Critical Theory: Hobbes, Locke, and Addison," *ELH*, 12 (1945):290–315.

12. See the discussion of Willis above in chapter 3. Yolton, *Thinking Matter*, 187 nn. 15 and 17, discusses *Spectator* nos. 86, 115, and 417 as an indication of the general dissemination of physiology. Hilbert H. Campbell has shown that the passage from no. 417 owes more to Malebranche than Descartes— "Addison's 'Cartesian' Passage and Nicolas Malebranche," *PQ*, 46 (1967):408–12.

13. See nos. 139, 243, and 274. "Guest writers" regularly quote Seneca in the Spectator's name—for example, Hughes, in no. 375. No. 397 summarizes the dispassion of Stoicism and then excoriates its lack of pity ("Love softened

by a degree of Sorrow") as an introduction to an exceedingly pathetic letter by Ann Boleyn (3,486).

14. No. 510, 4:312 (where Jonson's *Catiline* proves a passionate point). See also nos. 290 and 335, where first Steele, and then Addison, considers the passions in Philips's version of Racine's *Andromaque* in some detail; *The Spectator's* connections with the stage are discussed in Ketchum, 43–48.

15. No. 29, 1:121; cf. no. 18. See also Elioseff, 203–14, and, for a slightly more favorable view of opera, or at least of Nicolino, *Tatler* no. 115 and Joseph R. Roach, *The Player's Passion: Studies in the Science of Acting* (Newark: University of Delaware Press, 1985), 69.

16. No. 42, 1:180 (cf. the treatment of Corneille in nos. 39 and 44).

17. See Elioseff, 49–63, and Youngren, 276–83.

18. No. 147, 2:79; cf. no. 201; see also no. 541, where Hughes considers the effects of oratory on passion, and vice versa, and Gibbon's comments on rhetoric and sermons, below, chapter 8. As it happens, the manuscript of five numbers of the *Spectator* of most interest for the study of the passions survives in the Houghton Library at Harvard (MS ENG 772). The manuscript reflects, even more strongly than Bond suggests (2, 490n), the origins of some of Addison's papers as sermons. The essays on fame (nos. 255–57) move naturally and surely toward the inspection of the soul by God. The manuscript of no. 170 suggests that Addison added the quotation from Terence (2:170) sometime after he had written the essay—indicating that his conception of each passion could absorb, even summon, examples and illustrations long after the discussions had been composed. And when these examples came, they found their place readily in the existing discussion, because the early and late conceptions of the passions coincided perfectly.

19. No. 226, 2:378, 381 (cf. no. 244, where these are called "wise" pictures because all of our faculties are required to comprehend them). The passions figure in Addison's *Dialogues Upon the Usefulness of Ancient Medals* (London, 1726), 16, where Le Brun is mentioned, and minters are said to "have conjured up persons that exist no where else but on old Coins, and have made our Passions, and Virtues, and Vices, visible."

20. Ketcham, 13; this line of thought is also pursued in Richard Sennett, *The Fall of Public Man* (New York: Random House, 1978), 107–22.

21. No. 484, 4:218. Compare no. 538, where the silent scorn of the audience for an extravagant raconteur is analyzed.

22. No. 172, 2:180 (cf. the courtly puppet in no. 277; the cold civilities of the court levee in no. 193; the pride of the Spanish court in no. 394; and "Chezluy," a man without ambition, desire, or eagerness to please, who begs, for these reasons, to stay out of Pharamond's court in no. 480). In no. 97 Pharamond manages his own passions and tries to do so with those of his courtiers, and in no. 293 Gratian and Richelieu provide maxims for success at court. C. S. Lewis mentions, I think mistakenly, that "a *rapprochement* between the 'cit' and the courtier was an essential part of the Addisonian synthesis"; "Addison," in *Essays on the Eighteenth Century Presented to David*

Nichol Smith (Oxford: Clarendon Press, 1945); I quote from the essay as it is reprinted in James L. Clifford, ed., *Eighteenth-Century English Literature: Modern Essays in Criticism* (New York: Galaxy Books, 1959), 150.

23. No. 53, 1:225; this letter may have been written by John Hughes. The same idea is repeated in no. 73, by Addison. This consideration will also be extended by Hume.

24. No. 102, 1:428–29. This correspondent closes by announcing that he (one supposes) has "from my own Observations compiled a little Treatise for the Use of my Scholars, entitled, *The Passions of the Fan.*" Ketcham, 56–60, considers some of the other gestures then expected of women.

25. 4:351. The letter from a reader that inspired this paper survives. It was a son who brought the original consolation (5:236–37).

5. PHILOSOPHICAL DETACHMENT

1. For Rousseau, see Ernest Campbell Mossner, *The Life of David Hume* (Oxford: Clarendon Press, 1970 [1954]), 507–8, hereafter cited as "Mossner." Mossner considers Hume's ascription of these passions to himself in "Philosophy and Biography: The Case of David Hume," *Philosophical Review,* 59 (1950):190–91. For a more impassioned and ingenious reading of the Rousseau incident, see Jerome Christensen, *Practicing Enlightenment: Hume and the Formation of a Literary Career* (Madison: University of Wisconsin Press, 1987), 258–60. It is difficult not to suspect Hume's own passions, or at least his pleasures and his taste, of piquing his discussion of the embargo on French wines (*Essays,* I, 336; see n. 6 below).

2. I have noted some connections with Cicero and Addison, not because I want to see these names added to those of Hutcheson, Butler, Locke, and the other usual sources, but because these connections seem so pertinent to my own discussion. See Peter Jones, *Hume's Sentiments: Their Ciceronian and French Context* (Edinburgh: Edinburgh University Press, 1982).

3. The critics who deal with the passions in Hume include: Pall S. Ardal, *Passion and Value in Hume's Treatise* (Edinburgh: Edinburgh University Press, 1966); Annette Baier, "Master Passions," in *Explaining Emotions,* ed. Amélie Oksenberg Rorty (Berkeley: University of California Press, 1980), 403–23; Nicholas Capaldi, *David Hume: The Newtonian Philosopher,* Twayne's World Leaders Series, 48 (Boston: G. K. Hall, 1975), 130–50; idem, "Hume's Theory of the Passions," in *Hume: A Re-evaluation,* ed. Donald W. Livingston and James T. King (New York: Fordham University Press, 1976), 172–90; Jerome Christensen, *Practicing Enlightenment,* 66–93; Didier Deleule, *Hume et la naissance du libéralisme économique* (Paris: Aubier Montaigne, 1979), 56–70, 99–114, 156–60; Peter Jones, *Hume's Sentiments;* David Fate Norton, *David Hume, Common-Sense Moralist, Sceptical Metaphysician* (Princeton: Princeton University Press, 1982), 96–126; A. D. Nuttall, *A Common Sky: Philosophy and the Literary Imagination* (Berkeley: University of California Press, 1974), 93–111; Terence Penelhum, *Hume* (New York: St. Martin's Press, 1975),

89–110 (the book I find most in line with my own reading of Hume); John J. Richetti, "Hume," in *Philosophical Writing: Locke, Berkeley, Hume* (Cambridge, Mass.: Harvard University Press, 1983), 183–263; Norman Kemp Smith, *The Philosophy of David Hume* (London: Macmillan, 1941; repr. New York: Garland, 1983), 138–91; John B. Stewart, *The Moral and Political Philosophy of David Hume* (New York: Columbia University Press, 1963), 57–79; John P. Wright, *The Sceptical Realism of David Hume* (Manchester: Manchester University Press, 1983), 209–30; John W. Yolton, *Perceptual Acquaintance from Descartes to Reid* (Minneapolis: University of Minnesota Press, 1984), 165–203. Philosophers usually treat Hume's analysis of the passions etiologically and retain the medical connotations (e.g., Penelhum, 87, 96, 100). While the passions certainly do weaken philosophy, they can, as we have already seen, strengthen prose. If the passions and sympathy "infect" Hume's philosophy, they also enhance the lives—mental, social and emotional—of those who figure in and read his works. Inasmuch as they reside in human nature, and give that nature both life and art, perhaps Hume's own figure of "springs" is preferable to figures of disease.

4. The anonymous contemporary quotation is cited by Eugene Rotwein, "David Hume, Philosopher-Economist," in *David Hume: Many-sided Genius,* ed. Kenneth R. Merrill and Robert W. Shahan (Norman: University of Oklahoma Press, 1976), 120n. For Hume as historian, see J. C. Hilson, "Hume: The Historian as Man of Feeling," in *Augustan Worlds,* ed. J. C. Hilson, M. M. B. Jones, and J. R. Watson (New York: Barnes and Noble, 1978), 205–22; Leo Braudy, *Narrative Form in History and Fiction* (Princeton: Princeton University Press, 1970), 31–90; and Victor G. Wexler, "David Hume's Discovery of a New Scene of Historical Thought," *ECS,* 10 (1976–77): 185–202.

5. David Hume, *A Treatise of Human Nature,* ed. L. A. Selby-Bigge, 2d ed., rev. P. H. Nidditch (Oxford: Clarendon Press, 1978), 415.

6. P. 594; this example confirms Hume's assertion, mentioned below in conjunction with the essays, that sight is an essential circumstance of pity. See David Hume, *Essays Moral, Political, and Literary,* ed. T. H. Green and T. H. Grose, 2 vols. (London: Longmans, Green, 1882), 1:470 and 477, for examples of historical suppositions at work.

7. Richard Kuhns, "Hume's Republic and the Universe of Newton," in *Eighteenth Century Studies Presented to Arthur M. Wilson,* ed. Peter Gay (Hanover, N.H.: University Press of New England, 1972), 78.

8. P. 318; for other explicit statements of the uniformity of human passions, see David Hume, *Enquiries concerning Human Understanding and concerning the Principles of Morals,* ed. L. A. Selby-Bigge, 3d ed., rev. P. H. Nidditch (Oxford: Clarendon Press, 1975), 83.

9. Pp. 60–61; notice that Hume has smuggled into the mind a capacity for desire. This passage on the rummaging of the animal spirits delighted one of the few reviewers to pay attention to book 2 of the *Treatise.* See *History of the Works of the Learned,* November–December 1739, and Mossner, 120–23; Mossner suggests that this reviewer was Warburton. Hume's emphasis on the

function of the mind rather than on its structure, a feature of his work noticed by several recent commentators (e.g., Richetti, 242), should be seen as a part of the continuing discussion mentioned in chapter 3.

10. See Jones, *Hume's Sentiments*, 17–18, 96–97; Hume's distaste for anatomy is evident in the analogy that contrasts the accurate but hideous particulars of the anatomist with the more engaging art of the painter. He first employed this analogy in a letter to Hutcheson: "There are different ways of examining the Mind as well as the Body. One may consider it either as an Anatomist or as a Painter; either to discover its most secret Springs & Principles or to describe the Grace & Beauty of its Actions"; *The Letters of David Hume*, ed. J. Y. T. Greig (Oxford: Clarendon Press, 1932), 1:32–33; he repeated it at the end of the *Treatise* (621) and again in the *Enquiry concerning Human Understanding* (10). Yolton, *Perceptual Acquaintance*, 201, connects the analogy to Pope's *Essay on Man*.

11. Pp. 246–47. The famous billiard balls collide not in the *Treatise* but in the *Abstract* (see *Treatise*, 649) and then in the *Enquiry concerning Human Understanding*, 28–30, 78–79.

12. The French *ressorts* suggests the resilience and repetition of the passions, a feature of "springs" implicit in many episodes. Hume's springs are always mechanical, as nearly as I can tell; see, for example, I, 493, where he speaks of them rusting. See the quotation from Walter Charleton in chapter 3 and chapter 8, n.12.

13. For some indication of the difficulties Hume encountered in treating the self as both the subject and the object of passions, see Ardal, 17–19, 44–45; Capaldi, 182–83; Penelhum, *Hume*, 75–110, and "The Self in Hume's Philosophy," in Merrill and Shahan, *David Hume: Many-sided Genius*, 9–23; and Richetti, 218–26.

14. While Hume spoke highly of his "considerable Adjustment in the Boundaries of the Passions, which had been confounded by the Negligence or Inaccuracy of former Philosophers" (in a note to the *Enquiry concerning Human Understanding*, in *Essays* 2, 11n), few critics have been impressed. Ardal shows that the distinction between direct and indirect is neither consistent nor exhaustive (8–11) and discusses a serious flaw in the scheme of the four indirect passions (38) and several disagreements and confusions over the nature and number of the calm passions (93–108). See also Penelhum, *Hume*, 93–94, and Kemp Smith, 164–69. Those commentators who are not happy with Hume's classifications are not happy with one another's. None of them mentions the long tradition of previous attempts to supply such classifications. These continuing discussions are in themselves proof that Hume did not make these classifications unmistakable to begin with, that, having made them, he did not then employ them in ways that would clarify them, and that subsequent writers have been obliged to ignore, adjust, or quarrel over his classifications.

15. Pp. 290–91; for a discussion and extension of Hume's analysis, see Gabriele Taylor, "Pride," in Rorty, *Explaining Emotions*, 385–402.

16. Though it is not very sympathetic, the discussion of sympathy in Ardal (41–

59) is illuminating, as is Philip Mercer, *Sympathy and Ethics: A Study of the Relationship between Sympathy and Morality with Special Reference to Hume's "Treatise"* (Oxford: Clarendon Press, 1972).

17. Compare Penelhum, *Hume,* 89–90; Hume's own countenance, with its strange stare, was more dispassionate, and sometimes more baffling, than his works; see Mossner, 477, 529, 572. For Hume's pronouncement that Garrick was "the best Actor, but the worst critic in the World," a judgment provoked by Garrick's rejection of Hume's *Douglas,* see Mossner, 357.

18. P. 365. The image is taken from Locke, *Essay concerning Human Understanding,* 4.2.6. See Douglas Lane Patey, *Probability and Literary Form: Philosophic Theory and Literary Practice in the Augustan Age* (Cambridge: Cambridge University Press, 1984), 29–30, for a discussion of probability and clarity in this image. For some suggestive comments on the implications of the analogy of optics with perception and as a temptation toward scepticism, see Yolton, *Perceptual Acquaintance,* 10–12, 124–46, 181, 205; Kuhns, "Hume's Republic and the Universe of Newton," also discusses this issue. For the philosophical consequences of Hume's Newtonian framework in the analysis of causation and vivacity, but not in conjunction with the passions, see Capaldi, 95–129; and James Noxon, *Hume's Philosophical Development: A Study of His Methods* (Oxford: Clarendon Press, 1973), 27–123.

19. P. 356; cf. "My Father, who passed for a man of Parts, dyed, when I was an Infant; leaving me, with an elder Brother and a Sister under the care of our Mother, a woman of singular Merit, who, though young and handsome, devoted herself entirely to the rearing and educating of her Children" (*My Own Life,* in Mossner, 611). The capacity of passions to blend sometimes makes them more difficult to analyze than ideas, which compound only by conjunction. Thus pride and humility are "pure" passions, but love and hatred are invariably conjoined with benevolence or anger, the desire of happiness or misery for the person beloved or hated (366–68). The same desires unconnected with love or hatred produce, by the workings of sympathy, pity or malice. Pity, Hume adds in an aside that might recall the shipwreck, depends on the sight of its object and has little to do with our feelings of the instability of fortune or our own liability to the same misfortunes (369).

20. P. 399; cf. 119. Every commentator discusses Hume on the will; few of them agree. See, for example, Ardal, 81–92; Capaldi, 144–50; Kemp Smith, 433–41; and Penelhum, *Hume,* 111–30.

21. P. 436. The most thorough and most intriguing explication of Hume's ideas of time and the passions is Donald W. Livingston, *Hume's Philosophy of Common Life* (Chicago: University of Chicago Press, 1984), especially 120–30.

22. See the introduction to Selby-Bigge's edition of *Enquiries concerning Human Understanding and concerning the Principles of Morals,* xviii–xxii, xxxvi–xxxvii.

23. See also "Of Tragedy," where transitions and the double relation are added to the traditional explanations of the force of oratory. John Sitter has considered the dramatic shift in Hume's attitude toward eloquence when he came to write the *Essays* in *Literary Loneliness in Mid-Eighteenth-Century England* (Ithaca: Cornell University Press, 1982), 37–41; see also Wilbur Samuel

Howell, *Eighteenth-Century British Logic and Rhetoric* (Princeton: Princeton University Press, 1971), 614–16.

24. See I, 101, 132–33, and "Of Avarice" (II, 392–95), an early, feeble imitation of *The Spectator* which Hume withheld from later editions. He also withdrew several essays that discuss passions such as love and impunity allegorically and at length but not especially well.

25. See also "Of the Delicacy of Taste and Passion," I, 90–95, and "Of Essay Writing," II, 367–70. Several commentators have noticed the connections between Addison and Hume in treating aesthetics; see, for example, Jones, *Hume's Sentiments*, 204–5, n.17; Richetti, 231. For an extensive treatment of Hume's aesthetics, especially the schooling of taste and the "transformatory power of art," see Ralph Cohen, "The Rationale of Hume's Literary Inquiries," in Merrill and Shahan, *David Hume: Many-sided Genius*, 97–115, and "The Transformation of Passion: A Study of Hume's Theories of Tragedy," *PQ*, 41 (1962):450–64 (which contrasts Addison and Hume); and Peter Jones, "Another Look at Hume's Views of Aesthetic and Moral Judgments," *PQ*, 20 (1970):53–59, and idem, *Hume's Sentiments*, 93–135.

26. I, 164; this is one of several of Hume's ideas upon which Gibbon will expand. Eugene Rotwein, "David Hume, Philosopher-Economist," 122–25, discusses some of the ways in which passions produce economic actions, and Jerome Christensen, *Practicing Enlightenment,* deconstructs the discourse of avidity, 32–44.

27. I, 198; the masculine pronouns throughout this section are unavoidable. Ardal, 69–70, exonerates Hume from the charge of hedonism.

28. I, 217; Penelhum, *Hume,* 71–73 and 149–50, develops the implications of the division into primary and secondary qualities.

29. I, 259; Hume discusses the sympathies of the spectators at a gaming table in "Of Tragedy"; cf. Jerome Christensen, *Practicing Enlightenment,* 88–93.

30. David Hume, *The Natural History of Religion,* ed. A. Wayne Colver, and *Dialogues concerning Natural Religion,* ed. John Valdimir Price (Oxford: Clarendon Press, 1976), 31; I refer to these two works in these editions. I have also profited from Norman Kemp Smith's introduction and notes to his edition of the *Dialogues* (Indianapolis: Bobbs-Merrill, 1947).

31. P. 62; notice that Hume does not seem to confine himself to the tenets and practices of primitive or even polytheistic religions. Gibbon, too, objected to the unsocial passions of the monastery. Hume discussed the difficulties in ascribing sentiments to superior beings in a letter to Francis Hutcheson in 1740; see *The Letters of David Hume,* I, 40; see also *Treatise,* 224–25. Christopher J. Wheatley, "Polemical Aspects of Hume's Natural History of Religion," *ECS,* 19 (1986):502–14, discusses "Hume's sacrifice of philosophic decorum for the sake of polemic vigor" (511). See also Michael Morrisroe, Jr., "Rhetorical Methods in Hume's Works on Religion," *Philosophy and Rhetoric,* 2 (1969):121–38.

32. Pp. 64–66; cf. "Of Miracles," *Essays,* II, 95.

33. P. 257; cf. 161, where he relies on "Admiration," and 177, where he invokes

the direct, unmediated passions between the sexes, the ones that Hume ignored in the *Treatise*.

6. JUDGING, FEELING, AND FEIGNING

1. "An Essay on *Nothing*," in *Miscellanies by Henry Fielding, Esq.*, ed. Henry Knight Miller, Works of Henry Fielding (Middletown: Wesleyan University Press, 1972), 184; I quote the *Miscellanies* in this edition.

2. For Fielding I have relied on: Robert Alter, *Fielding and the Nature of the Novel* (Cambridge, Mass.: Harvard University Press, 1968); Martin C. Battestin, *The Moral Basis of Fielding's Art* (Middletown: Wesleyan University Press, 1959); Leo Braudy, *Narrative Form in History and Fiction* (Princeton: Princeton University Press, 1970), 91–212; Morris Golden, *Fielding's Moral Psychology* (Amherst: University of Massachusetts Press, 1966); J. Paul Hunter, *Occasional Form: Henry Fielding and the Chains of Circumstance* (Baltimore: Johns Hopkins University Press, 1975); Maurice Johnson, *Fielding's Art of Fiction: Eleven Essays on "Shamela," "Joseph Andrews," "Tom Jones," and "Amelia"* (Philadelphia: University of Pennsylvania Press, 1961); Henry Knight Miller, *Essays on Fielding's Miscellanies: A Commentary on Volume 1* (Princeton: Princeton University Press, 1961); and C. J. Rawson, *Henry Fielding and the Augustan Ideal under Stress* (London: Routledge and Kegan Paul, 1972). There is a very brief discussion of Fielding's artful representation of the passions in Barbara Hardy, *Forms of Feeling in Victorian Fiction* (Athens: Ohio University Press, 1985), 31–36.

3. "Remedy of Affliction for Loss of Friends," *Miscellanies*, 215. This is Fielding's most Ciceronian essay; see Miller, *Essays on Fielding's Miscellanies*, 228–71.

4. Hunter, 67–71, discusses the relationship between character and action. See also Ronald Paulson, *Satire and the Novel in Eighteenth-Century England* (New Haven: Yale University Press, 1967), 141–50. Alter discusses Fielding's architectonics and his reexamination of moral vocabulary (37–39, 69–118).

5. Douglas Lane Patey, *Probability and Literary Form: Philosophic Theory and Literary Practice in the Augustan Age* (Cambridge: Cambridge University Press, 1984), 208.

6. Henry Fielding, *Tom Thumb and the Tragedy of Tragedies*, ed. L. J. Morrissey (Berkeley: University of California Press, 1970), 35; II.viii.

7. Henry Fielding, *The Modern Husband*, IV.ii, in *The Complete Works of Henry Fielding, Esq.*, ed. William Ernest Henley (New York: Croscup and Sterling, 1902), 10.61, 63, hereafter cited as "Henley edition."

8. Henry Fielding, *The Author's Farce*, ed. Charles B. Woods (Lincoln: University of Nebraska Press, 1966), 89; the line was added in a revision.

9. *Covent Garden Journal*, no. 55, in *The Criticism of Henry Fielding*, ed. Ioan Williams (New York: Barnes and Noble, 1970), 175. Rawson, 192–93, connects this passage to its sources in Suetonius and develops the complexities of Fielding's attitudes toward the heroes (and, by implication, the pas-

sions of these heroes) of history. In passages employing physiology and deceit, however, Fielding's undermining of his hero is more straightforward than the generic and temporal complexities descried by Rawson.

10. Henry Fielding, *The History of the Life of the late Mr. Jonathan Wild,* Henley edition, 2.73. For the connections with the genre of criminal biography, see William Robert Irwin, *The Making of Jonathan Wild: A Study in the Literary Method of Henry Fielding* (New York: Columbia University Press, 1941). Rawson (147–65) discusses Wild's connections with earlier heroes. See also Allan Wendt, "The Moral Allegory of *Jonathan Wild,*" *ELH,* 24 (1947):318–19.

11. Many critics comment on this technique of Fielding; see, for example, Rawson, 105–9, and Robert H. Hopkins, "Language and Comic Play in Fielding's 'Jonathan Wild,'" *Criticism,* 8 (1966):216.

12. *Miscellanies,* 161; see also Rawson, 147–70, 178–208.

13. Pp. 199–200. In *Inquiry into the Causes of the Late Increase of Robbers, &c.,* Fielding cautions that the politician must, at executions, "raise an object of terror, and at the same time, as much as possible, . . . strip it of all pity and all admiration" (Henley edition, 13.123); see also Golden, 36–38, Rawson, 180–81, and Irwin, 10–11.

14. Henry Fielding, *Joseph Andrews,* ed. Martin C. Battestin, Works of Henry Fielding (Middletown: Wesleyan University Press, 1967), 326. The heading of this chapter (IV.xiii) mentions the "terrible Conflict in her Breast between Love and Pride," and the torments continue throughout it; Golden, 79–80, discusses Lady Booby's conflicting passions.

15. *Miscellanies,* 153; see also Miller, *Essays on Fielding's Miscellanies,* 189–228.

16. Henry Fielding, *The History of Tom Jones. A Foundling,* ed. Martin C. Battestin and Fredson Bowers, Works of Henry Fielding (Middletown: Wesleyan University Press, 1975), 45–46; I.v. The subtlety of the physiology is reflected in that of the syntax in another sentence on the same page, where the subjunctive provides a similar hint: "Her Orders were indeed so liberal, that had it been a Child of her own, she could not have exceeded them."

17. For Western's humours, see Alter, 91–94; Hunter, 178, comments on his compartmentalization of his passions.

18. *Miscellanies,* 137–39; see p. 125 for the distorting effects of pride, and *The Champion; or, The Evening Advertiser,* no. 52, for a graphic description of the physiology of contempt.

19. See, for example, XIII.xi and XV.iii and Johnson, 111–14. The *Covent Garden Journal,* no. 56, offers another discussion of blushing.

20. Pp. 189–90; IV.x. Parson Adams cites the anecdote of Socrates and the physiognomist from *Tusculan Disputations,* IV.xxxvii (*Joseph Andrews,* 182); Graeme Tytler, *Physiognomy in the European Novel: Faces and Fortunes* (Princeton: Princeton University Press, 1982), 144–51, discusses Fielding's distrust of hasty or platitudinous physiognomical judgments, as well as "physiognomical incompetence."

21. See chapter 1, above, for this hair-raising appliance.

22. Henry Fielding, *Amelia,* Henley edition, vols. 6–7, 6.121; III.iv. For some

reason, the passions in *Amelia* have been subjected to repeated study. See Tuvia Bloch, *"Amelia* and Booth's Doctrine of the Passions," *SEL,* 13 (1973): 461–73, and Frederick G. Ribble, "The Constitution of the Mind and the Concept of Emotion in Fielding's *Amelia," PQ,* 56 (1977): 104–22; see also Golden, 88–91; and Patey, 210–12, where all the signs, not just the passions, are uncertain. Frederick M. Keener, *The Chain of Becoming: The Philosophical Tale, The Novel, and a Neglected Realism of the Enlightenment: Swift, Montesquieu, Voltaire, Johnson, and Austen* (New York: Columbia University Press, 1983), 49–50, considers the "murkiness" of Booth's psychologizing and its connections to Pope's "ruling passion."

23. Hunter, 193, 201–7; Rawson, 74, 228–34.
24. *Tom Jones,* 580, XI.iii; 340, VII.iv; and see Golden, 50, 82–83, and Alter, 69.
25. Henry Fielding, *Miscellaneous Writings,* Henley edition, 16.236; see Rawson, 56.
26. *Journey of a Voyage to Lisbon,* 16.199; see also Miller, 253–71.

7. THE MORAL FORCE OF THE PASSIONS
IN *THE RAMBLER*

1. Samuel Johnson, *The Rambler,* ed. W. J. Bate and Albrecht B. Strauss, Works of Samuel Johnson, vols. 3–5 (New Haven: Yale University Press, 1969), no. 66, 3:351.
2. Most of the critics who mention the passions in Johnson's works treat them as part of some larger aesthetic or moral system. See: Paul K. Alkon, *Samuel Johnson and Moral Discipline* (Evanston: Northwestern University Press, 1967), 10–21; Walter Jackson Bate, *The Achievement of Samuel Johnson* (New York: Oxford University Press, 1961), 63–91; Leopold Damrosch, Jr., "Johnson's Manner of Proceeding in the *Rambler," ELH,* 40 (1973):70–89; Kathleen M. Grange, "Dr. Johnson and the Passions" (Ph.D. diss., University of California, Los Angeles, 1960); Claudia L. Johnson, "Samuel Johnson's Moral Psychology and Locke's 'Of Power,'" *SEL,* 24 (1984):563–82; Frederick M. Keener, *The Chain of Becoming: The Philosophical Tale, The Novel, and a Neglected Realism of the Enlightenment: Swift, Montesquieu, Voltaire, Johnson, and Austen* (New York: Columbia University Press, 1983), 38–40; Alan T. McKenzie, "Logic and Lexicography: The Concern with Distribution and Extent in Johnson's *Rambler," ECent,* 23 (1982):49–63; John B. Radner, "Samuel Johnson, the Deceptive Imagination, and Sympathy," *SBHT,* 16 (1974):23–46; Arieh Sachs, *Passionate Intelligence: Imagination and Reason in the Work of Samuel Johnson* (Baltimore: Johns Hopkins University Press, 1967), 44–45, 69–70, 74–79; Hoyt Trowbridge, "The Language of Reasoned Rhetoric in *The Rambler,"* in *Greene Centennial Studies: Essays Presented to Donald Greene in the Centennial Year of the University of Southern California,* ed. Paul J. Korshin and Robert R. Allen (Charlottesville: University Press of Virginia, 1984), 200–16; Robert W. Uphaus, *The Impossible Observer: Reason and the Reader in Eighteenth-Century Prose* (Lexington: University Press of Kentucky,

1979), 89–107; Robert Voitle, *Samuel Johnson the Moralist* (Cambridge, Mass.: Harvard University Press, 1961), 1–12, 50–54, 129–32; William K. Wimsatt, Jr., *Philosophic Words: A Study of Style and Meaning in the Rambler and Dictionary of Samuel Johnson* (New Haven: Yale University Press, 1948), 49–93.

3. Alkon, 10–11, discusses this distinction between "primary" and "adscititious" passions as central to Johnson's system.

4. No. 188, 5:221 (surely the shadow of Richard Savage lies over this essay?); see also no. 160, 5:88: "To raise esteem we must benefit others, to procure love we must please them."

5. No. 110, 4:223; see also Aristotle, *Prior Analytics*, 1.27.43b.

6. Samuel Johnson, *A Dictionary of the English Language* (London, 1755; repr. New York: AMS, 1964); all the definitions from the *Dictionary* are cited from this source.

7. No. 32, 3:176; Alkon, 10–14, discusses this uneasiness in conjunction with Locke. I return to this subject below, in discussing Johnson's physiology.

8. No. 130, 4:326; for an analysis of Victoria's "pathological narcissism," see Gloria Sybil Gross, "Johnson on Psychopathology," in *Greene Centennial Studies,* 271–87.

9. No. 172, 5:146–47; see also no. 86, which is full of the competitive episodes peculiar to authors, and Golden, 68–69, and 169, n.6.

10. Bate, *The Achievement of Samuel Johnson,* 63–91, and Paul K. Alkon, "Johnson and Chronology," in *Greene Centennial Studies,* 143–71, consider the richness of the temporal considerations in Johnson's work, though without reference to the strict temporal component of the passions.

11. *An Essay concerning Human Understanding,* 2.14.

12. No. 180, 5:182; James Boswell, who combined the emphasis of Descartes with the tendencies of sensibility, provoked a comparable pronouncement: "JOHNSON. 'Sir, as a man advances in life, he gets what is better than admiration—judgement, to estimate things at their true value.' I still insisted that admiration was more pleasing than judgement, as love is more pleasing than friendship. The feeling of friendship is like that of being comfortably filled with roast beef; love, like being enlivened with champagne. JOHNSON. 'No, Sir; admiration and love are like being intoxicated with champagne; judgement and friendship like being enlivened' " (*Boswell's Life of Johnson,* ed. George Birkbeck Hill, rev. L. F. Powell, 6 vols. [Oxford: Clarendon Press, 1934–50], 2.360).

13. No. 140, 4:377. For Johnson and Boerhaave, see above, chapter 2. For the intellectual context of Johnson's concept of the soul, see Gwin J. Kolb, "The Intellectual Background of the Discourse on the Soul in *Rasselas,*" *From Chaucer to Gibbon: Essays in Memory of Curt A. Zimansky, PQ,* 54 (1975):357–69; for the scientific context, see Richard B. Schwartz, *Samuel Johnson and the New Science* (Madison: University of Wisconsin Press, 1971); also Kathleen M. Grange, "Dr. Robert James' 'Medical Dictionary,' " *Psychosomatics,* 3 (1962): 1–5.

14. Samuel Johnson, *Sermons*, ed. Jean Hagstrum and James Gray, Works of Samuel Johnson, vol. 14 (New Haven: Yale University Press, 1978), 193–94.
15. See the textual notes to no. 77, 4:41. Johnson faulted Pope for confounding passions with appetites; *Lives of the English Poets*, ed. George Birkbeck Hill, 3 vols. (Oxford: Clarendon Press, 1905; repr. New York: Octagon Books, 1967), 3.174–75.
16. See R. B. Hovey, "Doctor Samuel Johnson, Psychiatrist," *MLQ*, 15 (1954): 321–35; Kathleen M. Grange, "Samuel Johnson's Account of Certain Psychoanalytic Concepts," *Journal of Nervous and Mental Disease*, 135 (1962):93–98; and Gross, "Johnson on Pathology."
17. Voitle, 56–58, discusses "interest" in conjunction with Johnson's altruism; see also chapter 1, above.
18. *Life*, 3.39; see also Jean Hagstrum, *Samuel Johnson's Literary Criticism* (Chicago: University of Chicago Press, 1952), 60–64, 137–52.
19. *Lives*, 1.180.
20. Samuel Johnson, *"The Idler" and "The Adventurer,"* ed. W. J. Bate, John M. Bullitt, and L. F. Powell, Works of Samuel Johnson, vol. 2 (New Haven: Yale University Press, 1963), 2.254.
21. *The Vanity of Human Wishes*, ll. 195–96, in *The Poems of Samuel Johnson*, ed. David Nichol Smith and Edward L. McAdam, 2d ed. (Oxford: Clarendon Press, 1974), 125; *The False Alarm*, in *Samuel Johnson: Political Writings*, ed. Donald J. Greene, Works of Samuel Johnson, vol. 10 (New Haven: Yale University Press, 1977), 319.
22. "Life of Dryden," in *Lives*, 1.342.
23. Note to *King John*, 3.1.68, in *Johnson on Shakespeare*, ed. Arthur Sherbo, Works of Samuel Johnson, vols. 7–8 (New Haven: Yale University Press, 1968), 415.
24. *The Letters of Samuel Johnson*, ed. R. W. Chapman, 3 vols. (Oxford: Clarendon Press, 1952), no. 163.

8. THE PLACE OF THE PASSIONS IN
THE DECLINE AND FALL OF THE ROMAN EMPIRE

1. *Portraits by Sir Joshua Reynolds*, ed. Frederick W. Hilles (New York: McGraw-Hill, 1952), 118–19. Incidentally, the passage of Gibbon that struck Boswell as most Johnsonian is the one below on the love of power (1:84–85); see *Boswell's Life of Johnson*, ed. George Birkbeck Hill, rev. L. F. Powell (Oxford: Clarendon Press, 1934), 4:389.
2. Edward Gibbon, *The History of the Decline and Fall of the Roman Empire*, ed. J. B. Bury, 7 vols. (London: Methuen, 1896–1902), 1:84–85.
3. For Gibbon I have relied on the following, none of which makes more than passing reference to the passions: Michel Baridon, *Edward Gibbon et le mythe de Rome: Histoire et idéologie au siècle des lumières* (Paris: Honoré Champion, 1977), esp. 709–30; Harold L. Bond, *The Literary Art of Edward Gibbon*

(Oxford: Clarendon Press, 1960); Leo Braudy, *Narrative Form in History and Fiction* (Princeton: Princeton University Press, 1970), 213–68; W. B. Carnochan, *Gibbon's Solitude: The Inward World of the Historian* (Stanford: Stanford University Press, 1987); Patricia B. Craddock, *Young Edward Gibbon: Gentleman of Letters* (Baltimore: Johns Hopkins University Press, 1982); Lionel Gossman, *The Empire Unpossess'd: An Essay on Gibbon's "Decline and Fall"* (Cambridge: Cambridge University Press, 1981); James William Johnson, *The Formation of English Neo-Classical Thought* (Princeton: Princeton University Press, 1967); David P. Jordan, *Gibbon and His Roman Empire* (Urbana: University of Illinois Press, 1971); J. G. A. Pocock, "Between Machiavelli and Hume: Gibbon as Civic Humanist and Philosophical Historian," in *Edward Gibbon and the Decline and Fall of the Roman Empire,* ed. G. W. Bowersock, John Clive, and Stephen R. Graubard (Cambridge, Mass.: Harvard University Press, 1977), 103–19 (this volume is hereafter cited as "Bowersock"); Martin Price, "The Inquisition of Truth: Memory and Freedom in Gibbon's Memoirs," in *From Chaucer to Gibbon: Essays in Memory of Curt A. Zimansky, PQ,* 54 (1975):391–408; idem, "'The Dark and Implacable Genius of Superstition': An Aspect of Gibbon's Irony," in *Augustan Worlds,* ed. J. C. Hilson, M. M. B. Jones, and J. R. Watson (New York: Barnes and Noble, 1978), 241–60.
4. Jordan, 157–58, 169–72.
5. Edward Gibbon, *Memoirs of My Life,* ed. Georges A. Bonnard (London: Nelson, 1966), 134; hereafter cited as *Memoirs.*
6. 1:17; see also Gibbon's note on the Romans' attempt "to disguise, by the pretence of religious awe, their ignorance and terror," Gibbon's source in Tacitus (*Germania,* c. 34), and 1:261–63, where the Goths embark "carelessly" on strange and inadequate Turkish craft. Gibbon was much impressed by the seamanship of the Saxons (1:333–34 and 3:39).
7. 1:129–30. The neoclassical bombast and "ridiculous fury" that Corneille put into Attila's mouth drew Gibbon's ire, presumably for similar reasons (3:474n).
8. See Carnochan, 79–86.
9. Gossman, 17; see also 67–69.
10. For the discussion of Gibbon's dispassionate nature, see, in addition to the *Memoirs,* Martine Watson Brownley, "Gibbon: The Formation of Mind and Character," in Bowersock, 13–25; Patricia Meyer Spacks, *Imagining a Self: Autobiography and Novel in Eighteenth-Century England* (Cambridge, Mass.: Harvard University Press, 1976), 92–126; Craddock; and Gossman.
11. 1:323; for Gibbon's discussion of the role of orators in the early Church, see 2:326–27, where he explores the effects of oratory on the passions of the congregation, and 3:158, where he considers the pathetic vehemence of Ambrose's sermon. See also 2:400–1.
12. For the "springs," see above, chapter 5, n. 12; and Frank E. Manuel, "Edward Gibbon: Historien-Philosophe," in Bowersock, 167–81, which discusses the ressorts in the *Essai:* "Gibbon's 'spring' is eclectic and fuses mechanistic and

vitalistic connotations without his having had much contact with contemporary medical controversies" (169–70).

13. Carnochan discusses the "ruling passion" on pp. 101–10.

14. "I need not blush at recollecting the object of my choice"; "his amiable character was still alive in my remembrance; each room, each walk was imprinted with our common footsteps, and I should blush at my own philosophy if a long interval of study had not preceded and followed the death of my friend" (*Memoirs*, 84, 184); compare Gibbon's comment on Julian's reaction to the death of Anatolius in n.21.

15. 5:487; see also Bernard Lewis, "Gibbon on Muhammad," in Bowersock, 61–73.

16. For a discussion of Gibbon's treatment of Julian, see Glen W. Bowersock, "Gibbon and Julian," in *Gibbon et Rome à la lumière de l'historiographie moderne*, Université de Lausanne, Publications de la faculté des lettres, 22 (Geneva: Librairie Droz, 1977), 191–217, and Carnochan, 110–20; Carnochan finds Julian more enigmatic than I do.

17. 2:285. His satire, *Misopogon*, "still remains a singular monument of the resentment, the wit, the humanity, and the indiscretion, of Julian" (2:485).

18. 2:501; even Julian occasionally had to resort to a rhetorical "donative" (see 2:492). Julian thought so highly of the powers of oratory that he prevented the Christians from teaching it (2:461).

19. 2:443. The same topic calls forth a singular instance of association: "The names of Christ and of Constantius, the ideas of slavery and of religion, were soon associated in a youthful imagination, which was susceptible of the most lively impressions" (2:433).

20. Francis Haskell, "Gibbon and the History of Art," in Bowersock, 194–95.

21. In the phrase that follows, however, Gibbon writes of the "amiable inconsistency" with which Julian regarded the death of Anatolius (2:516). In that phrase the passions assume a smaller, trickier place, the middle of a paradox, where they jolt the reader from admiration into thought.

INDEX